AF575097

Maine Odyssey

Maine Odyssey

Good Times and Hard Times in Bath

1936–1986

KENNETH R. MARTIN
RALPH LINWOOD SNOW

Patten Free Library
Bath, Maine 04530

First Edition
First Printing

Published by Patten Free Library
Bath, Maine 04530
(207) 443-5141

Project coordination
Wordsworth Editorial Services
Spruce Head, Maine
Design
Lurelle Cheverie, Rockport, Maine
Typesetting
Typeworks, Belfast, Maine
Printing
The Knowlton & McLeary Company
Farmington, Maine

Library of Congress Cataloging-in-Publication Data

Martin, Kenneth R., 1938–
Maine odyssey: good times and hard times in Bath, 1936–1986 / Kenneth R. Martin and Ralph Linwood Snow. — 1st ed.
p. cm.
Companion volume to: The Edward Clarence Plummer history of Bath, Maine / Henry Wilson Owen.
Bibliography: p.
Includes index.
ISBN 0-9620401-0-X: $30.00
1. Bath (Me.)—History. I. Snow, Ralph Linwood, 1934– II. Owen, Henry Wilson, b. 1875. Edward Clarence Plummer history of Bath, Maine. III. Title.
F29.B4M36 1988
974.1'85—dc19 88-17991
CIP

CONTENTS

PREFACE

Nineteen eighty-seven was a good time to write a fifty-year retrospective on Bath. The last history, written by Henry Foster Owen and completed in 1936, barely touches upon the Great Depression's impact on the Shipbuilding City. The half-century since its publication has also brought dramatic changes that need to be placed in historical perspective: boom and bust, regional growth, the triumph of the ubiquitous automobile, the decline and renaissance of the downtown, and the remarkable durability of Bath's major industry.

Normally, such a project would be undertaken by the local historical society. But Bath has no historical society. It has been the Patten Free Library that has moved to fill the breach, thereby adding research and publication to its previous achievements on behalf of genealogy and records preservation.

For some years, library corporators and trustees had intermittently discussed the possibility of a fifty-year history, but no funds existed for such a project. However, members of the library's History Room Committee were determined to nudge the project along by pegging it to one of three anniversary dates: the founding of the library in 1847, the construction of the first wing of the current library building in 1889, and publication of Owen's history in 1936.

With anniversaries on their side, the committee moved ahead, developing preliminary plans for raising the needed funds, laying down specifications for the history, and obtaining the approval of the Board of Trustees. Their proposal broke new ground in the affairs of the library, for the project would be started without assurance that its funding was available. That meant a library fund-raising drive.

Events moved quickly. In October 1986, the library trustees approved the project. Preliminary research and planning for the fund-raising program began the next month. By the time fund-raising began in the spring of 1987, the book was already under way. The funding goal was reached at year's end, and the complete manuscript was turned over to the library in January 1988.

In view of the tight time schedule and budgetary constraints, the book's specifications had to be detailed carefully. The volume was to be a readable, interpretive essay of about 115,000 words, arranged chronologically rather than topically, and was to place Bath events in a broad historical context.

The authors readily concede that the book contains all the pros and cons of its specifications, and we hope that it will be judged accordingly. Meeting those specifications forced us to make some hard decisions, the toughest of which was what to leave out. We, of course, assume full responsibility for these choices. Researching and writing the entire volume within fourteen months would have been impossible without the efficiencies of collaboration, computers, and photocopying.

In the interest of readability and concision, we have selected as protagonists individuals whose activities seemed most representative of the Shipbuilding City's variety. Our choices, therefore, did not always run to bigwigs. In every case, however, we have zeroed in on individuals who personified the issues and trends in Bath for the last half-century.

As the bibliography suggests, we were able to find a wide variety of material—published and unpublished—that has some bearing on the past fifty years in Bath. But the principal sources of information have been the official records—newspapers, city reports, and other printed studies, plus the minds and memories of fifty-five former and current Bath residents. Our interviews generated about 1,500 pages of transcript, which transcend their original purpose, providing a rich motherlode of historical information for future projects. The transcripts are available for research at the Patten Free Library's History and Genealogy Room. They constitute the nucleus for an important ongoing oral history program.

We believe that the Patten Free Library's successful undertaking of this history represents an important innovation in the way libraries interpret their bibliographic responsibilities. The project should serve as an encouraging model for community agencies elsewhere. Accordingly, we hope that the book's format and style will likewise offer an alternative to traditional town and city histories.

Throughout this project we have enjoyed the generous cooperation of many individuals and organizations. First and foremost, the Patten Free Library trustees and corporators, librarian Gary Berger, and his most helpful, cheerful, and cooperative staff were always ready to lend assistance. We especially appreciate the support of Gordon Struble, keeper of the library's History and Genealogy Room. Particular thanks go to Jane (Mrs. E. Barton) Chapin for her diligent chairmanship of the project from conception to completion. And the book would not exist but for the tireless enthusiasm of Chuck Richelieu and his group of volunteers, who performed fund-raising miracles.

We are grateful to John Carter, director of the Maine Maritime Museum, for making that institution's archives and microfilm reader-copier available at all times. Museum Curator Nathan Lipfert carefully read our typescript and offered valuable suggestions.

City Manager Peter Garland and City Clerk Beverly Henrikson were enthusiastic supporters of the project from the beginning. They and their staffs proved able to answer every question and every request with cheerful dispatch.

Campbell Niven, publisher of the *Times Record* (Brunswick), kindly gave us permission to quote from *Memories of Morse*, a publication of the Brunswick Publishing Company. *Times Record* staff, notably Sheryl Page and Editor David Swearingen, were especially helpful. Photographs from the newspaper archives have made a critical difference in this volume.

Bradley Hewes of Kennebec Camera contributed time, talent, and materials to reproduce the copies of all the photographs found in this book. George Baldwin and Ron Farr at Bath Iron Works also lent assistance in tracking down important photographs.

Whenever possible, we have credited the photographer whose work we use as well as the repository from which it came. Too many riveting pictures, alas, have become anonymous. It is quite likely that many—probably most—of the photographs in the first four chapters of this book are the work of Herbert Douglas, a man with an acute sense of Bath's changing scene.

Finally, for their editorial suggestions and good counsel, we acknowledge our wives, Barbara Martin and Christie Snow, without whom there would, simply, have been no book.

KENNETH R. MARTIN
RALPH LINWOOD SNOW
Woolwich, Maine
March 1, 1988

1

"We Still Had Our Pride"

Fifty years later, old-timers in Maine would still be talking about the Great Flood of '36; Bath old-timers in particular, because living along a straight and wide five-mile stretch of the Kennebec River had given them an especially good view of the flood's devastation.

The trouble started when it began raining on 11 March. Two days later,

MAINE MARITIME MUSEUM, BATH

Bath's downtown waterfront during the Great Flood of 1936.

Maine streams and rivers were perilously swollen. Accumulated snow and ice blocked the flow and made matters worse. Upriver from Bath, people headed for high ground, and the bridges that spanned the Kennebec and its long tributary, the Androscoggin, started giving way.

The Kennebec ice, flowing southward toward the sea with its accumulated wreckage, took almost a week to reach the Shipbuilding City. En route, it had carried away the Richmond-Dresden bridge, just a few miles north. Then, merging with the Androscoggin's flood, it neared the massive Carlton Bridge, which allowed U.S. Route One to span the Kennebec. Would the Carlton go the way of the other bridges? To prevent that, the Coast Guard Cutter *Ossipee* positioned herself north of the bridge for icebreaking duty. Meanwhile, Commercial Street, on Bath's waterfront, was covered by a foot and a half of water, forcing hundreds of flood-watchers to take precarious refuge on ramshackle downtown wharves. They got an eyeful. As the local press put it, there had not been such a spectacle "since the freshet of 1896. From shore to shore tons of ice, crowned with debris of every description, was swept toward the sea by the ebb tide. For some little time the . . . *Ossippee* [sic] faced the wrath of the floes. . . . But as the river filled at its widest points, the cutter put into the old Eastern Steamship Co. dock." The bridge held against the ice and assorted foreign objects: "Three tank cars, about one-half submerged, a large coal shed, a shanty with its chimney protruding above the ice field, [and] a dead cow, were among the sights."[1]

Once past the Carlton Bridge, the danger dissipated as the ice flood completed the last twelve miles of its journey to the ocean. Bath's houseboat colony was spared because residents there had adjusted their moorings for extra high water. The flood did, however, force postponement of the launch-

MAINE MARITIME MUSEUM

The U.S.S. *Drayton* slides into the Kennebec River from the Bath Iron Works yard.

ing of the U.S.S. *Drayton*, a newly completed destroyer perched on the ways at the Bath Iron Works, just south of the big bridge. Caught with vast quantities of uneaten hors d'oeuvres, the Iron Works donated them to hard-hit flood victims in Saco.

After a three-day delay, the *Drayton* was launched with appropriate pomp on 25 March. Attending dignitaries, who had arrived in Bath aboard a special sleeping car attached to the State of Maine Express, joined shipyard workers and other onlookers to witness the traditional bottle of champagne being broken across the sharp bow of the handsome warship. After an inevitable, momentary hush, the *Drayton* slid into the Kennebec to the festive accompaniment of tooting whistles, snapping pennants, and cheers from the assembled crowd.[2]

DESTROYER DRAYTON LAUNCHES FROM YARD OF BATH IRON WORKS

. . . The gift of the builders to Miss Barbara Drayton, sponsor [the thirteen-year-old great-great-niece of the destroyer's namesake], was a burnished copper card tray made from the plate from which the invitations were struck. She was also presented with a gold bracelet as a souvenir of the occasion.

. . . The sponsor looked natty in her navy costume of blue navy coat and navy blue skirt with stripes of white, and her tailored hat of navy blue that showed her becoming Dutch cut to advantage. She wore brown

MAINE MARITIME MUSEUM

> suede shoes and brown kid gloves, and carried a gorgeous bouquet of American Beauty Roses.
>
> For the first time in the history of launchings at the Bath Iron Works a loud speaker was set up in the launching stand. Not only did the assembled spectators have the opportunity of listening to the invocation . . . , but it enabled Pres. Newell to pass the word along in an audible voice when to release the destroyer. A second later and Miss Drayton smashed the bottle of wine . . . , and its foaming contents left a stain that proved to the crowd how well she had performed her duty.
>
> *BATH DAILY TIMES*, 26 MARCH 1936

If a *Drayton* VIP had had time to explore Bath before his Pullman car whisked him away, he would of course have noted the effects of the recent flood, and perhaps a few other distinctive aspects of the city. For example, flood or no flood, the Kennebec constituted an impressive body of water, about half a mile across at Long Reach, the tidal straightaway on whose west bank Bath was situated. The site and, from a distance, the city skyline were scenic in every season. But scenery had nothing to do with the city's location. Bath's side of Long Reach was deep and blessed with a sandy river bottom that made for good anchorage and a gently rising shoreline perfect for launching vessels. Small wonder that, in the eighteenth century, shipbuilding had taken hold here, especially with a ready timber supply growing right at hand.[3]

Shipbuilding and seafaring, in fact, had been the making of a vigorous, prosperous, and beautiful community. If, as was likely, a visiting dignitary knew something about shipbuilding, he would have been intrigued by reminders of Bath's maritime heyday. The city's rise to commercial importance had accelerated in the early nineteenth century. Between 1840 and 1850, its population had more than doubled, reaching 11,000. Meanwhile, Bath had acquired a look of conspicuous prosperity. Along the waterfront ran the noise and clutter of more than twenty shipyards.[4] Farther back from the water rose the status symbols of that productivity: huge, fashionable houses by the dozens, and hundreds of small, tidy homes whose architectural refinements distinguished Bath's blue-collar neighborhoods from those of most industrial towns. But the important symbols of well-being were seldom seen around town, for they were at sea. By the mid-1800s, about 500 commercial vessels were registered to the Bath customs district. A few years later, Bath's registered tonnage was fifth in the nation, behind New York, Boston, Philadelphia, and Baltimore.[5]

Growth was to prove that Bath's special locale was a mixed blessing. A very short distance from the water's edge, the shoreline sloped sharply upward to a series of stepped, north-south ridge lines that roughly paralleled the river. Thus, with its face to the river and its back against granite ledge, Bath had a tortuous history of construction, water, sewerage, and expansion problems. The longest thoroughfares—Washington, Middle, and High streets—ran along the ridge lines, connected by numerous cross streets that climbed and dipped. For the most part, the city was four blocks wide and four miles long; an ideal spot for shipyards but little else. For better or worse, it had to live with the consequences of its geographic uniqueness.

Bath's unique natural advantages diminished over time. As the wooden shipbuilding industry matured, its yards exhausted the ready timber supply, necessitating costly procurement of material from distant suppliers. Nonetheless, the city retained a competitive edge in wooden shipbuilding thanks to its pool of skilled, low-cost labor. But then, as changing technology and world trade patterns made iron and steel ships preferable to traditional vessels, Bath's know-how likewise lost its punch. Local shipbuilding was in serious decline by the late nineteenth century, and so was its handmaiden, shipping. Both were victims of aggressive foreign competition. A few city shipbuilders, seeing the writing on the wall, made the transition to steel construction (which was why, in 1936, a state-of-the-art warship such as the *Drayton* could be built on the Kennebec). Most yards simply folded. Entrepreneurial families invested their fortunes elsewhere.

Bath shipbuilding got a new lease on life during World War I, when demand for vessels of all types and sizes became ravenous. When the United States entered the war, Congress, alarmed at the woeful state of America's merchant marine, moved to revitalize it by commissioning literally billions of dollars worth of new vessels through a newly established Emergency Fleet Corporation. And, to alleviate the inevitable housing crunch in shipbuilding towns such as Bath, a United States Housing Corporation was created to erect instant neighborhoods for shipyard workers. All of this was very good news on the Kennebec. Thousands moved to Bath, and, in short order, the city took on the look and excitement of a boom town: traffic jams, tent communities, astronomical wages, round-the-clock production, and, for the duration of the emergency, almost superhuman effort. "The wartime state of mind is as impossible to reproduce by description as it would be for anyone who did not share it," wrote Colonel Henry Owen, Bath's official historian, in the 1930s. "People of all stations in life worked till they were ready to drop in war activities from which no personal advantage could possibly be derived, taking no thought of personal comfort, health or the abnormal demands of their private concerns."[6]

It didn't last. Hostilities ceased long before the mandated tonnage was completed, creating a peacetime glut of vessels that for years would discourage American merchant shipbuilding. The Bath waterfront once again grew quiet, the elaborate and still-new brick housing project at the city's North End became a drug on the market, and the wartime workers scattered to parts unknown. The Roaring Twenties did not roar in Bath. The city, in fact, had a substantial head start on the Great Depression, just around the corner. Meanwhile, World War I had forever changed the dynamics of Bath's kingpin industry. The Shipbuilding City's fortunes would henceforward be mortgaged not to the whims of international maritime commerce, but to the ups and downs of federal expenditure.[7] Few saw that reality, however, in the twenties or, especially, the thirties, when the despair of the Great Depression clouded all but the hardiest minds throughout the nation.

By 1936, Bath was a city whose legendary enterprise, wealth, and sophistication had fallen on very hard times, and a visiting dignitary could have read the signs everywhere. On Long Reach, where schooners, scows, square-riggers, and packet steamboats once participated in a daily, ever-changing parade, there was no commercial traffic except for an occasional collier or oil barge. The riverbank adjacent to the Bath Iron Works—the city's sole surviving shipyard—consisted mostly of rotting pilings or sagging, empty structures. Just north of the bridge lay the few square blocks that constituted Bath's downtown business section: a complex of narrow streets and aging, dignified, multistoried commercial structures, mostly brick, which (along with its trolley system) gave Bath a surprisingly urban char-

MAINE MARITIME MUSEUM

Looking north on Long Reach from the roof of the *Times* building. In the distance, a collier is unloading at the Coal Pocket.

MAINE MARITIME MUSEUM

Front Street at Lambard about 1936.

acter for so small a city. The two principal downtown streets were Front, running north and south parallel to the river, and Center, which ran perpendicular to the river. At the busy intersection of Front and Center streets was a small summit upon which stood the stately City Hall. From there, Center Street sloped down and up again for several blocks to another pinnacle topped by the Sagadahoc County Court House.

MAINE MARITIME MUSEUM

A few blocks north of the Carlton Bridge,
Maine Central locomotive 361 moves boxcars
along Commercial Street about 1941.

The downtown waterfront, once the scene of shipbuilding, steamboat landings, and, until recently, the Kennebec ferry slip, looked drab and worn. Its thoroughfare, Commercial Street, between Front Street and the Kennebec, ran for several blocks just a few yards from the river. Along Commercial stood an assortment of dingy industrial buildings dominated by the Kennebec Wharf and Coal Company (the "Coal Pocket"), at which visiting vessels discharged huge quantities of soft coal for local mills. Tracks of the Maine Central Railroad ran down Commercial Street to the Coal Pocket. Idle hopper cars, standing in the middle of Commercial Street waiting to load, were a common sight.

MAINE MARITIME MUSEUM

Looking north on Commercial Street. At left is the Torrey Roller Bushing Works.

A few woebegone buildings, leftovers from the maritime days, had been recycled. One was now a roller skating rink, another a plumbing supply firm. But any visitor would note the paint peeling from the walls of too many staring, vacant storefronts. Residential sections had a similar look; even some of the swank, old-money homes on upper Washington Street were having trouble keeping up appearances. In light of all this, the relative extravagance of the *Drayton* launching—Pullman cars, loudspeakers, hors d'oeuvres, and all—may have seemed frivolous.

It was not. The *Drayton*, in fact, was a floating symbol of two important national trends: the federal government's commitment to fight the Depression and President Franklin D. Roosevelt's almost singlehanded determination to rebuild the U.S. Navy. The *Drayton* was paid for not with the limited funds of the Navy Department, but with Public Works Adminis-

MAINE MARITIME MUSEUM

Looking west down Center Street from City Hall.

MAINE MARITIME MUSEUM

Looking east up Center Street toward City Hall.

tration monies, part of the New Deal's controversial program to put people back to work.[8] Uncle Sam would want more ships. Meanwhile, the U.S.S. *Lamson*, sister to the *Drayton*, was nearing completion at the Bath Iron Works. Having actually given up the ghost for a while during the twenties, BIW was back on its feet again, the best possible sign for the City of Bath.

Watching the *Drayton* slide into the Kennebec on that fine day in 1936, visiting dignitaries would have been aware of another symbol of possible better times: the eight-year-old Carlton Bridge looming over the launch site. Until it was built, rail and road traffic had had to traverse the Kennebec by ferry. Now, Route One was an unbroken ribbon linking Portland, nearby Brunswick, and Bath to such easterly towns as Wiscasset, Boothbay Harbor, and Rockland. Bath politicians and businessmen hoped that the bridge would establish their city as an attractive, convenient site for investors and shoppers on both sides of the river. There was even talk that Bath could become a tourist destination, although such talk seemed farfetched so long as the nationwide Depression ruled. But in 1936, for the first time, the license plates on Maine automobiles read "VACATIONLAND"; bridge traffic was picking up; and, hard times notwithstanding, cars and trucks were eclipsing other forms of transportation. Bath's trolley system was in financial trouble, as was the local Samoset Steamboat Company—the last, shrunken survivor of the packet-boat era. Few, however, could have foreseen the difference that automobiles soon would make in the quality of Maine life.

There was obviously room for optimism about Bath in early 1936, especially for the casual observer hearing such generalities as "New Deal" and "Vacationland." Full-time natives, however, had grounds to fret, for the city was reeling from years of economic hardship, groping with adversity on a day-to-day basis, without any organized plan. Bath's future, however it turned out, was in the hands of a small group of well-known citizens. Virtually all were male and were mutually acquainted. Some held elective office, some did not. Each was very influential. The differences and tensions among them were striking.

If Bath can be said to have had a local hero in 1936, that man was William S. (Pete) Newell, who had raised the Bath Iron Works from the dead and made it the city's biggest business. Newell, fifty-eight, clearly believed that what was good for his company was good for the community, and, by 1936, it began to look as though he might be right.

Although he was not a Bath boy—a point that was by no means trivial to natives—Newell had grown up close to the New England coast and its maritime industries. Interested in naval architecture, he had graduated from Massachusetts Institute of Technology in 1899, having meanwhile acquired on-the-job training at BIW. He joined the company full time in 1902.[9] His ability and personality earmarked him for a bright future. He became the protege of a corporate bigwig, and married a local girl, Caroline Moulton. By the early twenties, when American shipbuilding ran into trouble, he was BIW's works manager.

The Bath Iron Works seemed to have outlived its usefulness by 1920. The end of war contracts, the postwar shipping glut, and international agreements to limit the size of major navies painted a grim picture. With the last of its contracts completed and no new ones in sight, the company was unable to honor its obligations or devise a reorganization plan acceptable to its creditors. In August 1925, it delivered its last ship. In October of that year, it was sold for peanuts at public auction on the steps of the County Court House in Bath. The winning bidder was a New York junk dealer who scrapped out the yard and left the buildings empty.[10] When BIW fell silent, not a single Bath shipyard remained open. The future had never looked bleaker.

The losing bidder on that chilly October day had been Pete Newell, representing a small consortium of backers who felt that the company was worth saving. Newell had run out of funds just below the final bid, but he did not run out of confidence that, under new management—his own—BIW had the makings of future success. Here was an example of Newell's most formidable personal characteristics: boundless self-confidence and the unwavering determination to accomplish his objectives.

Another chance to pick up what was left of BIW appeared in 1927. This time Newell was successful, thanks to a triumvirate of investors: himself; Archibald Main, a Scottish-born naval architect with years of experience in British and American yards; and L. Eugene Thebeau of Bath, an agent of the Maine Central Railroad. Together they put up $25,000, which, after purchase, entitled them to 1,250 shares of preferred stock. Another $100,000 had been borrowed from the Henry Gielow Company, a New York naval architectural firm that intended to throw some yachtbuilding contracts to the reconstituted yard. As security, Gielow received 1,000 shares of preferred stock registered in the names of Newell, Main, and Thebeau. Small amounts of stock also went to such helpful individuals as Bath Mayor Charles Cahill, who agreed to a ten-year municipal tax rebate, and Walter Wyman, president of Central Maine Power.[11]

Newell's carefully assembled plan worked. The company refitted its empty buildings and went to work on Gielow's yacht contracts. Other contracts followed, and employment increased rapidly, with 122 on the payroll by early 1928. By the spring of 1929, the number had swollen to 500, and, a year later, there were 1,000 in the yard. Almost all of these employees lived in Bath, so it is easy to appreciate the local drama of BIW's recovery. In 1931, the company began to pay taxes to the city, despite its ten-year grace period. It also paid off the Gielow loan via credit memoranda for its yacht work.

Matters took an inevitable turn for the worse when the effects of the Great Depression reached Bath. Newell cut back drastically, keeping the ever-thinning ranks at work on whatever contracts he could find. By 1931, the company was surviving only because of massive layoffs; while a skeleton crew kept the fires going in the yard, the job situation in Bath became horrendous. At one desperate point, Newell needed a bank loan to meet his payroll. Bath's several banks were in better shape than most because of ultraconservative management, but, by the same token, they were not disposed to bail out shaky businesses. Newell approached the Bath Trust Company, onetime bank of the robber baron Charles Morse that had been rescued by its current president, Rupert Baxter. At times like these, Newell could be very persuasive. For his part, Baxter undoubtedly saw the dire consequences of a second BIW failure. He stuck his neck out and loaned Newell $50,000. As with the city's earlier tax rebate, that gesture would pay important dividends. Thus began a long, lucrative relationship between Bath Trust and BIW, during which Pete Newell became a director of that bank.[12] As of 1932, Newell was also president of the venerable Bath Savings Institution, a mutual savings bank.

MAINE MARITIME MUSEUM

Pete Newell displays his common touch at Bath Iron Works in 1937.

Meanwhile, the Newell team had resolved that BIW's only chance for survival lay in snagging Navy contracts. The timing was perfect for such a strategy, because, after a long, hard struggle, the U.S. Navy had received a congressional appropriation for new ship construction. BIW's size and capabilities dictated that it specialize in destroyers, a particularly cutthroat sector of defense contracting. Newell thus found himself pitted against bigger, more established yards that had solid Washington connections and a track record to match. Shaky BIW would have to convince the Navy, over competitors' propaganda to the contrary, that it could round up sufficient working capital to begin work on new destroyers. Or one destroyer.

The proposed contract required a credit line of $280,000—high finance, far beyond the range of local funding. With banks failing all over the nation, securing such credit was a formidable challenge even for a healthy company. But again, Newell was a determined man, and he was successful, an impressive measure of his reputation at that time. In late 1931, with no other work in sight, BIW was awarded a contract for one destroyer, the U.S.S. *Dewey*. Work on the vessel began after a forced ten-month hiatus in the yard.

That one destroyer contract was enough to inspire a parade up the entire length of Washington Street. It was also enough to put BIW on the naval map again and to secure its credit rating for future bids. Accordingly, in 1934, the company won a contract for two more vessels, the *Drayton* and the *Lamson*, both of which were nearing completion in early 1936. The company's backlog continued to rise, and there were more than 1,400 people at work in the yard by the end of that year.[13] In a town of 10,000, that meant that the worst of the Depression might be over.

Even as conditions improved, other financial events beyond its control threatened BIW. When the Depression deepened, the Gielow Company, undergoing hard times, had borrowed substantially from the Harriman National Bank in New York, pledging its BIW stock as security. The Harriman Bank never reopened after the federal Bank Holiday of March 1933, but its receivers put its BIW stock on the market. The stock was taken by Ross Judson, former president of Continental Motors, who sold some of it to a second party, Paul Buckley. Between them, Judson and Buckley then had a majority interest in BIW, but they deferred to Newell in management matters. In 1936, when it was clear that the company was on a firm footing, BIW recapitalized at $500,000, issuing new common stock at a one-to-sixty-five ratio for the old common and at a one-to-ten ratio for the old preferred, and went public.[14] Henceforward, the brightening future of the company was largely in the hands of Pete Newell and his managers.

Newell's resurrection of the shipbuilding industry was enough to ensure his influence in Bath. But it is important also to note the force of his personality. He was an extrovert, a master of the glad hand whose magnetism was undeniable. He was comfortable with people of any class and stood on no ceremony whatsoever. It is said he knew every BIW employee by name, and he often wandered about the yard, not to throw his weight around but to exchange ideas and pleasantries with his workers. A believer in a fair wage for a fair day's work, he rejected the widespread Depression practice of wage cuts, on the grounds that the working man was bearing too great a burden. He regarded unions with suspicion, but after they became a force at BIW, he accepted that fact and avoided adversarial relations.

Politically, Newell exhibited similar pragmatism. Though philosophically conservative, he was of course a major beneficiary of the New Deal. Accordingly, he cultivated a long list of helpful political contacts at the state and national level, with the help of BIW's corporate lawyer, John Carey, a Democrat who was influential in state party politics.[15] Newell supported candidates whose programs were closest to the interests of BIW, a policy that sometimes ran him afoul of Bath's predominantly Republican power structure. He also involved himself effectively in an endless series of civic and charitable causes. Since the inception in 1915 of the Bath Water District, a powerful municipal corporation independent of the city government, Newell had served continuously as a trustee. (Rupert Baxter, also a charter member, was another of the district's three trustees.)

Bath's peculiar topography made water supply a costly and difficult problem, so Newell's engineering talent had been vital to the Water District's success. For example, in 1938, the pipeline system that brought Bath its water from the east side of the Kennebec had to be repaired. When the work got underway, Newell went aboard the barge that was laying the pipe in the riverbed. Unable to satisfy himself about the underwater operation by talking to a diver, he took command of the situation, donned a suit and

HERBERT DOUGLAS; MAINE MARITIME MUSEUM

The Bath Water District lays new pipe under the Kennebec River in 1939.

helmet, and went down for a firsthand inspection. That dive did permanent damage to his hearing, but the pipeline was completed in due course.[16]

Newell's importance, however, led to accusations that he used his influence on the Water District and elsewhere to garner advantages for the Iron Works. And when, in 1940, the expanding company handily purchased a large tract of land belonging to the Water District, the transaction seemed to confirm his detractors' suspicions. A few months later, having declined to serve for another term as a district trustee, Newell saw to it that a hand-picked successor, BIW executive G. Baer Connard, filled his shoes.[17] For a man like Pete Newell, there was no real distinction between the health of Bath's biggest industry and taxpayer and that of the city itself. What was probably disturbing to his critics was that Newell had become Bath's most influential citizen without having to operate under the constraints that bound the city's elected officials. Another sticking point was the contrast between BIW's corporate performance and that of the city government.

Arthur Sewall began his second term as mayor of Bath with an inaugural address at the City Hall auditorium on a Monday night in March 1936. His speech revealed a public-spirited man outraged by the conditions he saw around him, but completely at a loss about how to improve them: "We must find out why it is that so many of our good people cannot earn a respectable living. I am convinced that something is wrong to have so many unemployed, both old and young. That is the real difficulty which faces us in this town and this country.

"We must use our influence to insist that this condition be overcome. . . . We are an important city in Maine and Maine certainly has influence in Washington. Washington will know what we are thinking and

MAINE MARITIME MUSEUM

Arthur Sewall, Bath's complex, intellectual mayor.

saying in this City of Bath. We have got to do some thinking and saying if we are going to control our destiny.

"This is a good world! The Lord has taught us how to make goods in vast quantities but we must have the wits to learn how to fairly distribute them.

"This is very different from the old days when we had hundreds of small businesses here in Bath. . . . In those days if a man lost his job there were several other jobs open to him and he did not have to be thrown out of employment and call on the city for help. There was a real balance of power in those days and the system was good.

"Please do not think I am a radical. I am only trying to attack this real problem from all angles, which is the first step towards its solution. I believe it is deeper than either the Republican or Democratic party and it is deeper than any local employer of labor.

" . . . On all sides there is much questioning going on; questioning of values, customs and standards. . . . "[18]

Sewall's frustrations are easy to understand. The mayor's job involved long hours of committee work, attention to financial detail, and, during the Depression, sticking to some very tough decisions as revenues fell and municipal services faltered. For all that, the city paid $400 a year. These conditions virtually dictated that the mayor be otherwise employed yet able to devote extraordinary amounts of time to his responsibility. Arthur Sewall was just such a man. Furthermore, he possessed other credentials well suited to small-town politics: a Yale education, a sense of public responsibility, and social prominence.

The Sewall name was magic in Bath. Arthur's forebears had enjoyed a worldwide reputation throughout the nineteenth century as owners and managers of a shipbuilding and shipping empire. Arthur M., the mayor's grandfather, had capped a successful career by serving, in 1896, as presidential candidate William Jennings Bryan's running mate. Sumner, the mayor's outgoing and charismatic younger brother, had been a fighter ace during World War I and a member of the postwar Lost Generation before settling down to manage his share of the family fortune and pursue an auspicious political career at the city and state level. In 1936, Sumner was a member of the Maine Senate, with greater things to come. Arthur's reflective, retiring personality contrasted sharply with Sumner's sociability, and it was a family joke that if the intellect of the former could be merged with the dynamism of the latter, the ultimate political candidate would result.[19]

After a brief, unhappy career as a Chicago bond salesman, Arthur had returned home to operate a dairy farm in the relative wilds of North Bath, but a heart ailment forced him to seek more sedentary work. Thus, still on the sunny side of middle age, he became president of the Bath National Bank ("The Sewall Bank"). His involvement with city politics was probably predicated on three factors: Christian devotion, which caused him to agonize over economic and social injustice; noblesse oblige, which made him somewhat self-conscious about the advantages he enjoyed; and the conviction that the world was on the verge of fundamental change. Like most Bath voters (and unlike his illustrious grandfather), Sewall was a registered Republican. But study and observation had convinced him that capitalism had widened the gap between rich and poor. That system, he maintained—in private, of course—had outlived its time, as the injustices of the Great Depression made clear. The future must necessarily be more socialistic.[20] Hardly a conventional outlook for a New England bank president, to say nothing of a Republican mayor. In public life, Sewall was inclined to favor causes that improved the condition of the poor and underprivileged. There were plenty of those around Bath in 1936, but not much with which to help them.

Sewall presided over a bicameral city government that met monthly. There were seven wards in the city, each of which elected one alderman and three councilmen. All aldermen, councilmen, and the mayor were elected on an annual basis. The principle of this system, which dated back to Bath's original 1847 city charter, was to make government responsive to the wishes of its constituents. Because neither aldermen nor councilmen received compensation for their service, they were presumed to be motivated toward community service and willing to meet their responsibilities on a moonlighting basis. The mayor chaired the Board of Aldermen but voted only in the event of a deadlock on the board. Councilmen elected one of their own to preside over the Common Council.

Like most city governments, Bath's was concerned primarily with deciding policy and budget for various departmental services, including schools, fire and police protection, roads, sewerage, parks, and relief for the poor. Policy proposals could originate in either house, but because both the Board of Aldermen and the Common Council had veto power, consensus on any matter was essential. City services were carried out by various departments whose performance, needs, and budgets were overseen by appropriate committees of aldermen and councilmen, meeting as often as was necessary to manage their affairs. Practically speaking, committee work usually meant long evening sessions every week. The mayor, first among equals, was a member of all committees. He also represented the city as a ceremonial dignitary.

The Bath city government derived the greatest portion of its revenue from real and personal property taxes levied upon its citizens. Consequently, it had to strike a balance between the community's needs and the taxes it could collect to fund them. The Great Depression had of course ravaged both the tax base and the city's services, a circumstance that must have been particularly galling to a man of Sewall's humanitarian inclinations.

While the Depression was a crisis that politicians and bureaucrats everywhere had to cope with, Bath had another long-term problem: a colossal public debt that bled off revenues and thereby reduced public services. The problem dated back to 1867. Bath had been hard-hit by the Civil War, which was ruinous to shipping. In search of alternative sources of prosperity, the city bought into a postwar plan to construct a coastal railroad, the Knox & Lincoln, taking stock in the proposed venture and lending its credit as well. The venture proved disastrous for Bath. The cost of blasting a right-of-way through granite ledge proved astronomical, and subsequent rail traffic was light. By 1884, Bath's railroad obligations had generated the highest per capita debt of any American city. When, a few years later, the Maine Central Railroad bought the Knox & Lincoln, Bath recouped about half of its investment, but the rest of the debt was to plague the city fathers for generations. By 1900, interest payments alone had cost the city $1 million.[21]

Over time, some progress was made toward reducing the debt, but in 1936, Bath was still five years away from an organized plan for its reduction and twenty-five years away from its elimination. Meanwhile, the burden had had two effects: It reduced the funds available for needed city services, and it served as an object lesson on the pitfalls of municipal indebtedness. It is not an exaggeration to say that many aldermen, councilmen, mayors, and influential taxpayers in Bath were haunted by the specter of the Knox & Lincoln fiasco.

More indebtedness could not be avoided, however. For years, Bath had frugally postponed replacement of its inadequate, century-old City Hall. But in 1928, it accepted a gift of land and $10,000, left to the city by wealthy philanthropist George Davenport, who had earmarked the gift for construction of a City Hall in memory of his father. Even with further assistance from the Davenport Fund, a trust the late benefactor had also established for charitable purposes, and monies already set aside by the city fathers, a new City Hall would cost many times the available resources; and the late twenties were hardly boom times in Bath. But the commanding location of the bequeathed lot on Front and Center streets was too good to resist. Accordingly, the city floated a substantial bond issue to build its new City Hall. The completed building was spacious, dignified, and architecturally harmonious right up to its gilded belfry in which was ensconced the "Paul Revere Bell," a municipal heirloom believed to have been cast at the illustrious Midnight Rider's foundry in 1803. But the building's completion had saddled Bath with more bonded debt.

In March 1928, just after the city fathers had resolved to build the City Hall, Morse High School burned, a total loss. The structure, a gift to his hometown from Charles W. Morse, the celebrated "Ice King," steamship magnate, and notorious bank manipulator, had been built in grand style and had rightly become an important source of school spirit and civic pride. The city, of course, could not flinch at the prospect of replacing a vanished high school. The building was immediately rebuilt in the manner to which Bath had become accustomed, but reconstruction had to be financed in part by still another bond issue. And over it all loomed Knox & Lincoln. Thus, by the early 1930s, the principles of debt reduction and debt avoidance were chiseled in stone.

A second, corollary principle held sway at City Hall: The tax rate must be kept as low as possible. Bath was primarily a Republican stronghold, where conservative fiscal policy had a good name. In addition, the political system was such as to encourage political activism and public service among the leading property owners: those who had the wherewithal to hold office, but who naturally would be predisposed against higher taxes. But the clincher was the Depression. It was simply not feasible in hard times to raise taxes, even though the need for public welfare was growing alarmingly in the city. Bath was full of small householders who could ill afford any great tax increase. It was also full of old, unrentable structures whose owners would regard them as not worth keeping if the tax bite increased. Most of Bath's structures were more than eighty years old, and, during the Depression, dozens were indeed torn down to avoid paying taxes.[22] In other cases, when the city took title to properties in tax default, it found itself the proprietor of unsalable real estate even as its tax base shrank. Harry Webber, editor of the *Bath Daily Times*, summed up the two principles of debt reduction and tax restraint early in 1934: "There is no question but that Bath must continue to run along economical lines for a year or two longer to get its debt reduced to a point where it should be, to attain a reduction in the tax rate and to get as great efficiency as possible for a minimum expense."[23]

Although Bath had not had an easy time of it during the twenties, the city government had stayed healthy. Expenditures did not exceed revenues; taxes, although on the rise, were low; and the rate of collection was high, averaging over 98 percent.[24] The apparent reason for this anomaly was that while Bath shipbuilding had almost ceased, Bath workers were able to find employment at more distant yards such as Quincy, Massachusetts, where the aircraft carriers *Lexington* and *Saratoga* were abuilding. Men so employed left their families at home, but, on an absentee basis, paid their taxes, sustained Bath merchants, and kept their children in local schools.

Many of these workers returned to Bath in 1928 and 1929, when the revitalized Bath Iron Works started hiring. Then the Depression clamped down hard. When BIW's business grew thin again, they were laid off, but this time there were few job opportunities elsewhere. By 1931, the city was operating $31,770 in the red, over and above its bonded debt.

The source of this operating debt was an increased expenditure for welfare purposes—much of it in public works under the title of "needy poor employment." There was, of course, no national system of unemployment compensation at the time, and Maine's needy poor were the responsibility of each municipality. Able-bodied welfare recipients were expected to do municipal work in return for their relief checks. Bath could receive reimbursement only if it could prove that a specific recipient was another town's responsibility or a charge of the state.

The welfare list lengthened along with the Depression, putting a huge burden on Bath's resources. Taxes rose slowly but did not keep pace. Neither did the collection rate, which dropped to 87 percent. The city was completely at the mercy of economic forces beyond its reach. Throughout the crisis, city fathers kept watch for light at the end of the tunnel. In early 1934, for example, Mayor Harold Small put on a bright face by announcing: "All cities for the past four years have been laboring under the same conditions as Bath with tax collections decreasing and poor department expenditures increasing. . . . But I feel we have weathered the storm very nicely and conditions are going to improve."[25]

The city fathers managed by cutting other expenditures such as education. In 1930–31, the school budget had been $112,056; five years later, it was down to $81,000, principally because of a reduction in teachers' salaries.[26] Policemen's vacation benefits were withheld. Other city employees' salaries were cut an average of 10 percent by 1936. How long could deteriorating roads, schools, and other public facilities hold up? Because Bath was reaching its legal debt limit, further bond issues were out of the question. During the 1935–36 fiscal year, Bath spent $78,538 on relief—more than $600,000 in 1986 dollars.

The Roosevelt administration's New Deal offered some forms of welfare assistance to struggling municipalities. Bath, however, missed out on the first of these, because they were in the form of grants, repayable at some future date. The city's fear of incurring further debt caused it to reject such assistance, despite assurances from state officials that Uncle Sam would almost certainly cancel the debt, as in fact happened.[27] Furthermore, among Bath's conservative elite, the paternalistic Roosevelt was usually seen as a traitor to his class and his programs as dangerously socialistic.[28] Displeasure with the New Deal was by no means confined to the upper crust. In 1934, though they labored in the city's one economic oasis, BIW workers protested federal labor regulations that limited their wages and working hours while Uncle Sam provided public works jobs for the unemployed. According to the *Times*, there were even rumblings of a strike. " 'We can't make a living wage,' said one workman. 'With destroyers under construction we are limited to 32 hours a week and our pay envelope won't begin to meet the demand of the butcher, baker and others.' This man was particularly incensed because he said he knew of men whom, under the Public Works Administration, are receiving a third more than he per week."[29]

Inevitably, hard times wore down Bath people's scruples about federal assistance. A branch of the National Re-Employment Office that had opened in Bath in September 1933 handled 1,900 job applications in the first six months of its operation.[30] Bath accepted help. By early 1934, the Civil Works Administration had 240 local people refurbishing schools, streets, and recreational facilities at Kelley Field, all on a short-term basis. It was enough to tide many families over, as one workman told the *Times*: " 'This has been a godsend to me. I hadn't worked for seven months and I hadn't taken aid from the city though I've a family of four depending on me. I'm behind but if this keeps up I'll get even with the world.' " The *Times*, no friend of the New Deal, admitted that "The C.W.A. has not put all the unemployed back to work. It probably won't. But it has temporarily staved off a mighty desperate situation in the City of Bath."[31] The desperate situation still had a long way to go, as Mayor Sewall's 1936 speech made

MAINE MARITIME MUSEUM

clear; but in the presidential election of that year, Republican Bath went for FDR.

Where could job-seekers find work in private industry? Although by 1936 the Iron Works was by far the largest employer in the region, the Shipbuilding City contained two other important industrial plants, the Hyde Windlass Company and the Torrey Roller Bushing Works. Both were venerable, family-owned concerns. Hyde, a corporate spinoff of the old BIW, was located on Washington Street just south of the Iron Works, where it manufactured precision deck equipment. Linwood Temple, who grew up nearby, recalled that the firm's reputation for high quality was "famous all over the world for . . . deck machinery and propellers. . . . I can remember in the early days when I was a youngster, you could walk down onto Washington Street from Hinckley Street and look up . . . , and there was a brass foundry going full blast: the greenish-blue-brown smoke coming out of the thing. . . . There were some good machinists there. They did good work."[32]

Torrey Roller Bushing, located in a Dickensian plant behind City Hall that backed onto Commercial Street on the downtown waterfront, was also a producer of specialized castings, some with marine applications. Like the Iron Works, Hyde and Torrey had been sensitive to the ups and downs of American maritime policy. But, unlike BIW, they had not shared much in the business upswing stimulated by the New Deal. Their employees were a small number of skilled specialists with long service records. Hyde and Torrey squeaked through the Depression by reducing their work force as needed.

Two other industries employed less-skilled workers. One was the Bath Box Company, operating out of a complex of rather large, flimsy-looking structures on the Kennebec shore below BIW and Hyde. Each summer and fall, the buildings were surrounded by millions of feet of timber barged downriver to the site. Marginally profitable, the firm sawed logs into boxboards and a few other basic wood products. Bath Box was a subsidiary of a Connecticut company, but it was managed by a member of the owning family, James Gillies, Jr., a Bath resident. According to Jim Temple (Linwood's older brother), whose father operated the company's towboat, "a good many people who lived in Bath worked at one time or another at the box company. . . . When a person got laid off at the Iron Works or Hyde Windlass, . . . or if they came home from working in some other shipyard, . . . they could come to the box company and earn enough, though wages were low, to keep bread on the table and to support their families. It was a sort of unemployment insurance at the time."[33]

The Congress Shirt Company, a maker of men's shirts, was situated in an old shoe-factory building on Middle Street in the downtown area. Most of its employees were women, an important fact in times when the male work force was suffering a severe job crunch. Congress Shirt, furthermore, was doing well enough in 1936 to contemplate expansion, a development that afforded the Sewall administration a chance to practice a little New Deal assistance of its own.

Learning that Congress Shirt intended to create about thirty new jobs if it could expand economically, City Council voted to take down a building at the old Kelley & Spear shipyard, a city-owned property, and move it at municipal expense to Middle Street, where Congress Shirt could lease it at advantageous terms. The expense was deemed a good long-term investment. The plan worked, and by 1937 Congress Shirt was contemplating still more expansion.[34] The city was also resourceful in finding other sources of revenue: It negotiated a lease of the Kelley & Spear yard to the Pejepscot Paper Company, and sold the old City Hall building on Center Street between Front and Water streets, vacant for nine years, for commercial purposes.[35] Late in 1936, W. T. Grant Co. opened for business near the former City Hall site. A new downtown department store was a sure sign that times were indeed changing for the better.

Meanwhile, the Sewall administration had assumed a more liberal view of Bath's financial management, deciding to go ahead with overdue municipal repairs. That meant that the city's operating debt was not eliminated and that its unpaid bills were transferred to the next year's budget as a "floating debt," a term it used to distinguish the overage from the dreaded bonded debt. The policy was, to say the least, controversial.

In March of 1938, after three consecutive terms, Arthur Sewall's place as mayor was taken by a fellow Republican, Donald N. Small, a former alderman.

Until the late thirties, the Republican majority in Bath was overwhelming. As Linwood Temple, who grew up in a diehard Democratic household,

MAINE MARITIME MUSEUM

Donald Small.

put it, "If you ran a dog as a Republican he would get elected."[36] A local joke had been that the Democrats could hold their municipal caucus in a telephone booth. But the New Deal and the resurgence of the Bath Iron Works had changed all that. For one thing, members of Bath's traditional power structure, such as Arthur Sewall and Donald Small, had grown wary of BIW's increasing influence over everyday affairs, which undoubtedly skewed Pete Newell and his cohorts, conservatives and otherwise, toward the opposition.

That anomaly confused the once-simple choices for members of both parties. Recalling those times, Linwood Temple described "sitting in the kitchen and watching them go through the ward lists and . . . the conversation was going, 'Well, that damn Bath Iron Works is going to run this election again.' That was the kind of conversation that went on. I don't think it was [because of] the management at BIW. I think it was because that was the largest employment in the city and the people there were a number of well-educated, prominent, and interested people. They wanted to run the city government, so they'd run on their own."[37]

The best example of a company man running on his own was Donald Small, Arthur Sewall's chosen replacement, who was a BIW draftsman. Like Sewall, Small was eager to preserve the city government's invulnerability to outside influence of any type. In 1938, however, mayoral candidate Small was surprised to find himself challenged by Archie Main, Pete Newell's partner in the historic BIW purchase and the company's general manager. Furthermore, Main was a registered Republican running as a Democrat. The meaning of all this was not wasted on Small. In March, he defeated Main by 508 votes after 3,240 voters—the largest turnout in Bath history—went to the polls.[38]

Donald Small, like Arthur Sewall, was a complex individual who worked because he wanted to, not because he had to. The Smalls were another of Bath's old-money families. Donald's father, the late Frank, had been a partner in the Percy & Small shipyard, Bath's last builder of wooden sailing vessels, and had served as mayor of Bath from 1911 to 1913. A boyhood accident had deprived Donald of the use of one eye, a handicap that made his work strenuous. Outspoken, mercurial, moralistic, and eager to change Bath for the better, Small, at age thirty-four, was more of a hard-nosed conservative than his intellectual predecessor. He was also a hard-nosed opponent of the endemic backscratching of local politics. His one-year administration was marked by a reduction of the city debt without any increase in the 45 mill tax rate, and by a concerted attempt to put local government on a professional basis.

During the early thirties, some city fathers had debated how to reform Bath's 1847 city charter. By 1939, the quirks of that charter were becoming difficult to overlook. The system had worked well in its day, but, its critics insisted, it simply did not meet the needs of twentieth-century administration, legal requirements, federal assistance programs, and financial demands. Furthermore, in a city of only 10,000, the bicameral system seemed needlessly ponderous. It was definitely controversial.

Bicameralism overpopulated the City Council, generating red tape and debate over the most basic issues. For example, every bill presented to the city had to be reviewed and approved by the Accounts Committee before payment. The charter included no civil service criteria for city employees, thus inviting local bigshots to promote their cronies for office regardless of qualifications. In the troubled thirties, as problems and budgets increased, there had been melodramatic battles in City Council over such appointments, during which personal animosities had flared.[39] Meanwhile, the preeminence of the Iron Works—by far the city's biggest taxpayer and a natural source of political talent—had heightened fears that the entire system might be dogged by factionalism between the company's proponents and their opponents.

Reformers insisted that the city government had to be insulated from partisanship. To accomplish this, they advocated the elimination of the mayor's office in favor of a full-time salaried manager, appointed by City Council, who would enjoy administrative control over municipal departments; coordinate their needs into a coherent, consistent budget; negotiate contracts on a competitive basis; and bring professional expertise to his responsibilities. The city manager system had been employed with good effect in many American cities, large and small. Its attractions were its impartiality, year-to-year consistency, and financial efficiency, which would help in restraining the tax rate.

Mayor Small had no interest in perpetuating his office. During 1938, he, former mayor Harold Small (now an alderman), and other City Council colleagues formulated a plan for a new charter based upon the city manager concept. The plan also included eliminating the bicameral system in favor of a body of five to seven representatives elected for staggered terms not by wards but by the city at large. Each representative would be paid $300 per year for his services. A second significant step toward professionalism was a proposal to establish a police commission that would maintain civil service standards in that department. During the discussion of proposed reforms in the Bath City Council, Small stressed that it was time to replace political methods with business methods.[40]

But to people unwedded to the idea of running government like a business, the proposed revisions looked undemocratic, even dangerous. Bowing to what they said was negative public opinion, most City Council members opposed the police proposal in January 1939. One alderman reportedly explained that the proposed police commission "looked to him more like putting the department into politics instead of removing it from same. He continued by alluding to the Bath Water District, controlled by three men and said 'many citizens objected.' "[41] Shortly afterward, the Board of Aldermen declined further discussion of charter reform, citing public objection to monetary compensation for Council service.

But the reformers were not to be denied. Harold Small persuaded Justus Miller, Bath's representative in Augusta, to present the proposals to the Legislature. There Sumner Sewall, now president of the Maine Senate, added his good offices, saying that the police revision "would help take the Police Department out of Politics."[42] The Legislature approved them, and they were added to a list of referendum issues to be voted on in September 1939. Donald Small, meanwhile, did not run for a second term as mayor, choosing instead to campaign successfully for alderman. His successor in the mayor's office was Arthur Sewall, who defeated BIW employee Robert Haskell in March.

Over the next few months, the pros and cons of charter reform were debated; but, as the *Times* reported with some satisfaction, the advocates of change were unable to arouse much sympathy.[43] In early September, on the eve of the referendum, fierce campaigning by members of the police department, along with considerable name-calling, likewise failed to generate much interest. Less than half of the electorate bothered to vote in the referendum. Those who did trounced the charter reforms. The idea of modernizing Bath's government was not going to go away, but clearly, interested citizens preferred the tried-and-true system, for all its shortcomings, to a streamlined, "businesslike" approach to politics.

The flap over charter reform was not simply a matter of political dialogue, but the product of personal animosities that were hard to hide in a spot as small as Bath; in fact, they were a constant source of material for the grapevine that sustained the city's hyperactive rumor mill. While not officially acknowledged, and seldom covered by the local press, they were a vital component of municipal affairs, and must therefore be included in any serious historical analysis. For example, these animosities had much to do with splitting the Republican establishment in 1939.

In 1987, John Morse, Jr., recalled a story he heard Pete Newell tell at a party at least fifty years earlier. According to Newell, BIW had just hired a man who had worked for Arthur Sewall. Why? "Mr. Newell commented . . . the guy found out he could make more money working in the Iron Works sweeping up horse buns out in the yard than he could working for Arthur Sewall. That pleased him no end!"[44]

In the close-knit social world of white-collar Bath, a story like that one might make the rounds until it became common knowledge. As far as Pete Newell and Arthur Sewall were concerned, it was also common knowledge that, while they remained friendly, they were philosophical and political adversaries. Sewall's suspicions about big business made him wary of a company interested in favorable property valuations, taxes, water rates, and the like, and able to use political clout to secure them. As Morse put it, Sewall "couldn't abide the fact that the Iron Works, because . . . they were creating jobs and boosting the economy in town when the rest of the state was in desperate straits . . . , were given preferential treatment in some minor regard."[45] Sewall's position, however, was neither popular nor very practical in the late thirties.

The Sewall-Newell standoff went back several years at least, and probably came to a head in 1933, when the defunct Harriman Bank's BIW stock was put up for sale for $200,000. Sewall's bank, Bath National, had considered the purchase. Should it take the plunge? During the discussion of pros and cons, John Morse, Sr., a Bath National director, pointed out that if Arthur Sewall's bank got a controlling interest in BIW, Pete Newell would almost surely leave.[46] Bath National paid Newell a colossal if indirect compliment by turning down the stock. That moment's historical alternatives doubtless aroused much "what if . . . ?" debate among local insiders.

The interplay of diverse personalities occasionally emerged from backstage into the spotlight, as in the case of the vest-pocket vendetta between Donald Small and Rupert Baxter.

In addition to his presidency of Bath Trust, Rupert H. Baxter, age sixty-eight, was a former president of the Maine Senate, a state GOP committeeman from Sagadahoc County, and a charter trustee of the Bath Water District. (He was also the brother of former governor Percival Baxter, Maine's grandest philanthropist at the time.) Around Bath, Baxter was Mr. Republican and a local kingmaker, shunning the limelight but enjoying immense influence as he pursued his own agenda. Take, for example, the time Bath Trust bailed the Iron Works out of its financial tight spot. Years later, Baxter's nephew by marriage, Bill Mussenden, whose father was treasurer of Bath Trust, recalled the story: "I guess you might say that saved the Iron Works. . . . The bank examiners, the next time they came around, criticized Rupert Baxter very heavily for making that kind of loan under those conditions, and Rupert told them to go to hell, nobody was going to tell him who he was loaning money to, if you don't like it, lump it!"[47]

But when Donald Small decided to run for mayor, Baxter was in a tight spot of his own. Small was a director of Bath Trust. So was Archie Main, who was running against him. As Mussenden recalled, "Poor old Rupert was in a bind, between a rock and a hard place. Who was he going to support, being a natural-born politician? He had to support somebody, and he opted for Archie Main. Don Small was furious. He resigned from the board, he drew his money out of the bank, and that was the beginning . . . of the Baxter-Small rift."[48] But it was not the end.

A credible but unsubstantiable story suggests that Baxter's decision might not have been too difficult to make. Baxter, who always operated on a quid pro quo basis, had earlier assisted Small, only to find that his help was unreciprocated when needed.[49] In any event, Small won the election without Baxter's influence, exposing a gap in the ranks of Bath Republicans.

Whether or not Baxter's influence played a role in defeating the Small administration's attempt at charter reform is not known. Whatever the case, Small opted out of the mayor's office in 1939 but won an alderman's seat. In October 1939, Baxter's trusteeship on the Bath Water District expired and he stood for reelection to that post by the Board of Aldermen. That generated a furor in which "Rupie" (as Small liked to call Baxter) and "That One-eyed Bastard" (to use Baxter's reciprocal endearment) squared off.[50]

In any year, the Water District was a touchy political subject for several reasons. Bath's peculiar geography being what it was, the city's water needs were the most expensive to supply in the state, a circumstance that was reflected in high rates. That alone would have been enough to cause grousing; but, in addition, the water rates were uneven. Customers could opt for metered or flat rates, the latter being advantageous to large users such as BIW. It is thus easy to see how Pete Newell's and Rupert Baxter's long-term trusteeships raised eyebrows. Moreover, because it was a separate, self-financing municipal corporation, the district's policies and decisions were out of range of the city fathers, some of whom characterized its trustees as high-handed and arrogant, despite the benefits of their political pull (as when they obtained federal funding assistance to replace the pipe under the Kennebec). Criticism of the Water District was an irresistible way to cut Pete Newell and Rupert Baxter down to size. Baxter especially, because, unlike Newell, he was not a public hero.

One night in October 1939, the Board of Aldermen met to vote on Baxter's vacant Water District seat. When Mayor Sewall opened the floor for discussion, what followed was so extraordinary that the usually discreet *Times* reported it in detail: "It was at this moment that Alderman Small asked permission to speak. 'It has come to my attention,' said he, 'that the rumor has been spread about town that a group of irresponsible young politicians is trying to upset the Bath Water District. No suggestion has ever been made that I would support Mr. Baxter, however. I think I can speak for the group that opposes Mr. Baxter's re-election that it hasn't the slightest idea of disturbing the water district or of any of its employees, but this group will continue until Baxterism in the water district is wiped out. I can't see where Mr. Baxter has helped the City of Bath except when he has been personally interested. Last year there were rumors that he was going to move to Topsham. Then he received a tax reduction. . . . A short time ago Chamberlain said Hitlerism must be driven out of Europe and I say that every vestige of Baxterism must be driven out of the City of Bath.' "[51]

Inasmuch as Small's remarks occurred less than five weeks after the German blitzkrieg on Poland, the reference to Hitler packed an explosive wallop all its own. Baxter's defenders responded in kind; then the six attending aldermen voted. They produced a three-to-three tie. At such times, the mayor was required to break the deadlock. Jim Temple, one of the aldermen present, recalled that "We forced Mr. Sewall to take sides, but he was reluctant to do so. But he voted against Rupert Baxter, and that was one of the reasons he didn't get reelected the next year."[52] County Commissioner Roscoe Bailey was elected to the Water District, ending Baxter's twenty-five years of service thereon.

The story, of course, was not over, as the municipal elections a few months later revealed. In early 1940, running for his fifth term as mayor, Arthur Sewall was again opposed by Robert Haskell. In the various wards, councilman and alderman slots were contested by a surprisingly numerous array of BIW employees. The strident campaign was a showdown between BIW and its detractors, between old-line and maverick Republicans, between the local GOP and a Democratic party invigorated by the New Deal. It also settled a few personal scores.

What further distinguished the 1940 campaign from its predecessors was a public display of personal sharpshooting. It was as if Small's published excoriation of Baxter—a breach of accepted etiquette and a political mistake to boot—had abolished the genteel politicking of previous years. This campaign went into overtime. So did the rumor mill. The *Times*, dutifully reporting every news plant and rumor, became a chatterbox of confusing items.

Campaigners and rumor-mongers alike (who in some cases were identical) dealt mostly with the smoldering issue of the incumbent government's reputed hostility to BIW, especially Mayor Sewall's alleged intent to raise BIW's tax assessment, a measure that would ostensibly have impaired the company's ability to bid competitively for new contracts. Item: BIW workers, worried about potential layoffs, were concerned with "installing a mayor, and city government, ready to cooperate with the shipbuilding firm making it possible to keep fixed charges down and enter the commercial market with bids that may be productive of contracts."[53] (Translated from *Times* journalese, that meant that BIW sought a city government prepared to keep taxes low so that the firm could bid competitively.) Item: In late February, the Republicans appointed an antigossip committee to offset the growing "whispering campaign."[54] Item: Donald Small publicly denied rumors that he was a candidate for Pete Newell's seat on the Water District board. (Newell was irreplaceable, said Small.)[55]

As Election Day drew near, the embattled Sewall took out an advertisement in the *Times* to squelch rumors of his hostility to BIW: "NOTHING COULD BE FURTHER FROM MY MIND."[56] Two days before the election, however, a Democratic notice in the *Times* proclaimed meaningfully that Pete Newell had come out for Haskell.[57]

Why had Newell permitted his name to be used for political purposes? The answer came on Election Day, only hours before the polls closed, when the Democrats breathlessly announced that, far from remaining aloof, the mayor had pressed city and state assessors to raise BIW's tax valuation. "Why, at the eleventh hour, did Mayor Sewall misrepresent these facts?"

asked a political advertisement in the *Times*. "Was it because Pres. William S. Newell of the Bath Iron Works had informed officials that if the shipyard tax were boosted it might injure their chances of obtaining destroyer contracts last May?. . . . Are You Going to Vote for a Man Who Is Definitely On Record as Trying to Stifle Bath's Major Industry?"[58] Perhaps taking a cue from Small's Baxterism remarks, the advertisement also pointed out that Sewall had simultaneously applied for a lower valuation for his farm.

Meanwhile, and despite the improving economy, Bath's major public issue was still the city's debt versus the city's needs. There was bipartisan agreement that Bath's debt situation was unacceptable. Democrats, however, charged that years of Republican administration had prolonged the city's financial crisis; Republicans countered that much of the city's debt—the City Hall and high school bonds—had been incurred in 1928, during the last Democratic regime.[59] Sewall stood on his administration's record of moderate debt reduction with no recent tax increase; Haskell said he could do much better. All of which sounded like old times, except that Sewall was up against more formidable foes than Haskell.

Part of the debate over city finances stemmed from the fact that they were inconsistently itemized from year to year, and therefore hard to analyze. There was no evidence of deliberate malfeasance. Confusion stemmed from such quirks as the time lag between a transaction and the processing of its paperwork, or the prorating of purchases over future years, a practice that was in fact illegal. Another bone of contention was the separation of bonded debt from floating debt, a bookkeeping device that conservatives denounced as City Hall eyewash. For example, the 1939–40 Sewall administration reported that it had reduced Bath's vaunted bonded debt by almost $14,000, a figure that lost some of its punch beside a concurrent floating debt increase of almost $4,500. In the words of Rupert Baxter, "a debt is a debt in whatever form."[60]

The debt issue got so muddled that, at the *Times*'s request for clarification, Sewall published a thumbnail rundown of his administration's finances, indicating that the city's total debt was $441,728, about $9,557 less than the year earlier. The mayor reminded citizens that the small overall reduction had been accomplished without raising the tax rate or valuations, "nor did the government make any large cuts in appropriations of the various departments. If one or the other had been done, we would have made a bigger reduction in the debt. I am of the opinion that next year's government will follow along the same general rules."[61]

But the opposition continued to make an issue of the floating debt's growth, prompting Sewall to publish a last-minute statement assuring voters that, all debts considered, Bath was safely below its statutory debt limit. It was probably fortunate for Sewall that this statement appeared in the *Times* on Election Day; any earlier and it would have been a disaster, for it revealed an astonishing arithmetical mistake. As itemized in Sewall's very brief advertisement, Bath's combined debt was $541,000, not $441,000 as erroneously totaled.[62] How many voters caught the mistake in the few hours between its publication and the closing of the polls is impossible to say, but its message that Bath's finances were in good hands would have backfired for any critic who could add.

Rupert Baxter could add. And he could write. In the wake of the recent discord between himself and other maverick Republicans, his letter to the *Times* in the election's aftermath must have seemed like poetic justice. Sewall's varying figures, said Baxter, were an attempt to "confuse the citizens. . . . For many years I have sought to learn the true financial condition but without results. Figures given me have not told the story and are so involved that only an expert could understand them. I would like a true and honest picture of the financial condition of the city—one that can be read and understood by the taxpayers, who are obliged to pay the bills. I would further recommend that partizan [sic] politics be adjourned and that the incoming administration set the house in order."[63]

Meanwhile, Robert Haskell, who in 1939 had lost to Sewall by 230 votes, had won the mayoralty race by a margin of 121. The Democrats, furthermore, could now claim three aldermen and six councilmen (plus one of each who had run on both tickets). The mayor and half of the City Council were BIW employees.

Analyzing the 1940 city election, *Times* editor Harry Webber affirmed that Bath's Democratic surge was not merely a reflection of the nation's trend in that direction. In Bath, he said, there was "no question but that a portion of the Democratic success was due to Republicans who either voted the Democratic ticket or failed to go to the polls to support their own party candidates."[64] His point was confirmed a few weeks later, when Pete Newell announced formation of a "Sewall for Governor Club," dedicated to assuring local support for the charismatic Sumner Sewall's Republican gubernatorial candidacy. Assisting Newell as vice presidents in the club were the heads of Bath's biggest businesses: Rodney Ross (Hyde Windlass), Bowen Torrey (Torrey Roller Bushing), James Gillies, Jr. (Bath Box), Arthur Price (Congress Shirt), and N. Sherman McQuade (Commercial Trading Company, a clothing manufacturer). Topping the list of the club's members was the name of the Honorable Rupert H. Baxter; also on board was Frank Nichols, publisher of the *Times*.[65] Incidentally, Sumner Sewall won the governorship in the November elections. At that time, Bath voters again declared for FDR.

In reviewing the city election, something else bothered editor Webber: the prominence of BIW as a political issue. He conceded that new city fathers employed by BIW could probably be expected to discharge their responsibilities with all Bath citizens in mind, but added that "the welfare of a city's industries is too important to be brought into the political picture, stirring up feeling and animosity which is not desirable." Making business a political football, wrote Webber, would discourage other industries from locating in Bath. "For that reason the writer hopes that in future campaigns it will not be necessary to bring the Bath Iron Works Corporation or any other industrial plant in the city into the political foreground."[66] Webber got his wish, although the now-booming Iron Works would thereafter loom large in the political background. And there was another point that Webber might have considered: Politics aside, what industry of any size would wish to locate in a city where, thanks to BIW, blue-collar wages were the highest in the region?

As was his custom, Webber avoided mentioning personalities, the third big factor in Bath's changing power structure. The omission was significant because the *Times* was Bath's most prominent broker of public opinion.

Frank B. Nichols, owner and publisher of the *Times*, was a charter member of the Associated Press and an innovator in the use of newspaper advertising. He had bought the *Times* in 1897 and, five years later, had founded the *Brunswick Weekly Record*. He maintained an office in the *Times* building on Front Street in Bath, just a few steps down from City Hall, where, at age seventy-two, he kept regular hours. (He would continue at his desk for another twenty years, becoming a legend in publishing circles.) Nichols also published the *Bath Independent*, a countywide weekly based mostly on items from the *Times*.

The *Times*'s schedule called for it to hit the streets in late afternoon, just as shipyard workers came off their daytime shift. Meanwhile, anyone walking along Front Street on weekday or Saturday afternoons could pause at

MAINE MARITIME MUSEUM

The *Bath Daily Times* office on Front Street.

MAINE MARITIME MUSEUM

Bath Daily Times Editor Harry Webber.

the plate-glass window of the *Times* office and read rushes of the day's news, pasted there by the newspaper's editor, Harry Webber. Webber, like Nichols, was an old-timer in the business. Valedictorian of Bath High School's class of 1889, he had spent most of his professional life in newspaper publishing, having once been owner of the successful *Independent*, which he had sold to Nichols. Since 1918, Webber had edited both of Nichols's Bath newspapers. Years of reporting and keen personal interest had made Webber an authority on local shipbuilding. His other interest, golf, had enabled him to publish an annual guidebook, *Golf in Maine*, which was the last word on the subject to its faithful clientele. He lived downriver in Phippsburg, where he was active in civic affairs. Much of his time was consumed by devoted care of his invalid wife.

John Morse, Jr., who grew up in a Phippsburg house just across the road from Webber's, was the editor's nephew by marriage. While attending high school, young Morse would sometimes go around to the *Times* office after school to hitch a ride home with Uncle Harry. Morse recalled noticing the close contact Bath's bigwigs cultivated with Webber: "He was the editor of the paper and he could make things happen or he could spoil something. So, people like Rupert Baxter and Arthur Sewall, all of the bank officers and the men who were active in city politics, mayors and council chairmen and lesser lights, always came in to pass the time of day and see what was going on, [or] maybe give him a tip."[67]

The *Times* employed a small staff of reporters for local news assignments and took national and world news from teletyped AP dispatches. Customarily, Webber wrote the daily editorials. Inasmuch as he and Nichols were both rock-ribbed Maine Republicans, the *Times* and the *Independent* affirmed conservative New England values, some of which had taken a beating during the recent Depression. Nonetheless, Webber retained a hearty distaste for FDR's big government. He also despised the growth of European totalitarianism, especially Hitler's, and did not hesitate to devote editorial space to issues of that magnitude.

The overall character of the *Times* and the *Independent*, however, was that of community "sweetheart" media. They did not indulge in adversarial reporting, nor did they acknowledge news about the personal foibles or troubles of Bath citizens, even if such items received notice elsewhere. When coverage of municipal affairs required attention to the friction and controversy therein, matters were presented as blandly and obliquely as possible, the effect further deadened by the papers' prolix, curiously roundabout style.

Complex local issues were usually packaged with a positive emphasis on the established way of doing things. During the controversy over charter reform, for example, the *Times* gave considerable space to blind items detailing possible pitfalls of the proposed new system, inconsistencies in its preliminary draft, and, as the referendum approached, the average voter's assumed indifference to the whole matter. In the perennial controversy over the Bath Water District, however, it lavished great attention on the merits of the system's design, its service, and the dedication of its overseers. Clearly, Nichols and Webber defined their responsibilities in terms of softening conflict and ameliorating damage in a close-knit community.

On the other hand, the *Times* and the *Independent* were, along with the rumor mill, the very stuff with which the community monitored and maintained its close-knittedness. Both papers were aswarm with tidbits about the comings and goings of Bath people and the local social calendar. Devotion to the *Times* was directly proportional to the importance a reader attached to such coverage. As Bill Mussenden recalled: "If you and your wife and another couple happened to drive to Portland, have lunch and come back, it would be in the paper. There were two or three old biddies who knew everything that was going on and they'd feed it into the newsroom down there. You couldn't do anything without it being in the paper. . . . I can see my father sitting [in his study] when he got home. He'd pick up the paper and he'd thumb through it—'Nothing in the *Times*!'—and he'd slam it on the floor. He'd do it night after night after night. The phraseology wouldn't vary a bit."[68]

A few examples from 1936 provide a whiff of the newspaper's social news blitz: A minstrel show was put on by the Jolly Minstreleers at the Masonic Temple in April; "applause was frequent and generous." The annual May Mother's Day tea at the Cosmopolitan Club was "largely attended." In July, to benefit the Elks' Charley Fund, a donkey baseball game was held at Kelley Field, and although "a family of 12 donkeys arrived in Bath Saturday evening and camped on the ball park grounds until Sunday, 13 left the city following the game as there was a new arrival in the family Saturday night." Items of this sort were occasionally treated as news if they involved the *Times*'s short list of favorites. For instance, when Mrs. Sumner Sewall scored a hole-in-one while golfing on a 1938 vacation at White Sulphur Springs, West Virginia, it made the front page back home.[69]

The *Times* was a remarkable newspaper because, on a daily basis, it provided Bath with continuity through a prodigious volume of coverage, trivial and otherwise. It was at its best chronicling the daily social transactions of its readership. It was also strong in editing and commenting upon world news. Its weak points were its bland, often Pollyannaish coverage of city problems and its reluctance to get down to cases about the ways and means of power in the city. As with any mass medium, its example and repetition sent an influential message about what was important and what was not.

Of course, any newspaper is both a cause and an effect of local attitudes. In Bath, the devotion of the press to chronicling life's small pleasantries was a reflection of the fact that many of the city's needs were attended to by friends, through unofficial channels. Bath may have been a place where everybody seemed to know everybody's business, but it was also a place where people looked after their own.

Jim Temple's early adulthood revealed a great deal about the strength of Bath's social infrastructure. When he graduated as valedictorian from Morse High School in 1932, he lacked the wherewithal to go to college, but he was financially assisted by the Davenport Fund, which earmarked part of its considerable outlay for deserving Bath students.

Temple attended the University of Maine at Orono, where, in October of 1934, he contracted poliomyelitis. He was kept alive in an iron lung rushed from Portland to Bangor under state police escort. During the next three months, as he lay virtually paralyzed from the neck down, people in his hometown mounted a community effort to get him effective treatment.

Friends of the Temples pulled Democratic party strings all the way to the White House to squeeze Jim into the crowded Georgia facilities of the Warm Springs Foundation, recently established by a group headed by polio victim Franklin D. Roosevelt. The Davenport Trust made a critical initial contribution toward his immediate treatment and also covered the cost of transporting him by chartered Pullman car to Warm Springs. He was accompanied on the trip by a local Red Cross nurse who contributed her services. To cover extended treatment, Bath's Rotary Club established a James B. Temple Fund Drive. Chaired by James Gillies, Jr., Jim's father's employer at Bath Box Co., the fund successfully touched sixty organizations and church congregations in the city. Benefit parties were thrown on Jim's behalf. The *Times* painstakingly reported on Temple's progress at Warm

Springs. "Everybody seemed to be concerned," Jim later recalled. "I was amazed. I knew very little about it during the time. It wasn't until I came home and saw some of the clippings that my mother had saved that I really learned what went on. . . . It seemed to be a community-wide effort."[70] And it all took place in the depths of the Depression.

Jim Temple responded dramatically to therapy at Warm Springs, although he would remain seriously handicapped. He returned to Bath in 1936 and went to work as a bookkeeper at Bath Box Co. He was, predictably, something of a local celebrity, especially among Democrats, and was elected to an alderman's seat in 1939, taking part in the debates on charter reform and the crucial vote on Rupert Baxter's trusteeship of the Bath Water District. Also in that year, he commenced a ten-year chairmanship of the city and county chapters of the March of Dimes. Having married and involved himself with Bath Box Co.'s new lumberyard, he did not run for city office again in 1940.

Temple's story is noteworthy for more than its human interest. It illustrates the community's internal strength and fundamental solidarity even in the worst of times. Such vitality was the corollary to the local rumor mill and the propensity to treat chitchat as news; Bath was a small enough place for someone's problems to become everyone's responsibility. Put another way—in the words of most of the Bath citizens who were interviewed for this study—Bath was a good spot to grow up in.

NEW SODA FOUNTAIN INSTALLED AT HALLET'S

Has All Latest Improvements and Will Prove Popular With Customers

Recently installed in A. Hallet & Co., 70 Front street, the new liquid-carbonic streamlined 12 foot soda fountain has received much favorable comment from both customers and employes. Built of stainless steel, with all the latest modern improvements, the corners of this new fountain are rounded,

MAINE MARITIME MUSEUM

that those working behind it will not tear their clothing or cut themselves on sharp edges. The latest method of refrigeration is employed, both for keeping ice cream and for drawing cold soda.

Among the features in this new type of fountain are two sinks . . . ; a running water disher vat; a refuse chute which goes direct to the basement; cold compartments electrically lighted whenever a door is opened; two draught arms to facilitate the drawing of soda during rush hours; six built in crushed fruit bowls; 12 improved syrup pumps; and bakelite, a non-conductor for either heat, or cold, covers for the ice cream compartments.

BATH DAILY TIMES, 31 MARCH 1939

POLICE BREAK UP BATTLE OF PUPILS

Capture of Class Banner Leads to Fistic Battles Between Seniors and Under-Classmen

Local police had a busy half hour Friday morning as Morse high seniors and under-classmen engaged in pitched battle in City Hall Square and adjacent byways following Thursday evening's larceny of the 1938 banner. . . .

After City Marshal Butler and his men had broken up several fistic free-for-alls in the heart of the business district, a dozen or more sophomores, said to be responsible for stealing the banner, took refuge in City Hall and the senior boys threatened to storm the building. Reminding the young men what had happened two years ago when the large plate glass window in the Bath Trust Co., was smashed during the inter-class rioting, Marshal Butler asked them to confine their warfare to the outskirts of the city and . . . had them taken to Kelley field.

Late in the forenoon the seniors cornered the majority of the sophomores who . . . fled from Kelley field to the nearby woods. Escorting the second year men to the park pond the graduates gave them their choice of walking through the pond or being thrown in. . . .

> Police recovered the banner early Friday morning and turned it over to Horace P. Herrick, principal of the high school. . . .
>
> In addition to their bath in the park pond, those sophomores unfortunate enough to fall into the hands of the irate seniors were submitted to a haircut that isn't going to improve their appearance at tonight's reception in the least. A furrow, the width of the clippers, that runs from the forehead to the nape of the neck decorates no less than 10 sophomores. . . .
>
> *BATH DAILY TIMES*, 17 JUNE 1938

By the end of the thirties, Bath schools were in shabby physical condition, thanks to the city's enforced financial austerity. "We didn't have all the athletic facilities in those days," recalled Linwood Temple. "If we wanted to play baseball or anything like that, we went out in the playground or got in a backyard lot. . . . But the schools, in my estimation, were more than adequate. The school rooms were light and cheery. We had the old-fashioned desks and things like that, but [there was] nothing really wrong with that. What was important was what was taught, and we got a very good education out of the Bath schools. I found that out over the years."[71]

Students may have been too busy in the classroom to notice the lack of amenities. As John Gilmore put it, "If you didn't behave you got whacked, I know that. And you didn't go home and tell your mother and father about it, either. . . . You did your year, whatever it was, and if you didn't know what you were supposed to know at the end of that particular year, then there was nobody in this world could ever teach you, because those teachers would drive it right into you. Boy! But, thinking back, we just had fun, raised hell like everybody else."[72]

Raising hell, recreation, and friendship were largely determined by which Bath grammar school a youngster attended. High school broke down parochialism, but there were still South End and North End gangs and subdivisions thereof, with the boundary running just south of the Carlton Bridge. In Bath in the thirties, a "gang" was a social group, based on the city's distended geography, and did not carry connotations of collective juvenile mischief. Or did it? Howard Kirkpatrick, who was raised on upper Washington Street, remembered that "Over on the North End, we had one group that we steered clear of, I suppose the same as today. They were rough and tough."[73] And Bill Mussenden recalled a South End incident from the early thirties: "When I was a freshman in high school, I went down to Winnegance Lake skating one night. I got over near the east shore . . . and the ice let go and I went in the water. I got myself out alright. There was a gang around. I said, 'Give me a hand, will you?' Somebody said, 'Aw, he's from the North,' and they all walked off."[74] In the adult world, "South End" and "North End" were sometimes used as verbal shorthand for blue-collar and white-collar, respectively, although there is little evidence that such distinctions meant much to the city's youth.[75]

In every neighborhood, there was always something to do. Much of the fun was seasonal. Arthur Sewall's son Bill, who spent his early years in rural North Bath, described how he and his buddy Mel Henderson lived Huck Finn-style in summer—rafting, fishing, and swimming at their campsites on Whiskeag Creek. The Kennebec was seriously polluted by the thirties, but that didn't keep John Gilmore and his friends from swimming in it ("It never bothered us any").[76] Howard Kirkpatrick described how he and his friends "built carts to ride around on, built locomotives out of fruit containers and boxes we got at the store, and we had the best time—better than anybody buying a bicycle or anything today."[77] At the city's southern tip, Stewart Day, Jr., and friends sometimes visited John Morse's sawmill, where logs were soaking in a tidal pond: "We used to go in there and jump logs. . . . In the winter we jumped ice cakes." Day and his friends used to keep an ice cake tied to the old Winnegance Bridge. "Long after the ice had gone, we would float all around the bay out there in the spring."[78]

Youngsters at loose ends on weekday nights could find recreational activities at the YMCA, but the sounding of the 8:45 siren meant that they were to be off the streets. Bath policemen took the curfew very seriously.

TIMES RECORD, BRUNSWICK, MAINE

Long lines at the Opera House.

On Saturday nights in season, there was Church League basketball at the Y; Bath was a devout basketball town.

Winter or summer, Bath people of all ages congregated in the downtown area on Saturdays to shop, have a snack or an ice cream soda, look each other over, and socialize. For small fry, the big attraction was the Saturday matinee at the Opera House or the Uptown, whichever theater was showing the best serial or cowboy feature. "Ten cents to get into the movies," recalled John Gilmore, "and [for] five cents, oh jeez, back then you could get real candy bars [or] what seemed like a monstrous bag of popcorn. Of course, you'd take your popcorn, go to the balcony and get the front seat, and then pop the kids on their heads. We spent half the movie keeping our eyes out for the ushers. . . . That was the Saturday ritual: go to the movies."[79]

BATH GIRL RISES FROM RIBBON COUNTER TO CINEMA STARDOM

A small town girl who made good in the metropolis returned to the Shipbuilding City Tuesday in the person of Miss Iva Stewart, Hollywood Cal., who jumped off the train nearly knocking her father's hat off as she greeted him. Miss Stewart, displaying none of the poise of the polished actress that she is, depicting only a charming young woman glad to be home again, was met by her

MAINE MARITIME MUSEUM

> father, . . . and her brother, John, and Managers Frank A. Vennett and Francis J. Gooch of the Opera House and Uptown respectively.
>
> Mr. Vennett greeted her and told her that during her stay in Bath she will have a 1939 Chevrolet at her disposal.
>
> . . . Her story, which from the screen angle has its inception in Bath, is that of an attractive young lady who, from behind a counter of the Woolworth store, dreamed of cinema fame. Then one summer's afternoon in 1933 she made the decision . . . to turn those dreams into reality.
>
> . . . She entered the ["Miss Maine"] contest and carried away the title. It led her to Atlantic City where as "Miss Maine" she was runner up for the title of "Miss America."
>
> . . . She studied dramatic art while an entertainer at the Paradise Club [in New York City] and during this period met three other young ladies who, like herself, had their eyes turned Hollywood way. . . . The quartet vowed to each other that they would stay together until they had landed a film contract and gone on to screen stardom. Today all four are under contract with 20th Century Fox and well along the path to fame they seek.
>
> Miss Stewart came under the Fox Company spotlight when she was selected as America's most beautiful girl in an evening dress.
>
> *BATH DAILY TIMES*, 14 FEBRUARY 1939

Bath's trolley cars attracted children like magnets. Until 1937, the Androscoggin & Kennebec Street Railway operated local streetcars that ran on a single track down Washington Street from one end of town to the other, except for a downtown diversion along Center, Front, and Oak. Northbound and southbound cars would edge past each other at a short section of double tracking on lower Washington near the Iron Works. A second line, whose downtown loop included Commercial Street (where cars could load at the Coal Pocket), linked Bath to Brunswick and Lewiston via Oak, Middle, North, and the old Bath-Brunswick Road.[80] The trolleys provided unlimited opportunities for pranks, generating a continual cold war between irked motormen and determined kids. A standard method of raising the critical cash for movie tickets or goodies was to hitch a free ride to town on the streetcar and recycle the unspent fare. Bath streetcars

MAINE MARITIME MUSEUM

Trolleys passing on south Washington Street.

mounted cowcatchers at each end, hooking the trailing one in an upward position while the car was in use. The raised cowcatcher provided a free perch for enterprising travelers, who considered the dime saved well worth the risk of injury. A favorite trick was simply to snag a passing car's pick-up pole and disconnect it from the high-tension wire overhead, causing the car to stop dead. Another was to grease the tracks on a grade and watch as the trolley lost traction. On the Fourth of July, a popular pastime was to chuck firecrackers in the streetcars' path.[81]

Boys will be boys, but there is no denying the Bath trolleys' mystique, then and now, or the void felt by many as they, like childhood itself, disappeared. Howard Kirkpatrick: "We had a bay window in the house . . . , and I loved sitting in that window and seeing all the goings-on up and down the street. The most spectacular thing I recall—and nothing has matched it since—was when the trolley came up Washington Street hill after an ice storm. There was ice on the wire and ice on the tracks . . . current had to

flow. . . . If you want to see something spectacular: [the arcing] as that trolley wheel came along that wire, and the arcing on the wheels on the car coming up Washington Street hill. There was nothing like it!"[82]

The trolley line had been in trouble for some years because of declining patronage, but the impending completion of the new Bath-Brunswick Road sealed its fate. In 1937, giving way to motor traffic, the streetcars were scrapped in Lewiston. In Bath, the tracks were quickly torn up and a locally owned bus line started service.

The construction of the new Bath-Brunswick Road, which became U.S. Route One, was, like the Carlton Bridge, a signal of the growing bond between automotive convenience and American commerce. On the old road,

MAINE MARITIME MUSEUM

Sign on the Old Bath Road.

drivers leaving Brunswick passed the snoozy crossroad of Cooks Corner, then turned northeast through several miles of rural landscape dotted here and there with produce stands and filling stations. Approaching Bath from the northwest, a newcomer might not suspect that a small city lay just ahead, for the northern outskirts had a rather wild aspect: outcroppings

of granite ledge, thick woods, and occasional farms. Settlement thickened as the route turned into Lincoln Street, which terminated at the Court House summit near the intersection of Center and High. Through traffic moved downhill two blocks on Center into the business district. To reach the bridge ramp, vehicles had to dogleg onto Washington and then Vine, near the main gate of the Iron Works, a maneuver further complicated by the Maine Central crossing at that intersection. Having crossed the bridge, motorists stopped to pay a toll on the Woolwich side.

Anyone taken by the bustle or sights of Bath could dally at one of several hotels. Best in the city was the new Sedgwick, an attractively adapted mansion diagonally opposite the Court House. It had opened for business to local fanfare in 1936 (with the captain of the U.S.S. *Drayton* as its first guest), suggesting that Bath might be out of the Depression. At the other end of the tourist spectrum was the American House, a large, once-proud, now-seedy antique on Water Street behind Front, which had a local reputation as a fleabag and brothel and looked it.

The old road did not take visitors through the grandest parts of Bath, and rush-hour traffic could be unpleasant. Some travelers undoubtedly were glad to pay their toll in Woolwich. In mid-1936, honeymooners Roger and Molly Luke passed through the city they would soon call home. According to Roger, "My wife took one look, because she was new at that time to the area, and said, 'This is the crummiest place I've ever seen, and I hope never to live here—ever!' And then, within little more than a year, we were living here."[83]

The old route also made it difficult for motorists to do business downtown. Yet, in 1934, when the State Highway Commission had recommended construction of a new Bath-Brunswick Road, Bath merchants pressed Governor Louis Brann to squelch the project. The new road was to proceed directly from Cooks Corner to Bath, straight across the boondocks of the New Meadows River and Witch Spring Hill. It would enter the city just west of the built-up area, feeding traffic onto Center Street just as the old road did, meanwhile depriving merchants and developers along the old route of their anticipated business.[84] What was the point? Aside from being a more direct route, the new road promised the same drawbacks as the old one, without any visible benefits. If, as was anticipated, volume increased on Route One, downtown Bath could become a traffic nightmare. Construction went ahead amid a storm of protests, alternate recommendations, and, later, some truly embarrassing moments as the new highway settled into mucky soil. It was operational by 1938.

Traffic was indeed getting heavier; during 1937, almost a million vehicles crossed the Carlton Bridge. In May 1938, Bath's city fathers at last instigated a few steps toward control, installing a traffic light at the critical Washington-Center intersection, creating one-way streets, and beginning a very long, uphill battle to enforce no-parking zones in the downtown. Editor Harry

Webber noted that the new regulations would "go a long way in undoing the reputation which the city has had, especially among visitors, of being the worst in the way of traffic control to be found in New England."[85]

It is trite but true, however, that traffic tie-ups are a sign of a city's life, and, commercially speaking, are much to be preferred over sleepy streets. Bath was alive again, and businesses, from BIW down, were improving. The trouble with Bath's traffic problem was that it discouraged tourists, held up work-weary BIW employees, and probably caused shoppers to search for less hectic places in which to do business. In 1940, with their work forces swollen thanks to accelerating defense work, BIW and Hyde Windlass disgorged 1,000 cars into the downtown every day at the four o'clock whistle.[86] In 1941, bridge tolls were eliminated, possibly inviting more traffic. With alternatives to the car and truck disappearing, Bath's traffic problem was here to stay.

WILL LIQUIDATE AFFAIRS AND SELL STEAMER VIRGINIA

Samoset Steamboat Company Will Not Operate Longer.

At a meeting of the stockholders of the Samoset Steamboat Co. . . . in this city . . . it was voted to liquidate its affairs and sell the steamer *Virginia* and wharf to Boothbay Harbor. It probably means the end of the good old steamboat days on the Kennebec and Sasanoa. The advent of the automobile and buses cut down the passenger business almost to zero. . . . Trucks have taken the cream of the freight business.

The Samoset Steamboat Co., was organized in 1928 after the Eastern Steamboat Co., an affiliate of the big Eastern Steamship Co., folded up.

Fortunately the debts of the company are not large and ought to be met by the sale of the steamer and wharf.

. . . All the stockholders were sorry to give up operating the line and had hoped to avoid this step. Two years ago, by having considerable excursion business, especially evenings, the line paid its expenses. . . .

BATH INDEPENDENT, 5 SEPTEMBER 1940

MAINE CENTRAL STATION IS MODERN IN ARCHITECTURE AND APPEARANCE

New Station Nears Completion

The new Maine Central railroad station . . . promises to be one of the finest and most modern buildings of its kind in the state. Topped by a cupola which will support a gold leafed weather vane model of one of Bath's own destroyers, the red brick station will not only afford a new and modern appearance from the outside but will be completely in accord with the newest designs in interior furnishings.

. . . Chrome chairs, streamlined, like the crack trains of some railroad system, will take the place of time honored benches. Concealed radiators will provide warmth and every inch of the decorations, plumbing and other equipment in the building, from the ticket office and waiting room to the rest rooms and phone booths, will be of the most practical type obtainable. When completed the interior will be not unlike that of many airport waiting rooms. . . .

BATH DAILY TIMES, 13 NOVEMBER 1941

Meanwhile, realizing that new shoppers might have to be enticed into Bath, businessmen established a Retail Merchants' Association. Sparked by Frank Vennett, energetic manager of the Opera House, the group quickly mastered the art of creating a quasi-event. During August 1938, it was Golden Harvest Days, in which shoppers were promised advertised bargains, a band concert, and a doll carriage and bicycle parade. (The parade winner in a field of nineteen entrants was a bicycle festooned with crepe paper and candy kisses.)[87] The practice of instigating seasonal sales events continued intermittently, but by 1940, business was in high gear without any need of gimmicks.

Bath's new prosperity was driven by defense contracts. The big news, as always, was the continuing expansion of the Bath Iron Works, but the European war and America's determination to rearm into an "Arsenal of Democracy" benefited other companies as well, notably Hyde Windlass. Even Bath Box Co. had bounced back from hard times by turning out cartons for smokeless powder under contract to the British government, and Congress Shirt constructed yet another addition to its busy factory. During 1941, a brick building was completed at Washington and Center streets to house a new Sears, Roebuck store and a First National supermarket, complete with parking spaces for 100 cars. Bath now had the large retail magnets to draw shoppers from both sides of the Kennebec.

The Bath Iron Works was a major benefactor of a $1.3 billion congressional naval appropriation in 1940. The bill's authorized ship construction was of such magnitude that it necessitated federal assistance to help shipyards enlarge their capacity. While other companies awaited the Navy Department's go-ahead, Pete Newell readied BIW for the onrush of new contracts. In mid-1940, he was alerted by a brief telegram from Secretary of the Navy Frank Knox, saying simply that he should prepare to expand. Rather than wait for matters to go through proper channels, Newell acquired a large tract of flat land in East Brunswick, a spot known as Hardings, where BIW began work on a massive new assembly shop. The land had been a property of the Bath Water District, and it is safe to assume that Newell's chairmanship of the Water District board facilitated its speedy sale. The Hardings plant was almost finished by the time the Navy Department authorized its construction subsidy.[88] The company also expanded onto a substantial tract of land adjacent to its riverside facilities that it had acquired from the Maine Central Railroad, of which Newell was a director. And across lower Washington Street, old structures would soon disappear to make room for Hyde Windlass's new office building.

Hard times were over, but years of depression had taken their toll on the city's physical appearance. Recollections vary about how woebegone Bath looked. The Lukes' first impression has been noted. According to John Morse, Jr., who would develop a very sharp eye for real estate in coming years, the city presented a drab appearance in the late thirties: "On every other house in Bath, the paint was peeling. They obviously hadn't been painted for years and they looked it. Blinds were falling apart, and many of them were vacant."[89] But Jim Temple recalled that while there were rundown sections in the city, "we still had our pride, and most people tried to keep their homes up. If they weren't employed, they would paint them."[90] The 1940 census revealed that almost 40 percent of Bath's housing needed major repairs.

For years, empty houses had gone begging, especially in the North End's Brick Project, built during the Great War to accommodate the temporary surge in Bath's population. The project had been bought after the war by a Portland entrepreneur, Arthur Spear, who hoped to cash in by profitable resales and rentals. It had been close to a ghost town throughout the twenties, and by the time of the Depression, rumor had it that Spear was letting some people live rent-free in the handsome but deteriorating houses to ward off vandalism.[91] For years, Spear and the city were locked in an ongoing dispute over unpaid taxes. A settlement was reached in 1940, when Bath was growing again.

Newcomers were often surprised by how far their real estate dollars went. That was especially true in the case of Bath's overabundant large houses, which continued to be white elephants even after prosperity returned. John Morse, Jr., remembered an interesting example from the late thirties involving John Cooke, who came to the city to take an executive position at Hyde Windlass: "Hite Stevens . . . was in the real estate business, so John hooked up with Hite. He took him around and showed him various houses that were for sale." One candidate was an immense, mansard-roofed house that, in the late nineteenth century, had been home to one of the city's leading shipbuilders. "It was run down somewhat then . . . but it was still a pretty imposing house. They looked at it and finally Cookie says, 'Well, I like that pretty well, don't you, Janice? I think that's a pretty good house.' He said, 'Hite, what's the price on that?' And Hite says, 'Well, I think probably you could buy that for about twelve.' Cookie thought it over for a few minutes, and he said to Janice, 'Well, what do you think? That doesn't sound too bad. I'm sure that we can get twelve thousand for our house [in New Jersey]. . . . and then we'd have the money to pay for this one.' Hite reared back and said, 'Twelve thousand? I meant twelve hundred!' "[92]

For the average worker seeking a place to live in Bath, however, the news was progressively worse. The expanding labor force had created an acute housing shortage in the city by 1940.

The political upset of 1940 took one year to right itself. Robert Haskell, Bath's new mayor, made it clear that the city's debt problem was his first priority, as it had been to his several Republican predecessors. His promised program of debt reduction included an increase in the city's annual reserve for deficits, to be covered by zealous collection of taxes and a cut in expenditures. Concurrently, he clarified the city's controversial bookkeeping by eliminating the disallowed and confusing practice of prorating purchases into the future. More accounting reform was promised.

In order to avoid raising taxes, City Council further tightened the municipal belt. Reducing expenditures inevitably got Haskell and his colleagues into trouble with those who complained about too much austerity. Bones of contention included a reduction in road maintenance; a plague of rats at the municipal dump that threatened playground safety at Kelley Field; and the city's abortive attempt to centralize its fire stations, which South Enders said jeopardized their neighborhood safety.

To make matters worse, a state report on Bath schools, undertaken at the request of the city's Board of Education, described them as crowded and deficient in heat, light, and ventilation. The study recommended consolidation of worn-out neighborhood grammar schools. Where would the money come from? Uncle Sam, if Congress passed the pending Lanham Bill.

The bill, which was indeed passed as America stepped up her military preparedness, would provide assistance to communities where federal defense priorities created a hardship. Bath was certainly one of these. Haskell prepared to lead a delegation to Washington to lobby for federal aid.

In early 1941, after complicated bookkeeping reform, Haskell's administration claimed to have reduced the city debt by almost $45,000.[93] Haskell had devised a five-year plan of debt reduction, but he did not have a chance to continue it.

The Republicans were determined to stage a comeback in Bath. In February 1941, at the city GOP caucus, ex-Mayor Donald Small successfully nominated former alderman Walter C. (Pete) Rogers, a hardware retailer and director of Bath Trust, for mayor. Small was an effective speaker, and he had learned a thing or two about discretion since his "Hitlerism" remarks in 1939. During his nomination speech, as reported in the *Times*, Small contended that Haskell and his fellow Democrats could never have been elected in 1940 without their unprecedented media campaign. "Who paid for it all?" asked Small. "Well, I've tried for a year to find out but I guess they are ashamed of their sponsor. They just will not file a report. . . . But until we find out let's call this power behind that party the Democratic Santa Claus.[94]

"In one of these Santa Claus sponsored advertisements in the *Portland Press Herald* . . . , they stated that the Bath schools were in deplorable condition. What did the present administration do to correct this after they were elected? They cut $3,000 off the school appropriation of 1939.

"Can anyone feel proud of that saving? Or is it a saving in any sense of the word?"[95]

Small couldn't resist one more shot at "that lovable old Democrat, R. H. Baxter." Referring to Baxter's 1940 post-election letter, in which he had described his unsuccessful attempts to get to the bottom of the city's murky finances and had called for an official investigation, Small stipulated that those annual accounts, like every city's in Maine, were routinely scrutinized by state-approved auditors; otherwise, not a soul had asked to examine them. Small's remarks were loudly applauded and seconded.

Haskell stood for reelection. Again, Pete Newell lent his personal prestige to Haskell's campaign, stating publicly that Haskell "has, I believe, proven by his record that my belief in him was justified."[96]

It was not enough. In the March election, Haskell lost to Rogers and the Democrats were swept out of both houses of City Council. Haskell learned of his defeat while en route to Washington to lobby for federal aid. He came home and turned over that chore to Mayor-elect Rogers.

Pete Rogers was sworn in at City Hall in March 1941, after his return from Washington. In his inaugural address, he pointed out that accelerating growth and rising population were bound to drive up municipal expenses, but that a tax increase would be intolerable to many property owners. But that did not necessarily mean shabby services; Rogers planned to hold the line on the correct expectation that the federal government would share Bath's financial burden. Pete Newell had helped open the right doors in Washington, said Rogers. Maine's representatives there were sym-

MAINE MARITIME MUSEUM

Walter (Pete) Rogers.

pathetic to Bath's needs, or, as Rogers put it, "extremely cordial to the delegation and untiring in their construction of a program, by which we were conducted to the various officials who are likely to be affected, if and when the Lanham Bill has its passage and from whom we received warm consideration, and courteous regard from the committee, which is considering the bill, although developments have not materialized to a point of surety, but we returned with the belief that there is no prospect of an improbability of our hope. . . . "[97]

Rogers may have been a poor speaker, but he was quite correct about federal assistance. The bill passed. Bath could squeak by without raising taxes as long as a national emergency endured.

Under Rogers's administration, immediate action was taken on the Knox & Lincoln bonds, which came due in 1941. A special committee on debt reduction paid off part of the debt from a sinking fund established for that purpose and refinanced the remainder through new bonds at a lower interest rate. Through an annual reduction of the principal, the committee expected to eliminate the debt by 1961. Chairing the committee was William Skelton of Bath Trust; another key member was the earnestly dedicated John Newell, Pete's son, chairman of the Common Council.

The GOP's recapture of City Hall pleased Harry Webber: "Bath, normally a Republican city but which occasionally wavers, demonstrated again Monday that it still lives up to its traditional Republicanism for in the annual municipal election the Republicans won what may be considered a clean sweep.

"The defeat of Mayor Robert H. Haskell, Democrat, who has served but one year, by Walter C. Rogers, Republican, who has served several years in both branches of the city government, came as a surprise to many who believed that Mr. Haskell might be given a reelection. However, the voters in no uncertain terms showed that they prefer Mr. Rogers should be at the head of the municipality for the coming twelve months and gave him a plurality so large that it proved one of the greatest victories a mayoralty candidate has achieved in several years. . . . The board of aldermen and common council are Republican, almost complete, and there is little doubt but that the new mayor and city government will have a fine opportunity to make a satisfactory showing during the twelve months ahead."[98] The election seemed to confirm Webber's contention that the 1940 upset had been caused by the defection of unhappy Republicans. In any event, Pete Rogers was a mayor most Bath citizens could live with: conservative, dry, familiar with the municipal ropes, and not disposed to seek publicity. He meant what he said about holding the line, notwithstanding the flood of new families coming to Bath for defense jobs.

With the election of Rogers, partisan politics tailed off sharply. One reason for that was the apparent resolution of issues that had divided citizens, notably the reality that the ever-expanding BIW was, unavoidably, the tail that wagged the dog. In addition, the city's financial condition had ceased to be the desperate problem it once was. But most of all, the onset of World War II submerged partisanship and personalities. By the time of Rogers's inaugural, outright war between the United States and the Axis powers was but months away. After Pearl Harbor, Rogers would be reelected annually for the duration of the war, an indication that Bath citizens preferred stability and conservative fiscal administration in times of crisis.

Many citizens, of course, remembered the city's frenzied growth during World War I, and the disastrous contraction thereafter. It had taken two decades to recover from the doldrums of the Depression. Now, the city stood knowingly on the edge of another such cycle. Given the pervasiveness of its defense work, Bath was sensitized to the deteriorating world situation; talk of war and preparation for war had been lively for years. Yet the city stood on the edge with no municipal plan other than its two principles of debt reduction and tax restraint, its belief in the inherent strength of its citizens, and its almost complete dependence upon federal expenditure as the source of prosperity.

Notes

1. *Bath Daily Times* (hereafter cited as BDT), 19 March 1936; *Bath Independent* (hereafter cited as BI), 20 March 1936.
2. BDT, 26 March 1936.
3. David B. Marentette, "An Historical Geography of Bath, Maine: 1600–1920" (unpublished doctoral thesis, University of Oregon, 1983), pp. 20–24.
4. William Avery Baker, *A Maritime History of Bath, Maine and the Kennebec River Region* (2 vols., Bath: Marine Research Society of Bath, 1973), I, 423–24.
5. Henry Wilson Owen, *The Edward Clarence Plummer History of Bath, Maine* (Bath: The Times Company, 1936), p. 188.
6. Ibid., p. 324.
7. Marentette, p. 324.
8. Bill Caldwell, *Rivers of Fortune: Where Maine Tides and Money Flowed* (Portland, ME: Guy Gannett Publishing, 1983), p.46.
9. Garnett Laidlaw Eskew, *Cradle of Ships: A History of the Bath Iron Works* (New York: G. P. Putnam's Sons, 1958), pp. 124–26.
10. Ibid., p. 121; Ralph Linwood Snow, *Bath Iron Works: The First Hundred Years* (Bath: Maine Maritime Museum, 1987), pp. 210–12.
11. Snow, p. 223.
12. Caldwell, p. 142; William F. Mussenden, Interview, Bath, February 1987.

13. BDT, 31 December 1936.
14. Snow, p. 311.
15. James W. Temple, Interview, Wiscasset, ME, February 1987.
16. John R. Newell, Personal Communication, 15 January 1983.
17. G. Baer Connard, Interview, Bath, May 1987.
18. Arthur Sewall, Inaugural Speech, Bath, 16 March 1936; quoted in BI, 19 March 1936.
19. William D. Sewall and Melvin B. Henderson, Interview, Bath, May 1987.
20. Ibid.
21. Owen, pp. 233–34; BDT, 2 June 1936.
22. BI, 12 March 1938.
23. BDT, 10 February 1934.
24. *City of Bath, Maine: Annual Report* (published annually, Bath: City of Bath, 1926–1930).
25. BDT, 19 March 1934.
26. *City of Bath Annual Report*, 1935–1936.
27. BDT, 25 February, 1938.
28. J. Temple interview.
29. BDT, 29 March 1934.
30. Ibid., 16 March 1934.
31. Ibid., 6 January 1934.
32. Linwood E. Temple, Interview, Bath, April 1987.
33. J. Temple interview.
34. BDT, 26 March 1936, 6 April 1937.
35. Ibid., 30 October 1936, 9 June 1937.
36. L. Temple interview.
37. Ibid.
38. BI, 10 March 1938.
39. See, for example, the controversies over the cemetery and park department (BDT, 3 May-15 June 1934, 7 June 1935); and the Overseers of the Poor (ibid., 7 June 1934, 10 October 1935).
40. Ibid., 12 January 1939.
41. Ibid.
42. Sumner Sewall, quoted in ibid., 23 February 1939.
43. BDT, 9 September 1939.
44. John G. Morse, Jr., Interview, Phippsburg, ME, February and June 1987.
45. Ibid.
46. Ibid.
47. William B. Mussenden, Interview, Bath, February 1987.
48. Ibid.
49. Morse interview.
50. "Rupie": Morse interview; "That One-eyed Bastard": Mussenden interview.
51. BDT, 5 October 1939.
52. J. Temple interview.
53. BDT, 27 February 1940.
54. Ibid., 28 February 1940.
55. Ibid., 29 February 1940.

56. Ibid., 2 March 1940.
57. Ibid., 2 March 1940.
58. Ibid., 4 March 1940.
59. Ibid., 1 March 1940.
60. Rupert H. Baxter to Harry C. Webber, Bath, n.d. (ibid., 5 March 1940).
61. BDT, 2 March 1940; see also *City of Bath Annual Report*, 1939–1940.
62. BDT, 4 March 1940.
63. Baxter to Webber.
64. Editorial, BDT, 5 March 1940.
65. BDT, 4 April 1940.
66. Ibid., 5 March 1940.
67. Morse interview.
68. Mussenden interview.
69. BI, 30 April, 14 May, 23 July 1936; 26 May 1940.
70. J. Temple interview.
71. L. Temple interview.
72. John R. Gilmore, Interview, Bath, April 1987.
73. Howard W. Kirkpatrick, Interview, Woolwich, ME, April 1987.
74. Mussenden interview.
75. W. Sewall-M. Henderson interview; Donald A. Spear, Interview, Bath, June 1987.
76. Gilmore interview.
77. Kirkpatrick interview.
78. Stewart Day, Jr., Interview, West Bath, February 1987.
79. Gilmore, interview.
80. P. L. Pert, Jr., "End of the Line," *Times Record* (Brunswick, ME, hereafter cited as TR), 15 May 1987; Kirkpatrick interview.
81. Kirkpatrick and Day interviews; Raymond C. Small, Interview, Bath, May 1987.
82. Kirkpatrick interview.
83. Roger M. Luke, Interview, Bath, February 1987.
84. BDT, 8 May 1934, 23 July 1938.
85. Editorial, BI, 20 May 1938.
86. BDT, 20 April 1940.
87. BI, 25 August 1938.
88. Eskew, pp. 197–98; Caldwell, p. 46.
89. Morse interview.
90. J. Temple interview.
91. Spear has related the vicissitudes of ownership in his peculiar little book, *I Bought a White Elephant in Maine: An Adventure in Homes* (N. p.: Published by author, n.d.).
92. Morse interview.
93. *City of Bath Annual Report*, 1940–1941; BDT, 27 February 1941.
94. A 1987 search could not unearth the report in question.
95. D. Small, quoted in ibid., 12 February 1941.
96. William S. Newell to the *Bath Daily Times*, Bath, 18 February 1941 (ibid., 1 March 1941).

97. Walter C. Rogers, Inaugural Speech, Bath, 17 March 1941, ibid., 18 March 1941.
98. Editorial, ibid., 6 March 1941.

2

"Ships For Uncle Sam"

Edwin L. Emmons of Bath was probably the world's oldest drum major, and certainly one of the best dressed. Thin and straight as a pole, and a twinkle-toed master of jaunty steps he had learned on the vaudeville circuit, "Eddie the Drum Major" had been a fixture of Shipbuilding City parades for forty years. Eddie, who worked at a variety of minor city jobs—he was for years Bath's truant officer—had spent a small fortune on his collection of splendid costumes, and he liked nothing better than to strut his stuff down Front or Center Street at the head of a marching column. He got many a chance to do so, for Bath people loved parades and would stage them at the drop of a hat.

Eddie was seventy-eight when he led Bath's Army Day parade on 8 April 1939. He shared honors with a winsome teenage South Portland majorette, and his retinue included Bath's own National Guard unit, Battery H of the 240th Coast Artillery. Also marching were footsoldiers and a band of the Fifth Infantry, detachments from two visiting Coast Guard cutters, a show-stopping drum and bugle corps from Portland, Bath's police force, and contingents of the American Legion and Veterans of Foreign Wars, including a few who had served in the Spanish-American conflict. The official occasion was the launching of the U.S.S. *Sims* at the Bath Iron Works, but the parade was part of a widening series of exercises promoted by military and veterans' organizations to popularize American preparedness for war.

Over the previous year and a half, Bath citizens had had ample opportunity to reflect upon the drift toward global war. And they seemed interested. In January 1938, for example, they filled the Morse High School auditorium to hear an upsetting lecture on the rise of Japan delivered by

MAINE MARITIME MUSEUM

Eddie Emmons, the world's best-dressed drum major.

Herman Krafft, a former professor at the United States Naval Academy. Introduced by Pete Newell, Krafft expressed regret that the U.S. Navy had ever opened up Japan to Western trade and technology: "Sometimes I think it would have been just as well to let the Japanese stay where they were. . . . "[1] Later in the year came FDR's nationally proclaimed Navy Day, followed by Mobilization Day and Preparedness Day, all duly observed in Bath with concerts of martial music and lectures on the need to rearm by political, military, and business VIPs.

Talk of military increases might naturally fall on receptive ears in a community so devoted to naval construction, but concern deepened with the outbreak of European hostilities. In September 1939, just two weeks after war broke out in Europe, Bath Rotarians gathered at the Hotel Sedgwick to hear Sumner Sewall, president of the Maine Senate, former fighter pilot, and pioneer in commercial aviation, express the urgency of strengthening the nation's defenses: "We must arm to the teeth. We must build and maintain a Navy which will command with absolute certainty our ocean approaches, and our air force must have such striking power that an attack on our shore would be unthinkable. With such forces of National Defense,

HERBERT DOUGLAS; MAINE MARITIME MUSEUM

Charismatic Governor Sumner Sewall making a wartime speech.

diplomatic blackmail is futile and attack suicidal."[2] Most of the talk stressed that America could avoid war by the deterrent of defensive power. But no one was ever coy about who the diplomatic blackmailers or aggressors might be.

BATH BUILT SHIPS
MAY BECOME JAP MUNITIONS

All Three Steel Square-
Riggers to Be Junked
and Metal Shipped to Japan

Three of the last square-riggers, built by Arthur Sewall & Co., of Bath, are bound for Japan where they will be scrapped, their metallic ingredients to be used, so the story runs, in the manufacture of Japanese munitions. All are four masted steel barks. . . .

To those Shipping City people of a generation ago, it will undoubtedly be ironic, that these vessels, sent forth from Bath when the city was glorified in its production of commercial ships, should now be in possession

> of . . . a Japanese corporation, for no other purpose than scrap metal.
>
> The *Star of Shetland*, built as the *Edward Sewall*, was the first constructed. In 1889 Arthur Sewall & Co. sent this craft into the Kennebec waters. She was built for the Alaska Packers Association [sic] . . . for use in the fish trade.
>
> The *Star of Zealand*, originally the *Astral*, was built in 1901 for the same firm [sic] and was originally employed as a freighter. The *Star of Lapland*, ex-*Atlas*, followed up in 1902, also a freighter for the same firm [sic]. . . .
>
> *BATH DAILY TIMES*, 8 DECEMBER 1934

Although nominally neutral, the United States became ever more interested in stopping the Axis powers in Europe and Asia. Around Bath, the best evidence of this was the new destroyer program. After the approval of the Atlantic Charter in August 1940, new Bath-built vessels were plugging the defensive gaps caused by the transfer of obsolete U.S. destroyers to the Royal Navy. The Iron Works, meanwhile, continued its phenomenal growth, bulging with ship contracts and perpetually seeking more workers.

If anyone in the Shipbuilding City had somehow remained oblivious to the gathering war clouds, events of September 1940 would have made him take note. Early in the month, Mayor Haskell received a communication from the mayoress of Bath, England, asking Yankees to help their sister city raise enough contributions to buy one Spitfire fighter for the Royal Air Force. At the same time came news that the Maine National Guard had been federalized. Bath's Battery H, which had lately moved into a new armory in the North End, was assigned to Fort McKinley, in Portland. And in mid-September, Congress adopted the Selective Training and Service Act.

Like most National Guard units, Battery H had not undergone rigorous training. Linwood Temple recalled that "When I joined, it was kind of something to do socially. . . . A group of us young fellas said we would join [for] something to do in the evenings. We would drill one night a week. . . . When we finally got the authority to build a new armory out on North Street Extension, . . . we did some volunteer labor with that thing. We had a basketball court; that was a nice wooden floor at the time. . . . The National Guard at that time was like a volunteer fire department. It was a social group. But we drilled pretty hard . . . , and had some fun, too."[3]

Military times were changing, however. On 20 September, 8,000 cheering people lined the downtown streets as Eddie the Drum Major led Bath National Guardsmen in a farewell parade. That night, at a farewell party in Columbian Hall, Mayor Haskell presented the battery commander, who in civilian life was the city police marshal, with an inscribed sword: "To

Captain Joseph A. Butler from Mayor Robert H. Haskell."[4] Early in 1941, the 240th Coast Artillery moved to Texas for further training.

The Sagadahoc County draft board opened an office in the Bath Trust building. In February 1941, its first nine inductees (seven from Bath) took the train to Boston to begin their military service.

WINDOWS OF EIGHT JEWISH OPERATED STORES SMEARED

Tires of a Fruit Produce Truck Are Slashed

Show windows of five stores in Bath's business district, all Jewish owned, were smeared with varnish in the early hours of Saturday morning and the tires on a fruit produce truck, also Jewish owned, were slashed.

Victims of the vandalism included the clothing store operated by Max Kutz on Elm street, a furniture store; three establishments on Center street, the Boston Shoe Store, Bath Department Store and Markson Brothers. The truck . . . was owned by Sam Prawer, wholesale fruit dealer, and was parked in front of Prawer's place of business on 260 Front street.

. . . Police announced that later developments Saturday morning showed that three other Jewish-owned stores had also had their windows smeared with the varnish. They were Julius Gediman's clothing store, Jay Povich's second-hand furniture store and Morris Petlock's meat market, all located on Center street. . . .

The police learned that there was a similar occurrence in Lewiston a few weeks ago when a mixture of paint and grease was applied to show windows.

BATH INDEPENDENT, 12 SEPTEMBER 1940

By the spring of 1941, the Bath Iron Works had 4,150 people in its employ, which amounted to a weekly payroll of about $200,000—$1.45 million in 1986 dollars. Seventy percent of the workers were Bath residents. Contracts in hand would take three years to complete, and more expansion was planned. In April, Pete Newell told the Retail Merchants' Association that

MAINE MARITIME MUSEUM

Expansion at BIW, 1941.

the number of workers could well reach 6,000 by 1942. "Added to this must be the payrolls of the Hyde Windlass Co., Torrey's and the other industrial plants throughout the city, all of which gives Bath a payroll that is equaled by but few other communities. We are fortunate that ours is a line of work needed by national defense. We are enjoying the flood tide while other communities who have no national defense industries are experiencing the ebb."[5] Newell advised merchants, who were characteristically more preoccupied with downtown parking problems than with glamorizing their stores, that by practicing competitive pricing on attractive merchandise, they could keep a great portion of the Iron Works payroll right in Bath. Newell and BIW brass, meanwhile, were themselves preoccupied with cofounding (along with Todd Shipyards Corporation and Henry J. Kaiser) a new facility in South Portland designed to build merchants ships for Britain.

The Japanese attack on Pearl Harbor in December 1941, prompting America's entry into the war, accelerated the production whirlwind. By the middle of 1943, there were 12,000 people working at BIW, and the city's population was estimated at close to 20,000. The surge in downtown business was enough to make a merchant momentarily forget the lean years of the thirties, when Bath consisted of 10,000 souls. It was also enough to arouse nostalgia for the traffic jams of 1940.

As war production was nearing its peak, the great American author John Dos Passos came to Bath to observe its impact upon the city. His visit was part of a nationwide sweep to gather material for a magazine series on America's home-front mobilization. On that trip, Dos Passos, famous for his left-wing politics, was so impressed by the prodigious grassroots energy of Americans caught up in the war effort that he apparently began to reconsider his own political values, commencing a long and famous ideological

MAINE MARITIME MUSEUM

Wartime work at Hyde Windlass.

trek toward conservatism.[6] What Dos Passos saw was a nation of people performing productive miracles out of collective will—not propaganda, force, fear, or slavish devotion to a system. The City of Bath was one of those miracles.

It was a rather grimy miracle. Dos Passos watched thousands of purposeful workers emerge from BIW and Hyde at the blowing of the afternoon whistle. Part of the crowd piled into cars already wearing out from the long

MAINE MARITIME MUSEUM

A shift change at the Iron Works about 1943.

highway grind to and from work, somehow snaking their way onto the bridge toward farmhouses and villages near and far. Others lined up for commuter buses. The rest, local people, diffused into the narrow, littered streets of Bath, heading for home. For many of these, "home" was a euphemism for a prefabricated dormitory, a glorified shed, a tarpapered trailer, or a tenement rescued from demolition by the new housing crunch.

Here were people who toiled long hours under trying working conditions, but who took home high wages, especially if they were willing to work overtime, which everyone seemed to be. Dos Passos asked a white-collar type at City Hall what the work force did with all its earnings, inasmuch as there was little time to enjoy life and not much to splurge on. He was told that Bath people were "bailin' themselves out": paying off mortgages, buying homes and furniture, taking care of long-neglected dental work, eating and drinking more and better than they had for years.[7]

Dos Passos was surprised by the contrast in Bath between boomtown squalor and staid New England elegance, noting that the city seemed overwhelmed by the onrush of change. But he was in a hurry, and, after noting a few trenchant images, moved on to inspect other wartime miracles.

The widening role of women in the Bath work force made an impression on Dos Passos. Until 1942, Pete Newell had been unwilling to hire women except for office positions at BIW. But realizing that the local male labor supply would soon be exhausted by wartime expansion and the draft, he dropped his opposition. (Another reason for that decision was that welding had largely replaced riveting in ship construction, so sheer physical

MAINE MARITIME MUSEUM

Women fill critical gaps in BIW's work force during World War II.

stamina had ceased to be essential in many jobs.) Women quickly showed that they could excel in a variety of construction jobs, and their employment in heavy industry was correctly perceived as an important social change in Bath. A female personnel director at BIW gleefully told Dos Passos that the phenomenon culminated the revolution that had begun with the women's suffrage movement, " 'and nobody's had a parade or anything.' "[8] Even with the addition of local women, the local labor supply was exhausted. By December 1943, when the Iron Works labor force peaked at 12,042, fully three-fourths of its workers were commuters from out of town.

By any standard, productivity at BIW was miraculous during World War II. A first-rate management team and the advantage of timely expansion gave it an edge, as did the skills of its established work force, which provided a nucleus for newer workers. From top to bottom and from old-timer to newcomer, the work ethic prevailed. Accordingly, BIW's labor costs and overhead were less than those at other yards, enabling the Iron Works to turn out destroyers for hundreds of thousands of dollars less yet show a greater profit than any competitor. Between 1939 and 1945, BIW cut its average construction time by 70 percent. At its peak of production, the company was launching a destroyer every seventeen days.[9]

QUARTET . . . BEAT THE WORLD'S RECORD TUESDAY . . . AT IRON WORKS

Four of the happiest, proudest and most tired men one could imagine were the quartet which made up the riveting crew that established a new world's record at the Bath Iron Works Corp. Tuesday as they left the yard after completing their rigorous eight hour grind.

One large blister occupied the place usually taken by Ross Ambrose's thumb but the man who handled the gun throughout those eight hours didn't mind. And Walter McKinney, the holder-on, and Leston T. Harrington, the heater, and young Horace M. Melville, didn't mind either as they gazed smilingly at the blisters on their palms.

. . . Starting at ten minutes after five Tuesday morning in a mist so heavy the river could hardly be seen from amidships on the destroyer on which they worked, the men heated, tossed, held and smashed rivets until noon. With only a half hour rest for lunch they were back at it again and going strong until 2:10 when the final minute ticked away.

Through the morning the mists held and the dampness was welcomed by the four men. But near noon the sun came out in burning brilliance and the rivulets of perspiration became streams of water pouring down their faces and soaking their clothing.

But the men did not once slacken their pace for they knew that they were well on their way to that much sought after record. At the half way mark . . . more than 900 rivets had been driven. With that encouraging knowledge the men continued to go at top speed and at the finish the count was 1768 rivets.

. . . Will other teams compete for the record now? . . . Very likely. The crew that established the record here yesterday has this to say. "It's all right with us if some other teams want to better the record. But if they do it the way we did it here Tuesday they'll know they've been somewhere before they get through."

And the Iron Works continues to build ships for Uncle Sam and to smash record after record as they do it. . . . A riveting crew establishes a new world's record for an eight hour shift. Axis papers please copy.

BATH INDEPENDENT, 2 JULY 1942

BATH BUILT DESTROYER SUNK BY JAPANESE IN KULA GULF

First announced casualty of our new advance against Jap sea power in the southwest Pacific is the U.S. destroyer Strong . . . , which was a 1942 product of the Bath Iron Works. The Strong, 2,100 tons and modern, was sunk by Jap torpedoes while engaged in the Navy's bombardment of enemy positions at Villa and Bairoko, on opposite sides of Kula Gulf in the New Georgia group. Normal complement of the Strong was estimated at about 250 officers and men.

BATH INDEPENDENT, 15 JULY 1943

Even before Pearl Harbor, Bath's housing was stretched beyond its limits, and some working families were living in quarters that would have been disdained during the depths of the Depression. During 1941, when it became clear that private enterprise could by no means cover emergency needs, the federal government pressed for construction of a new project using Lanham Act funds. City fathers resisted on the grounds that such housing would be a tax-exempt burden on the city's services. With John Newell's help as chairman of the Common Council, a federal representative won support for a new project by promising that Uncle Sam would build the project's roads, sewer and water facilities, and, after completion, would pay Bath an annual maintenance fee to offset city expenses. The federal government also promised a new elementary school (Huse School, named in honor of John E. L. Huse, Bath's first World War II fatality). Funds from Washington also completely underwrote an addition to Morse High and provided $265,000 for an addition to Bath Memorial Hospital.

The new development's location was dictated by its need to be within walking distance of BIW and Hyde, and by the layout of the new Route One, which had reoriented Bath's axis of growth.[10] Hyde Park, as the project was called, was located on purchased farmland near the west end of Center Street and Route One. An entire forty-acre neighborhood went up with surprising speed in the last half of 1941. The 200 low-rent dwellings owed their character to the sometimes-eccentric workings of the federal bureaucratic mind: They were built of brick because the bids submitted to Uncle Sam had all been above the federal limit for wood structures; furthermore, they were built southern style, on slabs, with their heaters crammed onto the ground floor. ("Somewhere in Georgia," quipped a Bath newspaperman years later, "there's a housing project with full basements.")[11] In February 1942, families began moving in.

More Lanham Act funds were forthcoming. Early in 1942, Uncle Sam authorized construction of Lambert Park, a North End complex of "temporary" two-family houses and dormitories to house 1,235 men, two to a room. The Federal Housing Authority also subsidized the conversion of large, single-family homes into multiple apartments, while a Fair Rent Commission office kept watch for rent gougers. Entrepreneurs opened trailer camps. Pete Newell publicly appealed to Bath citizens with spare rooms to make them available to service personnel, who were not eligible for housing in federal projects. Such measures eased but did not end the severe housing shortage.

By mid-1942, every livable space in Bath was occupied, as well as a few that were less than livable. Vacation cottages and slapdash summer camps were pressed into service. Possibly the low point in emergency housing was the refurbishing of the transformer shed at the old Percy & Small shipyard site: one room, ten feet square, with a woodstove for heat and no plumb-

MAINE MARITIME MUSEUM

Lambert Park, Uncle Sam's response to Bath's severe housing shortage.

ing whatever.[12] It rented. Dos Passos described a few junkyard shacks cobbled together from assorted scraps by "hopeless individualists."[13]

Traffic had become a nightmare. Plans had been made to construct an underpass at High Street and a separate approach to the Carlton Bridge for through traffic, but the project was held up indefinitely by wartime shortages of materials. Wartime rationing of tires and gasoline, imposed in 1942, reduced traffic somewhat but threatened to keep out-of-town employees from reaching Bath. In response, BIW instituted and coordinated a ride-sharing program that became the best in the nation by 1943, averaging 4.57 riders per vehicle and involving 9,500 employees. By 1943, when wear and tear on nonreplaceable automobiles began to take its toll, the company had its own transportation department under Edward Edgren. Edgren treated transportation like the crisis it was, matching riders, finding critical tires and gasoline coupons for drivers, and keeping parking lots open in all kinds of weather. Edgren's most creative step was to lease thirty-seven Navy buses and put them into regular service to and from outlying towns. The bus arrivals and departures coincided with the three daily shift changes at BIW.[14] Keeping tired and wheezy buses on the road year round was no small task, and the success of the wartime bus service was a vital ingredient of BIW's phenomenal efficiency. It also went a long way toward reducing pressure on the municipality.

MAINE MARITIME MUSEUM

Defense workers' dormitories in Bath, built in 1942.

LIEUT. JOHN HUSE IS BATH'S FIRST CASUALTY OF WAR

Parents Get Word That He Has Been Killed

The war in the Pacific was brought home to Bath in all its grim reality and tragic consequences early Thursday with the brief announcement . . . of the death of . . . 1st Lieut. John E. L. Huse, Air Corps, U. S. A., on February 3, 1942. . . .

Lieut. Huse left San Francisco on Oct. 17 [1941] in one of the Army's huge four-motored bombers and arrived in the Philippines a few days later. Further than this the family had no knowledge of his location, but believed it possible that he had seen service on the Malayan peninsula.

Lieut. Huse was born in Bath, May 2, 1916. He graduated from Morse High School in 1934, studied for one year at Stanton Preparatory Academy . . . for his preparation for entrance examinations to the United States Military academy at West Point. . . .

. . . While at Morse High School Lieut. Huse was an outstanding student. He was

MAINE MARITIME MUSEUM

co-valedictorian of his class, attaining an average rank of 97 which has seldom been exceeded or equaled. He was president of his class and took an active part in practically all school activities. . . .

BATH DAILY TIMES, 19 FEBRUARY 1942

POSTHUMOUS MEDAL PRESENTED FIRST LIEUTENANT JOHN E. L. HUSE OF BATH. . . .

In the blazing sunlight of Maxwell Field, Alabama, a few days ago, two young women stood soberly at attention. . . . Medals were to be awarded posthumously to two Army Air Force officers killed in action. Widows of the two officers were there to receive the awards.

One of the two women standing quietly there on that great field . . . was Mrs. Nell B. Huse, widow of First Lieutenant John E. L. Huse who was this day being decorated posthumously with the Silver Star for gallantry in aerial action. Lieut. Huse . . . was shot down over Java in the Jap's first attack on the Dutch Island.

. . . The award . . . is a hint to some of the action he must have experienced. The posthumous award of the Purple Heart a few months ago was another hint that Lieut. Huse had met the enemy before that day

TIMES RECORD

> over Java. With full military honors, he was buried at Malang, Java. . . .
>
> His younger brother, Robert M. Huse, is now a private with a detachment of the 9th Weather Squadron, stationed on some little, treeless, bushless island many miles off the coast of South America.
>
> *BATH INDEPENDENT*, 15 JULY 1943

In the spring of 1942, General Sherman Miles, commander of the First Corps Area, admonished citizens of coastal New England to be alert for spies. "An attempt may be made to land enemy agents from axis [sic] submarines operating off our shores. Such agents . . . may betray themselves through their unfamiliarity with the locality. If you see a strange face in an unlikely spot and have sound reason to believe the person is acting suspiciously—notify your police at once."[15] Miles warned citizens to avoid hasty decisions, advice that Bath people had taken to heart three months earlier, when shots were fired on the Carlton Bridge.

Shortly after Pearl Harbor, a military guard had been placed on the bridge to thwart possible sabotage. In the wee hours of a January morning in 1942, a sentry noted that a big black sedan, having traversed the bridge from Woolwich, had crossed into the eastbound lane and stopped overlooking the busy yard of the Iron Works. That looked suspicious. The guard hailed the driver, who gave no answer but blinked his lights. Was he perhaps signaling someone? The soldier fired a round overhead. More blinking lights; then another shot from the soldier, who approached the vehicle. Its driver, staring into a rifle muzzle, spoke with a decided accent. A foreign agent?

Bath policemen, who took the prisoner into custody for questioning, got to the bottom of the mystery. According to the local press, "The driver identified himself as Harry Argiroulas, Brunswick restaurant proprietor, and told police that the second time his lights blinked it was accidental. No explanation was offered for the first blinking other than to acknowledge the presence of the guard who the driver said he saw but didn't hear until he fired. He said he had stopped to watch welders at work on the ships at the Bath Iron Works Corp. After producing satisfactory identification he was released."[16]

Although the bridge incident had its comic side, it revealed the depth of uneasiness in the early days of the war, when the coast supposedly swarmed with U-boats, and spies or saboteurs might be operating under citizens' noses. Rumors flew at all levels. Charlie Burden, still in knee pants, got word that Japanese paratroopers had stealthily landed in the Oak Grove Cemetery. Unable to arouse any support from the local constabulary, he and his playmates conducted their own sweep through granite rows of the enemy's drop zone, satisfying themselves that Bath people could sleep peacefully for at least another night.[17] Meanwhile, adults prepared for strategic warfare. The importance of the Iron Works raised serious concern that the Shipbuilding City would be a target for Axis bombers. Accordingly, an air-raid signal was installed at City Hall, and, as in other cities, Bath civil defense units enforced total blackout security during air-raid drills. At Morse High, students pitched in for the war effort by building model airplanes for the Navy's aircraft recognition training. A human interest article on Morse's festive 1942 commencement that ran later in a national magazine offered the wistful observation that graduates were moving "toward battle lines, toward field hospitals; toward jobs in factories. . . . Some of them will work and fight—some of them will die"; and those who attended that commencement had been handed programs printed with blackout instructions.[18]

Later in the war, British fighter pilots training at Brunswick's new naval facility liked to show off the right stuff by flying their Corsairs full tilt between the cable supports of the Carlton Bridge.[19] The worrisome thing was that they performed the maneuver upside down. The reassuring thing was that such cocky displays put the local military situation into perspective: The Allies had the upper hand, and the front was a long way from Bath. Fears of outright enemy attack (always a remote possibility at best) had eased.

Bath's ability to increase homefront production was challenged by the departure of hundreds of its citizens for military service. Experiences of Bath men and women in uniform deserve a book unto themselves, for they transcend the limitations of this study, for which a few representative examples must suffice.

During the thirties, there was an airstrip in East Brunswick where Herbie Simpson kept a biplane. On Sundays, people looking for a thrill used to congregate there to watch recreational parachute jumps, or perhaps take a spin themselves. That was how Stewart Day, Jr., got a boyhood birthday surprise. "Everybody knew I wanted to fly," he later recalled, "so . . . my grandmother and grandfather gave me a ride." After that, young Day was hooked on airplanes. It was probably natural, then, when the South End gang went to Portland to enlist in the Navy in 1942, that Day, nineteen, surprised his buddies by signing up for Air Corps training. Since graduating, Day had been working at BIW, but "I joined up because I thought it was going to be over quick. I thought it would be over before I got a chance to do anything. That was a mistake, there."[20]

Day trained as a tail gunner in heavy bombers and was assigned to "Mary Pat," a B-17 in an Eighth Air Force bombardment group stationed at Great Ashfield, England. "I liked flying every minute. We never had any second thoughts. I was on my first mission and began to think it was serious because one of our planes tipped his wing up into the propeller of the other one and lost about four feet of the wing. When I saw that flying by, I thought it was getting pretty serious along about then." Mary Pat took part in the celebrated Regensburg air raid, where the action was the thickest: " . . . they flew everything against us that they could fly . . . , and they never quit until we went down through the Brenner Pass, down through Italy [to North Africa]. We lost about eighty planes altogether, between ditching in the ocean and one thing and another. The most planes I ever saw go down at once was twenty-six all going down at the same time . . . , it was probably on that raid. . . . They used to stay away when we were bombing France—they weren't too aggressive—but when we started bombing Germany, why then they were really aggressive. . . . They used to fly us right over Hermann Goering's Flying Circus boys all the time, right over their airfield, to stir them up . . . so we could shoot them down. By shooting them down, you eventually wore them out; that's how they got rid of them. But they took a lot of us with them. They had yellow-nosed ones and red-nosed ones; you couldn't mistake them. When their airplanes were up there, you knew they were up there. They used to fly so close, [that] if I knew what [the name of] the person was, I could have told you who was flying the airplane."[21] During his combat service, Day knocked down three attacking German fighters.

Day's last mission was against German submarine pens at Bordeaux in December 1943, when Mary Pat was hit by antiaircraft fire. "The day they shot us down, they blew a hole through the side that you could walk through, in the radio room. Blew the tail off right over my head. . . . I don't know how I got by that one; just lucky, I guess. They got our ball turret man and two waist gunners. The radio man was hit, but a lot of those twenty millimeters went through his legs, blew out the bulkhead, set us on fire. . . . " Mary Pat was ditched about a thousand yards off the French coast. Crewmembers managed to get their wounded buddies into liferafts before their plane sank, but they were hit by hostile small-arms fire from onshore as they tried to get onto a beach. Day, who was wounded, and two others survived, thanks to the arrival of a German air-sea rescue plane. After hospitalization and interrogation ("I told them I was spare crew and didn't know where I was going or anything else"), he was shipped to Krems, Austria, to sit out the war in Stalag 17. For the next year and a half, he and other sullen POWs subsisted largely on thin fare: rutabagas, boredom, Red Cross parcels, deception, and whatever vegetables they could scrounge from slave laborers toiling in the adjoining fields.[22]

Public relations organs of the American armed forces supplied civilian news media with items about native sons' combat service, which allowed homefront readers to keep tabs on the war in a personally meaningful way. The ongoing tale of Day's aerial victories, his subsequent loss over France, and his reappearance in a Nazi prison camp was probably the biggest cliff-hanger to appear in the *Times* during World War II, but it was by no means the only dramatic one. The *Times* and the *Independent*, of course, also covered the exploits of servicemen home on furlough. For example, when Norman Seekins arrived in Bath in May 1943, after seeing action on the U.S.S. *Salt Lake City*, he told a reporter that the old cruiser and her men had " 'tackled the enemy at Wake, Wotje, Marcus, Guadalcanal, and the Savo Islands' . . . and that they believed 'they have sunk more ships than any other vessel in the history of the United States Navy.' "[23] Seekins himself wore five battle stars and was on his way to officers candidate school.

BATH'S SONS PLAY THEIR PARTS IN THIS GREAT WAR

Sons of Bath are on the far flung battle fronts in this World War II. They are performing with credit to themselves and to their country, and in their letters to relatives in this country complain not at all about conditions on foreign soil and all seem anxious to get a whack at a Jap or a Wop or a Nazi as the case may be.

Take young Jackie Spellman, for instance. Jackie is the son of Mr. and Mrs. John Spellman . . . , formerly of this city. . . . He is a sergeant in the air corps and his squadron, up to the first of the year, had been in 41 raids. . . . Spellman's squadron consists of light bombers and the men live in huts and pup tents on a field attacked almost daily by the Luftwaffe when not attacking Germans in Tunisia.

. . . There is no recreation, no place to go and nothing to do but fly, eat and sleep. Rations for weeks come out of cans and there was no surprise element. Always it was hash. . . .

BATH INDEPENDENT, 14 JANUARY 1943

LIEUT. ARTHUR F. CAIN, JR., MISSING IN ACTION OVER THE PHILIPPINES

Pilot of a P-47 Thunderbolt Had Named Plane for His Home Town, "Bath, Maine"—Was on Combat Mission over Luzon

Mrs. Shirley S. Cain recently received word from the War Department that her husband Lt. Arthur F. Cain, Jr., has been missing in action over the Philippines since Jan. 17.

Pilot of a P-47 Thunderbolt fighter, Lt. Cain named his plane after his home town, The Bath Maine. Condemned because of its number of combat hours, this plane was left behind in New Guinea.

A member of the 69th Fighter Squadron, Fifth Air Force, he was based at Leyte and Mindoro, but was over Luzon on a combat

TIMES RECORD

> mission at the time he was reported missing. . . . He was cited for meritorious achievement while participating in sustained operational flight missions in the Southwest Pacific Area. . . . In the course of these operations, strafing and bombing attacks were made from dangerously low altitudes, destroying and damaging enemy installations and equipment. Lt. Cain is the son of Mr. and Mrs. Arthur F. Cain of 36 Bluff Road. Their other son, Pfc. Raymond E. Cain is now in the Pacific with the 4th Marine Air Wing. . . .
>
> *BATH INDEPENDENT*, 8 MARCH 1945

When Battery H had been called up in 1940, Linwood Temple chose not to "sit in Portland Harbor." He worked for a while under draft deferment at BIW, then joined the Navy. By the summer of 1945, he was a machinist's mate with a flying boat unit in the Philippines. "We were being trained as pioneer groups," he related later. "We were going [to be] in the invasion of Japan. After the first wave, we were going to set up the pioneer groups for the brass and things like that. We were not particularly happy about it. But, I can remember that night in August when Truman said, 'Drop the Bomb,' and they did. We were happy people! Many people now think it was a crime to do that, but if you are in the war you fight to win. You use what you have at the time to do it. We would have had millions of men killed in the invasion of Japan. I might not be here."[24]

Staff Sergeant Stewart Day, Jr., meanwhile, had been liberated by the Allies, but not before he underwent a few more harrowing experiences. As advancing Soviet troops approached, the Germans evacuated POWs to the west by rail and foot. Day's group of several hundred POWs trekked under the fretful but ineffectual eyes of elderly guards, as the Third Reich collapsed all around them. "We raided everything we could raid on the way when the Germans weren't looking. If the road was full of chickens . . . we grabbed them. We stole pigs, pigeons and everything we could get hold of to eat. Vegetables. Polish women were planting potatoes. . . . When we went through . . . we'd grab a bag. Jeez, they almost fainted! . . . We marched 300 miles over the mountains there toward Germany. We ended up near Braunau, where Hitler was going to make his last stand. They were going to use us for hostages for bargaining purposes, but it never materialized because Patton's Third Army swept through there and cleaned them out before they got organized. . . . They got through marching us and they dumped us into a wooded area. . . . We had to make our own shelter, and stayed there for three or four days before Patton's Thirteenth came in and took over, recaptured us you might say. Then we took the Germans and marched them into the nearest town and dumped them off. About that time, I was getting anxious to return home." Day, who had plenty to be bitter about, had meanwhile seen much more: "I probably hated the Germans. . . . We knew what they were doing. I know one time when we were on the march we met a bunch of those SS marching Jews along the road—Hungarian Jews. . . . I counted twenty-six dead . . . where they shot them in the head. . . . If they dropped out, they shot them." Once, Day caught sight of a distant death camp "with the smoke coming out of the stacks. We didn't know about the burning at that time. . . . But we knew that they were killing the Jews."[25]

In July 1945, after an airlift to England and a transatlantic crossing on an LST—"the worst ride I ever had in my life"—Day arrived home. "I kind of held low, you might say. I went to Popham Beach and everywhere I wanted to go. I stayed away from crowds and stuff, and it finally wore away. I guess a couple of years went by before I settled down; all that experience, I guess. I wasn't too talkative. . . . It took a couple of years to get over it, to settle down."[26]

Although they may not at first have noticed, weary veterans returned to a city itself much changed by war. Given over to care and feeding of its swollen population and the daily influx of thousands of working commuters, Bath's prosperity was obscured by cramped, boomtown conditions. Just south of the bridge, adjoining the expanded sprawl of the Iron Works and Hyde Windlass, was the Barbary Coast, a scuzzy warren of hole-in-the-wall lunch counters, takeout beer joints, and streetwalkers, all cashing in on workers' fat times and servicemen's determination to paint the town red. The general effect was shabby and trash was everywhere.

Even in the downtown business section, merchants had succumbed to the lure of the fast buck and the problems of wartime shortages. There was no need to glamorize merchandise or make shopping a pleasure; customers

MAINE MARITIME MUSEUM

Bath's seedy Barbary Coast.

with money in their pockets but no time to spare bought whatever was offered without quibbling. Traffic inched past cars parked in every available space on and off the littered streets. Lines at the liquor store on Front Street were the longest in the state. Taking it all in, a professional educator deemed the region generally unfit for decent youth: "The rise in criminal tendencies among adults and minors alike cannot be ignored. The war years with their emotional violence, disorganization of social mores and customs, upheavals of home and community, have wreaked a heavy toll. . . . How, then, can these evils be combated—the lure of the uniform for the light-minded girls, the intriguing possibilities of unsupervised hours for restless boys? What can detract from the fascination of the shining cocktail bars, the sordid road houses, the juke boxes, the floods of colorful magazines of doubtful benefit, the risque books and motion pictures that present a bewildering kaleidoscope of possibilities to minds hectic with the onward rush of war and the repercussions of peace? Take a walk down Center or Front Streets in Bath, Maine, any night in the week, and really observe what surrounds the pedestrian. There one has a cross section of the youth of America."[27]

The youth of Bath—more numerous, of course, than in the thirties—were also more likely to be at loose ends with both parents working. To stem the tide of juvenile aimlessness, the city created three supervised playgrounds during the war, but otherwise, youngsters were to a large extent on their own. Sports activities at Kelley Field were off limits for many, however, because the place had become a hangout for rats overflowing the nearby city dump.

It was not even necessary to go to Center and Front streets to get a slice of the racier side of wartime life. Pity the poor North Enders living near the armory, where blaring, all-night dances for the BIW swing shift kept

MAINE MARITIME MUSEUM

A servicemen's dance at the Bath USO.

policemen busy and householders tossing in their beds. Stanley Hunter, whose job at the Oakhurst Dairy required him to rise early, remembered that armory revelers would "get down the road and holler and whoop and swear. They'd been drinking—I presume they had or they wouldn't talk the way they did. . . . We didn't complain too much, but the neighbors up at the corner, they only lasted a couple of weeks, I guess."[28] A neighborhood petition to City Council brought an end to the dances.

Visiting servicemen, most of whom were naval personnel getting advance training on new destroyers, could attend downtown dances held by the United Service Organizations (USO). But the "lure of the uniform for the light-minded girls" was indeed a serious problem. Chester McCabe, Bath's public health officer, was charged with identifying streetwalkers and having them tested for venereal disease. In 1945, he reported that several females had been institutionalized, and that 129 cases of VD had been diagnosed in Bath. A year later, he reported 135 such cases.[29]

Bath's quality of life suffered mightily from wartime shortages and rationing, although there were innovative ways to remove some obstacles. Young John Gilmore, whose social life revolved around his car, began to take the war seriously when Uncle Sam instituted gasoline rationing. To keep mobile, he connected with a friend whose business entitled him to a generous allotment of fuel stamps and who had his own connection at a Woolwich filling station: "If there was a certain person on duty over there, there was no problem. I would take my car over there with Frank; he'd have the stamps and we'd get gas. If we couldn't, his father had a big truck that he used to haul wood to Pejepscot [Paper Co.] on; he'd get that filled up and come over to Bath. We'd take a siphon hose and siphon it out of the truck and put it in my car."[30]

Roger Luke's problem was more serious: His wartime work for Hyde often took him out of town, leaving Molly housebound with the children, unable to devote the requisite time to food foraging. "At the end of the war, my wife went to the doctor and he said, 'I've never seen a worse case of malnutrition.' . . . Well, with two young children, and I was away a lot. . . . Well finally, I went to a man who was a pattern maker [at Hyde Windlass]. He had some cows 'way down in Phippsburg. I said, 'Look, can't I buy some cream?' I said, 'If I can at least get some cream, at least I can churn butter.' He said, 'What's the matter?' and I told him about Molly, and so we got everything we needed. We got good, rich milk."[31]

By the autumn of 1944, *Times* editor Harry Webber was exasperated with the citywide look of neglect: "During these wartime days Bath is not the attractive little New England city we have known in the past. The city in many sections is dirty. Even the mayor and members of the city government have admitted this. Then why not have a cleanup this fall and start drastic enforcement of the law against any person, or persons, who may throw rubbish and garbage into any city street, lane or other property not designated as a city dump?"[32]

The slovenly attitudes that annoyed Webber were partly attributable to the fact that Bath filled every day with hurried people who lived elsewhere and may have known nothing of Bath's days as an "attractive little New England city." But much of the problem was beyond the effective power of individuals or local government: ubiquitous parked cars, which prevented proper snow removal in winter; overcrowded housing, which strained Bath's fragile sewer system in every season; and wartime shortages of critical maintenance equipment and materials, which thwarted the best municipal intentions.[33]

City fathers coped with the situation manfully on a day-to-day basis, for they could see the worsening effects of wear and tear, and they resourcefully exploited governmental largesse for the duration of the national emergency. Nonetheless, they quite misunderstood the inflationary impact of high wages and wartime shortages on the city, and thus made no accommodation with these phenomena. As a consequence, Bath came out of World War II in shabby shape, without the financial wherewithal to cope with postwar adjustments. All this despite the grim lessons of the city's post-World War I tribulations and continual discussions about the need to prepare for peacetime.

Although the federal government imposed fairly rigid price controls, wartime prices and wages rose substantially. At BIW, base wages increased no less than 22 percent in real terms (that is, adjusted for inflation). In view of the lack of consumer goods and housing supplies on the wartime market, that meant that the average worker was substantially increasing his or her disposable income. Uncle Sam's policy in those years was to soak up as much surplus income as possible through war bond sales and taxes. Yet in Bath, the local tax bite, expressed in constant dollars, fell about 10.5 percent during the war—a formidable compliment to the local principle of tax restraint. In 1940 and 1941, when the prewar boom was on, real operating expenditures had dropped below the value of 1939's in terms of constant dollars; after Pearl Harbor, they climbed in annual steps until 1946. When federal assistance is considered along with inflation, it is apparent that Bath taxpayers had an easy ride during World War II.

Even adjusted for inflation, expenditures for education rose at a phenomenal rate, because enrollment increased 35 percent during the war years. High industrial wage scales and rents necessitated competitive salaries for teachers, and keeping Bath's post-Depression facilities operative was likewise expensive. "Probably no other phase of city government has felt the impact of war conditions more than the School Department," read Bath's annual report for 1942–43. "Schools not only teach the ABCs but also serve as agencies of democracy in salvage campaigns, defense stamp sales, draft registration, rationing, civilian defense education, Junior Red Cross, special wartime courses including administering the National Defense Welding School." Wartime outlays for schools increased 196 percent in actual dollars, or more than 100 percent in constant dollars. Nonetheless, the school department was conducting a holding action as facilities grew creakier by the year.

Sewerage was the second-largest municipal expense in the war years. The nature of Bath's terrain and soil, as well as the city's long, narrow layout, presented a real challenge in waste disposal as the population doubled. The municipal sewer system had developed slowly, spreading from the downtown core to virtually all the built-up areas by the thirties. There were no treatment plants; raw sewage was simply discharged from several outfalls directly into the river. Much of the system was old and inadequate, and even before the onset of war, open sewers and cellars filled with waste from backed-up mains were facts of life in the city. By the end of the thirties, the mushrooming population caused sewer problems to multiply, creating a distinct threat to public health. It was not until 1942, however, that the city government began to overhaul, extend, and improve the sewer system. In 1943, the highway and sewer department reported that "probably more money has been spent on sewers in Bath in the past year than in the preceding 25 years. . . . "[34] That, of course, was a relative statement. The city did indeed devote a larger percentage of its budget to sewerage problems, but when the figures are adjusted for inflation, it is apparent that Bath's wartime sewerage expenditures actually decreased below the 1939 level. Expenditures proved inadequate to meet the problem. Such conservatism may be explained partly by the shortage of critical paving products, which discouraged street excavation.

Wartime pressure made the city dump pestilential. Enormous rats roamed vast piles of unburned trash, and on burning days, acrid smoke permeated the city's northwest neighborhood. The situation was neglected until state public health officials condemned the site in July 1944. An alternative dump site was hastily acquired and, after an enforced cleanup, the old dump was closed.

On a more creative note, the city established a federally assisted recreational program, equipping and supervising three playgrounds. Such a program was the personal mission of Edward J. (Red) McMann, a mail carrier and father of five. McMann attended virtually every City Council meeting to promote his objectives and state his views of municipal affairs on no uncertain terms, thus earning the reputation throughout Bath's seven wards as "the councilman from Ward 8." McMann's hobby was politics, which he pursued with a passion. By the forties, he had built up considerable political influence without holding an outright office. "He didn't have to," explained Jim Temple. "He was always pushing someone else who owed a little credit to him for his help, and when it was time to call in the chit . . . , he had several in various places. . . . "[35] McMann's brash persistence made

MAINE MARITIME MUSEUM

Red McMann.

him controversial around City Hall. Willie McCabe recalled that he "was very set in his ways. If he had an idea in his head, there wasn't much way you was going to get it out. But Red McMann probably did more for the children in Bath, as far as recreation goes, than any other man that I can think of, because he was really dedicated. It didn't make no difference if it was a kid in Bath who needed clothes or something [else]. When Red found out about it, somehow it was produced."[36] After the war, the city took over the USO hall for use as a recreational center for young people, and McMann served as recreation commissioner. Recreation, however, would always be considered a frill by postwar City Hall economizers, who readily cut its budget in favor of other priorities. The programs would have died altogether without McMann's perennial championship.

More assertive leadership could have improved Bath's financial condition and equipped it to spruce up its shabby infrastructure in peacetime, but the municipal government maintained only a holding action against current need, a policy that generated its own set of problems. Wartime growth required city fathers to spend more of their annual budgets for police and fire protection. Conduct of the police force became a hot issue, as departures for military service caused a rapid turnover in the office of marshal (chief), and City Council members volubly promoted their personal favorites for the office. The force, meanwhile, was too small to cope with the city's expanding problems. It was repeatedly criticized for its tolerance of parking violations, which merchants insisted was poison to business. In 1941, the forceful Deputy Marshal Percy Kingsbury had publicly advised his patrolmen that "our job is a task in which it is almost impossible to make friends . . . but nevertheless you have a job to do and you're going to do it," a gesture that was surely designed to mollify critics.[37] Under pressure, discontented patrolmen demanded that City Council award them a 30 percent pay raise or face en masse resignations. They settled for 21 percent late in 1942, but after that, it was open season on the force.

QUARTET OF BATH POLICEMEN ARMED WITH NEW REISING SUB-MACHINE GUNS

The new sub-machine guns added to the department's equipment a few days ago were first tried out by members of the police force Thursday afternoon and proved most successful. And the men found them much to their liking. . . . The men fired 20 shot clips in almost less time than it takes to draw a deep breath.

With the addition of the sub-machine guns and the now assured two way radio the police department will be virtually as well equipped as many of the larger departments in the State and certainly on a par with any small department. . . .

BATH DAILY TIMES, 11 DECEMBER 1941

TIMES RECORD

Alderman Charles A. Shepard, proprietor of a shoe store on Front Street, demanded better police work. "Every ordinance of the City is being broken many times daily and nothing is being done about it," he reportedly told City Council in January 1943. "There's been too much talk and not enough action. The only activity in the police department is so little that I could do it and run a shoe store too and I don't know anything about police work."[38] Those were fighting words to the police, who in an open letter to Bath citizens stated that "the police department is, has been, and always will be a political football as long as it is controlled by its politicians." As to the charge that they were loafers: "We feel that we as a body of 11 men answering anywhere from 250 to 400 complaints per month, by telephone alone, do fairly well along with the many other duties. . . .

"The FBI states that every city should have one officer for every 1000 population. According to that we should have at least nine more men to aid in the work we are now doing ourselves."[39]

A remedy for the political football problem was on the way, however. In March of 1943, the citizens of Bath, in "as lackadaisical a city election as can be remembered here," approved a bill to establish civil service standards for city employees.[40] That effectively reduced City Council's pressure on patrolmen, but relations were strained throughout the war because of arguments over the force's inattention to recommended professional standards. Alderman John Newell characterized the situation as a "comedy," reportedly adding that the police "pay no attention to anything the mayor says."[41]

Remarks like Newell's about the mayor's authority spoke once more to the issue of whether or not Bath's old charter was equal to new demands. During 1944, City Council commissioned John Carey to draft another version of a charter reform proposal for discussion and possible acceptance. The resulting document was more of a compromise with tradition than the ill-fated proposal of 1939 had been. Its provisions included retaining the Board of Aldermen as Bath's unicameral government, and strengthening the office of mayor into that of a quasi-manager by giving him appointive power over department heads. To reduce absenteeism and encourage familiarity with public issues, aldermen under the new charter would receive modest fees for their service. The old discrepancy between the date of the fiscal year and the election year (a relic of the days when elections were postponed until winter subsided) would be eliminated and, in the interest of clarity, phraseology would conform to usage in new ordinances.

Carey worked hard to sell the new plan, telling City Council that Bath was probably the last city in Maine still making do with a horse-and-buggy charter: "To maintain the present charter is costing money. It is like a man who needs medical attention but puts off an operation through fear. After he finally takes the step and fully recovers he wonders why he hadn't done it before."[42] But some councilmen and aldermen still thought the operation was worse than the disease. After two lengthy debates in early 1945, they could not come to terms. Some thought monetary compensation was improper or that the mayor would become too powerful; others said the time was wrong for the requisite charter referendum, what with native sons away in the service and the city full of newcomers insensitive to Bath's particular circumstances. What was the hurry? Bath could get by with the old system at least until the war was over.[43]

Dramatic Allied advances in 1944 and 1945 accelerated local concern about postwar readjustment. From its very inception, everyone in Bath had known the boom wouldn't last, and in fact the city began to shrink long before the end of hostilities. At the Iron Works, people were let go as improved productivity reduced manpower requirements. Between 1943 and V-J Day, the company payroll dropped from 13,000 to 9,000 and Hyde's fell from 1,000 to 400. For years there had been talk about how to prepare for Bath's peacetime readjustment. After his reelection in March 1942, Mayor Pete Rogers stated publicly that the postwar period "does not present a pleasant anticipation, for when the postwar condition does arrive, currency will not be so liquid as at the present time."[44] Bath, therefore, should exploit its prosperity to prepare for a slump. But to Rogers and his City Council colleagues, that meant merely upgrading the city's equipment wherever possible and, more important, whittling down the public debt without overburdening the taxpayer.

Given the wartime conditions, they and the city department heads did a creditable job on both counts. For example, the city leased restricted or unavailable big-ticket items such as vehicles from the federal government, then bought them outright at low prices when victory was in sight and Uncle Sam wanted to clear the books. At such times, City Hall conservatives did not flinch at departmental overdrafts. It had also become regular practice intentionally to overspend annual education budgets because the federal government would always make up the difference.

Meanwhile, Rogers and his colleagues made impressive inroads against the city's indebtedness, wiping out the floating debt in 1944 and reducing the bonded debt to below $200,000 by 1945.[45] But there were rumblings about the need to do more, notably to establish a reserve during those good times to help with problems of the inevitable postwar slump. That could only be accomplished by raising taxes, a measure the city government was of course loath to take. Tax restraint remained in force: The mill rate rose from 45 to 48 between 1941 and 1943 but stayed put for the duration of the war. Even if taxes had been raised, it is doubtful that resulting monies would have been used for more than further debt reduction, for that constituted Bath's highest priority for achieving stability. As Rogers inimitably put it in 1943, "a belief which I entertain, and especially as concerning a community such as our own, which is obligated by a heavy indebtedness which must be liquidated, is that a good post-war plan would eliminate, or in the least reduce this embarrassment to the greatest possible minimum, prior to the advent of post-war conditions."[46]

Not many argued. The elections of March 1943 (in which city civil service standards were approved) were held when Bath's population was almost twice what it had been just a few years earlier, yet only a handful of citizens showed interest. It was a new low in voter apathy, said the *Times*: "Walter C. Rogers . . . was reelected mayor for a third term Monday as Republican candidates in every ward strolled into office unopposed by any Democratic nominees. With the election in the bag anyhow, only 658 voters wended their way to the polls and many of them were interested mainly in deciding the referendum issues."[47]

In 1944, there was enough dissension in Republican ranks to prompt a few write-in votes, but not enough to make a difference. Nor did the national debate over FDR's fourth-term intentions rub off in the Shipbuilding City: "The matter of a fourth term locally was without controversy and with very little interest as Walter C. Rogers, Republican, was reelected mayor for the fourth consecutive year in a nonchalant city election Monday. Only 460 persons in the entire city were interested enough to go to the polls . . . which saw the entire list of Republican candidates unopposed for the second straight year."[48] In November 1944, Bath voters favored Roosevelt over Thomas E. Dewey by more than four to one.

How Bath would find the ways and means of confronting postwar problems had started to nag civic leaders, however. What could be done to attract more industries? And what if federal grant support evaporated along with defense contracts as soon as peace was established? Early in 1944, City Council established a five-man committee of councilmen and aldermen, including John Newell and Roger Luke, to coordinate ideas about coping with the future. In February 1944, former mayor Harold Small, a kingpin in the charter reform movement, spoke the unspeakable to City Council: "It is my belief that if local industries were to pay larger taxes in current and prosperous times it would be a good thing." After all, he continued, the city had given businesses tax breaks during the Depression. And, since defense plants contracted on a cost-plus-profit basis, they could legitimately pass any higher tax bite on to the federal government as part of their operating overhead. "In this way the city could build up a reserve with which to work when and if dull times set in."[49]

Small had a point, but he was also exhuming the conveniently buried prewar squabbles about corporate influence and responsibility. Higher corporate taxes could only have been achieved via a revaluation of industrial property, a measure that BIW especially would have regarded as a disaster. Much of the company's expanded property, paid for by the federal government, could well become a liability as soon as peace broke out and warship construction stopped. Accordingly, higher taxes would increase BIW's overhead at a time when competition would be cutthroat, possibly worsening the anticipated postwar slump in Bath. That may explain why BIW paid the city an unpublicized "supplementary tax" of $15,000 that year.[50] The tax rate stayed put.

By early 1945, the Allies were closing the ring around Berlin and storming ashore at Iwo Jima. In Bath, where newspapers were full of talk about an impending victory, the question of how to wean the city from its wartime economy still loomed. Mayor Rogers himself was on record as saying that "conditions which we are about to be confronted with . . . are much too gigantic for the average mind to anticipate," but the Bath city government still concentrated on eliminating city debt as insurance against the future.[51]

Cutbacks at BIW and Hyde were providing a whiff of things to come. To wrestle with these issues, civic organizations formed discussion committees and exchanged dialogue. The result was mostly talk, not action, probably because action meant money and money meant higher taxes, but the voters were stirring again.

In February 1945, Mayor Rogers prepared to run for his fifth consecutive term. At the city Republican caucus, he was renominated on grounds that he had guided Bath throughout "trying times." But there was some outright opposition: Harold Small was nominated by Carl French, who countered that the times had hardly been trying. On the contrary, said French, they were prosperous times, ones in which the city had had the opportunity to prepare for a dropping population and a drooping economy. Bath needed to depart from its conservative, pennypinching habits, said French, and elect a mayor "not subject to pressure groups and not afraid to get the money required."[52] Here again was the issue of corporate responsibility to the city, along with the implication that Rogers had been in office long enough.

Rogers prevailed and won the nomination over Small. As before, the Democrats did not field a single candidate for city office. Small, however, decided to run alone on the "Citizen" ticket as an alternative to Rogers. The principal issue of the election was Small's advocacy of aggressive taxation.

Harry Webber of the *Times* stuck to the principle he had espoused in the *Times* five years earlier: that the role of business should not become a political football. In sharp contrast to the 1940 campaign, 1945's was almost devoid of publicity, paid or otherwise. An advertisement on Small's behalf spoke weakly to the rumor that he was anti-business, pointing out only that tax assessments were beyond any mayor's official jurisdiction, as though that explanation would somehow dispose of the tax issue.[53]

More than four times as many voters turned out for the March 1945 election as had done so the year before. Rogers won, 1,097 to 766. During 1945, BIW paid the city another "supplementary tax" of $18,000.

Within a few months of the election, the question of how to plan for the postwar future had disappeared. The future had arrived.

WILDLY ENTHUSIASTIC CROWDS JAM THE BUSINESS DISTRICT TUESDAY NIGHT

Thousands Gather to Add to Noisy Demonstration Due to Surrender of Japan

It was a spontaneous and orderly demonstration that occurred in Bath when word came last evening of the unconditional surrender of the Japs. The first street demonstration noted by the writer happened near Legion hall when a neighbor appeared on his walk ringing lustily a large bell, and telling people that the President had just announced the capitulation. A little lad with a set of sleighbells joined him, jingling merrily the sweet toned bells. Soon an occasional motorist came along tooting his horn vociferously, and in just a few minutes the swelling notes of noise-making and the increasing traffic brought a real demonstration into being.

Someone called the B.I.W. and asked why the whistle was not blowing and the operator replied they had not heard the news. But soon the deep throated whistle at the yard was heard adding to the increasing crescendo of happy sound. . . .

Church bells added to the volume of the sound as did the increasing number of autos, and the whistles of other industrial plants of the city. A reporter sat in a Times window and watched the throng gathering, and the auto traffic increasing. . . . Cars went by the Times office at the rate of 1500 an hour for more than two hours. And all of them added to the din of the celebration. . . . A young girl went past, riding a bicycle. Two "pigtails" of hair-braids hung down her back, decorated with a red ribbon, and she wore a gaily colored shirt which wafted in the breeze as she sailed along.

Quantities of paper wafted down from the windows and fell in showers upon delighted passers-by. Soon the street was littered with the papers and it looked like snow as the breeze and the motion of the cars wafted it across the road. A group of young people, dressed in fantastic garb, went by in a car, their laughter filling the air. Cars with gay streamers; others decorated with all sorts of colors, and with long strings of large oil cans tied on behind, passed in an apparently endless procession. The din kept increasing from all sorts of noise-makers attached to the cars or carried by their passengers.

. . . far into the night there came echoes of the celebration as now and then horns were heard and the jolly voices of people homeward bound were heard in laughter and chatter. Bath will not forget for many a day and year, the spontaneous demonstration aroused by the news of the ending of the war and the triumph of a just cause.

BATH INDEPENDENT, 16 AUGUST 1945

BATH'S TWO LARGEST INDUSTRIES FEEL EFFECTS OF WAR NEED DECLINE

Vice President Main of B.I.W. Denies the Rumored Heavy Layoff—Hardings Plant Not to Close

The effects of the sharply lessened demands of the armed services upon American industry that followed the end of the war in the Pacific are being felt by the city's two largest employers. . . . Eight thousand men and women are on the payroll at the Bath Iron Works today, as opposed to 9,000 a month ago. The company's wartime peak was 13,000. At the Hyde Windlass Company's plant, "substantial cutbacks" have forced reduction of the employment level from a wartime high of 1,000 to less than 400. . . .

Rumors that the Bath Iron Works would lay off 1,700 more employees last week were denied in a statement by Archibald M. Main, executive vice-president of the ship-

> yard, who said also that the company was not contemplating closing the Hardings fabrication plant, "now or in the near future, insofar as could be foreseen. . . ."
>
> Stabilization of the Bath Iron Works' employment level depends . . . upon such factors as the Navy Department's delivery schedule of destroyers now under construction at the shipyard, the avoidance of other cutbacks, and the degree of success attending the company's efforts to win commercial shipbuilding contracts. . . .
>
> The drastic employment reduction forced upon the Hyde Windlass Company by the sudden change of international events was caused primarily by what company officials described as "substantial cutbacks." Another reason was that the company's wartime, three shift production was geared several months ahead of the nation's shipbuilding program, in order to assure continued prelaunching delivery of Hyde quality machinery to the various shipyards depending upon it. . . .
>
> *BATH INDEPENDENT*, 5 SEPTEMBER 1945

In late 1945, both BIW and Hyde promoted new contracts to keep active, so the postwar slide was not nearly so steep as some had feared. The increasing layoffs at BIW were mostly at the expense of out-of-towners who had predominated on the wartime payroll. Discontinuation of bus service by the company accelerated attrition, as did a regional job market that stayed far stronger than that of the Shipbuilding City. Another stabilizing factor was the "52–20 Club": Uncle Sam's proviso that returning veterans could draw twenty dollars a week for a full year after discharge. This stayed a rush on the labor force, despite the fact that veterans rated preferential hiring benefits at places such as BIW. For example, Stewart Day used 52–20 for his necessary unwinding process. And John Gilmore, back home after a stint in Europe as an artilleryman, decided to take his time: "Hey, you could draw twenty dollars a week for fifty-two weeks. I drew that for six weeks and then I went to work. They started bumping in the yard: If you were a veteran you had preference. Well, I was probably twenty-three or twenty-four, and I was going to bump a poor old devil fifty-five years old; and I mean that's all he had done all his life, and he didn't have anything. I said no. I was single. . . . I could go out and draw my twenty dollars. I said, 'No, I'm not bumping him. It's my turn, I will go.' I think for two or three weeks I was out. Then I applied for a job with the telephone company and went to work with them."[54] By the spring of 1946, BIW's work force was below 4,000 and hometown people were beginning to feel the pinch.

The adjustment period could have been worse, but it was hardly satisfactory, and the city fathers had not developed strategies other than debt reduction to cope with problems. Because the work-force attrition had largely affected out-of-towners, Bath's critical housing shortage remained, especially after the city started condemning the seedier habitats that could no longer be justified by the emergency. Another crisis that did not go away was the overpopulation in the schools. Lurking perpetually in the background was the perennial issue of debt reduction and low taxes. All of which constituted a weak hand with which to improvise a future. Hindsight affords an inescapable comparison between the years of the Depression and those of the war. In the thirties, with no precedents to fall back on, city fathers had done a lot with a little. In the early and mid-forties, the opposite was the case. Was there a political solution? Could other industries be enticed into the city? Who would pay for refurbishing Bath's worn-out facilities?

As ever, Bath was out of phase with most Maine communities. Joys of the long-anticipated end of World War II were clouded by uncertainty. Peace had halted the industrial crescendo that had revitalized the city while others were shuddering in depression. More than ever, Bath needed some innovative, possibly unique, solutions.

Peacetime had interesting consequences for some of Bath's favorite sons. Early in 1946, Pete Newell was appointed to President Truman's commission to observe the effects of the Bikini A-bomb test. Governor Sumner Sewall was appointed military governor of Bavaria in occupied Germany. And Eddie the Drum Major died at eighty-six. His last parade was on Memorial Day, 1946.

NOTES

1. Herman Krafft, quoted in BI, 20 January 1938.
2. S. Sewall, quoted in ibid., 5 October 1939.
3. L. Temple interview.
4. BI, 26 September 1940.
5. W. Newell, quoted in BDT, 4 April 1941.
6. Robert C. Rosen, *John Dos Passos: Politics and the Writer* (Lincoln: University of Nebraska Press, 1981), p. 105.

7. John Dos Passos, *State of the Nation* (Boston: Houghton Mifflin, 1944), p. 12.
8. Ibid., p. 15.
9. Snow, p. 317.
10. Marentette, pp. 145–46.
11. David L. Swearingen, Interview, Brunswick, ME, May 1987.
12. William Donnell, Personal Communication, Bath, 1971.
13. Dos Passos, p. 12.
14. Snow, pp. 320–22.
15. General S. Miles, quoted in BI, 16 April 1942.
16. BI, 22 January 1942.
17. Charles E. Burden, M.D., Interviews, Woolwich, ME, March-May 1987.
18. Toni Taylor, "High School Graduation, Bath, Maine: 'Like a Mighty Army . . . ,' " *McCall's*, June 1943, p. 15. The commencement program is reproduced in Richard Aldridge, ed., *Memories of Morse, 1904–1979: A Seventy-Fifth Year Tribute to Morse High School in Bath, Maine* (Brunswick, ME: Brunswick Publishing Co., 1979), pp. 112–14.
19. *Captain's Log: A Twelve Month Personal Calendar Accompanying An Intimate History of the Area In and Around Bath, Maine* (Bath: Bath Area Chamber of Commerce, n.d.), p. 35.
20. Day interview.
21. Ibid.
22. Ibid.
23. Norman Seekins, quoted in BI, 27 May 1943.
24. L. Temple interview.
25. Day interview.
26. Ibid.
27. Glenn Kendall, "Study of School Community: Summary of Results of Workshop Course conducted at Bath by Prof. Glenn Kendall, Winter of 1945–1946" (typescript [copy], 1946, Patten Free Library, Bath, ME, hereafter cited as PFL).
28. Stanley R. and Vivian Hunter, Interview, Woolwich, ME, February 1987.
29. *City of Bath Annual Report*, 1944–1945, 1945–1946.
30. Gilmore interview.
31. Luke interview.
32. Editorial, BI, 5 October 1944.
33. *City of Bath Annual Report*, 1943–1944; BI, 14 September 1944.
34. *City of Bath Annual Report*, 1942–1943.
35. J. Temple interview.
36. Willard H. McCabe, Interview, Bath, June 1987.
37. Percy Kingsbury, quoted in BDT, 12 July 1941.
38. Charles A. Shepard, quoted in BI, 12 July 1941.
39. Bath Police Department to the Citizens of Bath, published in ibid.
40. BDT, 2 March 1943.
41. John Newell, quoted in BI, 13 January 1944.
42. John Carey, quoted in BI, 19 March 1942.
43. Editorial, BDT, 6 February 1945.

44. W. Rogers, quoted in BI, 19 March 1942.
45. *City of Bath Annual Report*, 1943–1944, 1944–1945.
46. W. Rogers, quoted in BI, 30 August 1945.
47. BDT, 2 March 1943.
48. Ibid., 8 March 1944.
49. H. Small, quoted in BI, 10 February 1945.
50. BDT, 20 April 1957. This news item concerns BIW's 1957 offer to pay a supplementary tax in lieu of revaluation, and precedents therefor.
51. W. Rogers, Inaugural Speech, Bath, March 1945, published in *City of Bath Annual Report*, 1944–1945.
52. Carl French, quoted in BI, 22 February 1945.
53. BDT, 2 March 1945.
54. Gilmore interview.

3

"Small Town Stuff"

By 1946, Dominique Tardif was one of the best-known, best-liked people in Bath. He had come to the Shipbuilding City in 1929, a year after graduating from high school in Lewiston, to manage the Wisemann Farms dairy store, located near the main entrance of the newly reopened Bath Iron Works. An ice cream salesman is bound to be popular, but Tardif's wholesome good humor, good looks, and ingratiating manner with people of all ages and stations made him even more so: "I called on every store in Bath. Now remember, there were no refrigerators or freezers, so every housewife had to be in one of these stores between nine-thirty and eleven o'clock every morning to get the food for the day . . . , and so this is how I got to know people. And then I went to every basketball game. At that time basketball was big. . . . Every high school kid that had a dime at that time came and I sold the ice cream. . . . Pete Newell quite often walked from his home and would always stop in, and it didn't make any difference that probably the next noontime I would deliver the ice cream to his house at the back door. Pete Newell was just great."[1]

Tardif lived in Ward 6, Bath's Democratic ward. In 1937, on his second try, he won a seat in City Council. A year later, he was elected to the state legislature in Augusta, where, despite his party affiliation, he was included by Senate President and aspiring governor Sumner Sewall in the Republicans' state committee meeting. When the Sewalls threw a party at their upper Washington Street home, Tardif "would deliver the ice cream to the back door, go home and change my clothes, and then come in and be in the receiving line because I was a member of the Legislature. I think the people in Bath accepted that."[2]

In 1940, Tardif took advantage of an opportunity that temporarily ended his political activism: "I had made a deposit in the Bath Trust Company six mornings a week from 1929 [on], and about the second year I was in the bank I said to Bill Skelton who was the vice president, 'Gee, I'd like to have a job in here.' I can see him now. He roared, 'Ha, ha,' so as to say, 'Who the hell do you think you are?' The third time I said it, Bill said, 'Dom, I don't know of anyone that we'd rather have in here than you.' " An opening occurred in June of 1940. "At Wisemann Farms the telephone rang. . . . 'Baxter here. Want to see you at the bank.' . . . So I walked to the bank. Sixteen directors and there was only one I didn't know. I had done business with Dura Howard who owned Howard's two cigar stores, and Charlie Cahill who owned New Meadows Inn and the Colonial Cafe. They were my good customers. Pete Rogers, Pete Newell, Archie Main; I went around the table and there was only one by the name of Sawyer who spent most of his time in Florida, he was the only one I didn't know. So I got back to where Baxter was and he said, 'Want you to come to work next morning.' So it had worked. That was in 1940, and I couldn't have run for any office because Baxter and I used to argue: 'Goddam Democrats!' every time he'd come in. . . . So there was no way I could have ever done anything. I forgot politics completely."[3]

Tardif stayed at Bath Trust until 1946, when he accepted a position with Equitable Life Assurance. That freed him to pursue his political avocation. Meanwhile, Bath's Democratic party had awakened. Tardif was nominated to try to unseat Pete Rogers, who was running for a controversial sixth term, and a slate of Democratic candidates was proposed for City Council. The 1946 race would be the last municipal partisan political contest in Bath history.

"When I decided [to run]," Tardif later recalled, "I just went to everybody. . . . I talked with Don Small . . . who . . . was a boss in the Iron Works. . . . So, I stopped him and he said, 'Yes, Dom?' I said, 'Don, I know you're a good Republican and I know that you've been mayor, and I know that you have to be with the party, but I'd love to have your vote and Marjorie's.' 'Haw, haw!' He laughed and laughed, but he said, 'Thank you for asking me,' and off he went. Now I didn't win by a landslide but I did get elected. . . . "[4]

The campaign was straightforward and clean, and it brought out a record 3,009 voters. Tardif won by a margin of only sixty-one. "The defeat of Mr. Rogers by so small a margin," wrote Harry Webber, "indicated that a great many of his fellow citizens would have preferred that he should continue in office for another year. However, any man who serves as mayor for five terms builds up a considerable number of those who want a change and when the Democrats selected Mr. Tardif . . . they picked a man who has an army of friends, stands well in his home community and who many believe will give an excellent administration."[5] The Democrats also gained three of the seven alderman seats and three of the Common Council's twenty-one. Despite the rumblings of the year before, Rogers and his team had apparently been caught off guard. Rogers called for an inspection of the ballots, which indicated a slightly better showing for Tardif. There was no official recount. The lame duck Council, having boosted the mayor's salary from $400 to $1,000, quickly reduced it again.

Tardif was a team player, however, and not disposed to take positions far afield from conventional wisdom in Bath. At his inaugural, he acknowledged the city's large debt, which, though declining, retained "enough of the ancient shadow to warrant our being concerned this year as much with caution as with enterprise." As for enterprise, Tardif called for modernization of the city's faltering school facilities and a revamping of the city charter.[6]

The perennial issue of needs versus revenues had threatened to become divisive; in fact, petitions had been circulated in the city calling for no tax increases. Yet when City Council held a hearing on the need for higher revenues, only a handful of citizens attended. Accordingly, the city passed a budget almost 4 percent higher than the previous year's, necessitating a 3 mill increase in the tax rate. In the meantime, a controversial revaluation of the city was undertaken, which further increased the tax bite for some. Revenues reduced the bonded debt by about $17,000 (leaving a remainder of about $150,000), but overdrafts created a new floating debt of close to $13,000.

With the lifting of federal price controls, the nation had commenced a disturbing inflationary spiral. Bath was now in a two-way squeeze: The predicted postwar contraction was forcing people out of jobs and onto the city's welfare rolls; but the unemployed stayed put in Bath. So did their children, dashing hopes for a postwar reduction in school overcrowding. A concurrent decline in federal aid forced the city to assume a greater share of responsibility for its hard-pressed schools. And, in the midst of these financial and economic uncertainties, the city installed downtown parking meters as a means of traffic control, provoking outraged merchants to protest that Bath was discouraging downtown shoppers.

Tardif's popularity probably suffered during his tenure, but he had meanwhile been transferred to Lewiston, so he did not run again in 1947. Nor did the Democratic party advance a slate of candidates for city government. The Republicans nominated Donald Small for mayor. Eastham (Bud) Guild recalled that "there was a meeting up to City Hall to enter nominations. . . . And there was a group from down in the shipyard, I think in the drawing room. . . . Well, they were trying to get in the city government somehow or other, so they had their followers out in the corridor planning their strategy. Another group [was] in the auditorium at City Hall. The next thing we knew, somebody nominated Don Small as mayor, and somebody seconded it, and somebody said they wanted the nominations to cease and it was all over before these people came into the hall. It was really quite comical."[7]

The 1947 mayoralty election was Bath's last. In March, Small, running unopposed, was elected by 1,021 voters. Small was as hard-nosed as ever about fiscal matters and resolutely set against higher taxes. Accordingly, when the city financial committee proposed a budget almost $10,000 higher than the previous year's, he vetoed it, reminding City Council that revenues were bound to be lower and expenses higher than anticipated. Small refused to have anything to do with another jump in the tax rate.

To protect their special interests against fiscal surgery, pressure groups came to the fore, notably a well-organized Parent-Teacher Association (PTA), determined to get funding for capital improvements and higher teacher salaries. To this end, the school department's request showed a 17 percent increase for 1947–48. Because the school system was undeniably in need of improvement, its increased needs were met through judicious reductions in other departmental budgets—and by clever rearrangements of figures, including application of the previous year's overdue Lanham Act monies to the coming year and raising the figure on anticipated excise tax revenues. By such devices the city was able to reduce but not eliminate increased expenses.[8] Bringing the schools back to a competitive standard would prove a long and hard task, becoming a perennial source of antagonism between education professionals and dedicated parents on one side and beleaguered city fathers on the other.

HIGHWAY DEPARTMENT BIDS GOODBYE TO HORSES

The era of city horse drawn vehicles came to an official close in Bath Wednesday with the sale of the City's proud teams. For many years they have worked faithfully in foul and fair weather . . . . But with the coming of the automobile, labor with the assistance of the horse saw its days numbered. Recently the Highway and Sewer Department of Bath advertised for bids on the remaining four horses and all equipment drawn by them. . . . High bid of $600 came from A. S. Morris of Wiscasset. . . .

Included in the sale was four horses, two sets of harness, two sidewalk plows, two snow scoops, one hay fork, one jigger, two dump carts, one Studebaker wagon, one tank wagon and one set of wheels, straight axle.

Mr. Morris plans to employ the teams in the woods. . . . At present he is doing extensive lumbering and logging operations for the Central Maine Power Co., and feels that his purchase will fit into the work very nicely.

Still, it was a solemn group at the City stables who witnessed one more final step in the march of progress, the end of the horse and buggy day forever.

BATH DAILY TIMES, 10 MAY 1947

FLYING SAUCERS APPEAR IN SKIES OVER THIS CITY

Those much talked of flying saucers have at last hit Bath, or rather passed over the city! Four reliable citizens report seeing four mysterious looking silver discs travelling at great speed in the western sky at about 10.15 Monday morning. They were Lewis E. Spicer, Joseph Legendre, attendant at the city boat landing floats, George Nelson of Washington street and Steve Doty.

These men swear it was not the heat but that they actually saw these objects from the wharf at city landing where they were standing. They described them as being silvery in color and appeared, from where they were, to be about the circumference of the upper rim of a ten-quart water pail. They seemed to be travelling at a great height and travelling in regular formation . . .

. . . The first report of these flying saucers came about a year ago when airplane pilots in the west and southwest parts of the United States reported seeing them. After that reports began to come in from all parts of the United States. . . . After a while there was a falling off of the reports . . . until they had nearly been forgotten.

The atmosphere in this vicinity Monday morning was exceptionally clear with few clouds in the sky. . . .

BATH INDEPENDENT, 22 JULY 1948

Attending to the schools was a long-overdue problem in Bath; so was revamping of the city's charter, an idea that had finally come into its own in the postwar era. It is worth noting that Bath's last three mayors—Rogers,

Tardif, and Small—all supported charter reform. With the end of the war and the return of Bath's native sons, there were no reasons to postpone taking the issue to the people.

What remained to be done was an exercise in public enlightenment, because the issue was indeed a complex one, and because city fathers presumed substantial grassroots hostility to the idea. During Tardif's administration, a ten-part public program to explain and discuss charter reform, led by a Bowdoin College political scientist and presented as a free extension course of the University of Maine, was initiated at Morse High. The program clarified the long-standing issues of legal consistency, fiscal economy, and functional simplicity, making a strong case for a city manager system. The *Times*, won over, also promoted the proposed system.

Tardif had replaced an inactive charter committee with a more dedicated one, chaired by William Turpie, a Hyde Windlass employee. The finished charter, passed by both houses of City Council, went to the voters in a referendum on 8 September 1947. Of the more than 3,000 registered Bath voters, 965 participated in the referendum; 610 said yes.

Here was a milestone in city government, for the approved charter was a true break with the past. Gone was the bicameral system. Instead, Bath would employ a single deliberative body consisting of fourteen councillors, two from each ward, who ran without party affiliation and served staggered two-year terms. (In the first election, scheduled for February 1948, two would be elected from each ward; the recipient of the higher number of votes would serve for two years, the runner-up for one, in order to maximize the benefits of experience.) Councilmen would elect one of their own to serve as chairman and to act as the ceremonial head of the city government.

The mayor's office was abolished. Instead, City Council would appoint a professional city manager who would be the sole command link between city departments and the elective Council and who would make all appointments to city offices, subject to approval of the Council. While the manager was accountable to the city fathers, the various municipal departments were henceforward isolated from direct action by councillors, who were required to address all municipal matters to the manager. As chief purchasing agent for the city, the manager would prepare the annual budget and present it to Council. The expectation was that a professionally trained manager would save the city money, end the problems of cronyism and interference with daily municipal affairs by political figures, spur higher performance standards among city employees, and reduce the backbreaking load of committee red tape. The new charter was an auspicious way for Bath to start its second hundred years as a city.

THOUSANDS WITNESS PARADE OF PROGRESS OPENING CENTENNIAL WEEK CELEBRATION

. . . Fair skies and cheering thousands greeted the nearly two-mile long "Parade of Progress" which formed on North street, proceeded over Washington street, Center and Front streets, through the business district and to the Park where it was disbanded. Dozens of colorful floats, six bands and bugle and drum corps, ancient automobiles and new ones, comedy floats, marching organizations, fire and street department equipment and the men that man them made up a parade that topped anything undertaken in Bath in many years.

. . . A great crowd had gathered on the City park and along both sides of Washington street, an hour before the parade was due to start. It was a colorful crowd, and the bunting flying everywhere in the breeze, the hundreds of colored balloons carried by the children, many of which broke away and fluttered over the park, together with the decorated reviewing stand and other booths along Washington street, which gave much color to the scene and added much beauty to the area. The crowd waited patiently for the coming of the procession. . . . Its approach was heralded by the stirring and martial music of Dunlap Commandery band, which headed the procession. . . . A group of State Police on motorcycles then followed

MAINE MARITIME MUSEUM

A hundred years of progress: a float in Bath's centennial parade, 1947.

> and behind them came . . . the massed colors of the Regular Army, the Navy, the patriotic bodies and the National Guard. . . .
>
> . . . Division Three presented many interesting floats and displays. . . . [There] were cars bearing former mayors Walter C. Rogers, J. Edward Drake, Arthur Sewall, Robert H. Haskell, Dominique J. Tardif and Fred W. Quimby, one-time acting mayor.
>
> Next was a pair of Guernsey oxen and cart. . . . The oldest car of the ancient car group was a 1913 "Car-Nation". . . .
>
> The Bell Manufacturing Co. had an attractive crepe paper covered float of yellow and blue. A zipper press with Miss Mary Bernier operating was displayed atop the float. . . .
>
> *BATH DAILY TIMES*, 28 JULY 1947

Elections for the new Council were held in February 1948. Winners included the first woman to serve as an elected official in Bath—Etta Thurlow, office manager at Bath Box. Among the other members were Pete Rogers; Stanley Hunter, former president of the Board of Aldermen; Arthur Gediman, an incumbent member of the Common Council; and Rodney Ross, Jr., assistant superintendent at Hyde Windlass. Ross was to Hyde what John Newell was to BIW. Although he lacked Newell's dedication to business, he had a similar commitment to public service.

The search for a qualified city manager produced a first-rate candidate: Ralph F. Mittendorf, who had served more than six years as manager of Ironton, Ohio, his hometown. Participation in a family banking business had given Mittendorf additional executive experience. In middle age, he projected a pleasant, modest demeanor and a sense of humor, all of which would come in handy in the Shipbuilding City. His starting salary of $7,000 (about $33,500 in 1986 dollars) was undoubtedly more than the earnings of most councillors during their business lives. He would have to prove himself and, to some, vindicate the new system by his performance.

The most important issue in Bath during 1948 was the shakedown of the new charter. Bath's first manager took office at a time when the city was facing up to long-neglected problems with its infrastructure, when resistance to higher taxes was gospel, and when the new charter was still viewed with hostility even by some city fathers. Would an outsider with, possibly, his own managerial agenda, create new problems? As Harry Ring, city clerk at the time, later put it, "The people of Bath as well as some of the council members were very skeptical of the system itself. But I think as time went on, they saw the fact that our taxes did not take a big jump and that business was conducted as usual, if not better. Then they swung around to the manager form. I think those who were working [for the city] under the system liked it much better because this way you had a single person to answer to and it did work out well. The bicameral system did a good job. I'm not saying it didn't; it did. But the manager form was more direct for business operation."[9]

Throughout the long debates about charter reform, much had been made of the need for "businesslike" conduct in city government. That word covered a multitude of issues ranging from accountancy to personal behavior. To take the former example: Although much progress had been made, Bath's fiscal accounts were still complicated, inconsistent, and subject to time-consuming, often meddlesome committee review. To take the latter: Council discussions over departmental conduct had not always followed "businesslike" conventions. Ring, who had to attend all Council meetings, recalled that "I had seen one or two circumstances in the old days where they really came to fists or fights over certain issues, which wasn't in the best interest of the city of Bath."[10]

The new manager could not stop fractiousness among city councilmen, but as an outsider, he was forgivably aloof from local emotionalism, a position he carried off with unflappable diplomacy. Mittendorf's responsibilities placed him administratively between city fathers and the various city departments, where some had made a practice of special pleading and kibitzing, making him a single, full-time agency for the ranking of priorities and the evaluation of departmental performance. Furthermore, as was his responsibility, he drew up a five-year capital improvement plan that was to serve as a general guide and thus eliminate much year-to-year bickering over priorities. His first budget, for 1948–49, was more than $25,000 under that of the year before, which allowed Bath to attend to some improvements without disturbing the tax rate. And, at the end of that fiscal year, the city enjoyed a cash surplus of $40,000, much of which was outright operational savings. That was probably the most telling vindication of the new system. It was certainly an impressive start in Bath for Ralph Mittendorf. Mittendorf was aware that, despite his performance, there was a group unalterably wedded to the old system, and he "suspected that a few members of . . . council were with this group. Every plan will have some opposition . . . , but the staunch supporters of the council-manager form were far in the majority."[11]

The establishment of the new system had another important effect on Bath politics: It eliminated altogether the two-party character of elections. Henceforward, candidates for municipal office would run on issues, not party affiliation. Thus, the reality of the Republican predominance in Bath or the image of the Democrats as underdogs ceased to pertain to city elections. The change was almost certainly salutary.

Mittendorf's above-board financial conservatism fitted the Bath tradition, but the enemy of this policy, as in earlier years, was inflation, which eroded the value of city revenues by the month. Something had to give, and it proved to be the tax rate. In 1949, faced with undeniable municipal needs, notably the ever-climbing school budget, City Council raised the rate. By 1951–52, the rate had reached 58 mills; it dropped back one mill the next year, then continued to climb. By the mid-fifties, even Bath diehards were resigning themselves to an annual tax hike.

Bath's economy, which had mushroomed dramatically at the end of the thirties, began to shrink in like manner after World War II. Most apparent was the slackened activity at BIW. Within a year after V-J Day, the Iron Works payroll dropped from 9,250 to 1,250, a shrinkage that involved employees living in Bath as well as those from outlying towns. The corporate contraction proceeded in orderly fashion, and a worse crash was prevented when BIW was permitted to finish a few now-redundant vessels ordered by the Navy late in the war. Management also secured a contract for a fancy yacht and a large French order for fishing trawlers to replace wartime attrition. But the national steel strike of 1946 delayed construction, causing a sharp turn for the worse in profitability and increasing unemployment in Bath.

Luckily, BIW had emerged from the war with a substantial cash reserve. Between 1946 and 1950, it was able to fight speculative trading and uphold the value of its stock by paying dividends that, although much below the wartime boom rates, were extravagantly high for a company that was now losing money.[12] The corporate strategy was to stay active and retain its skilled labor pool by taking whatever contracts could be found, even at a loss, and diversifying into the manufacture of such heavy industrial items as structural steel columns, turbine exhaust casings, and pumps.[13] Apparently realizing the volatile nature of visibly dabbling in city politics, the Iron Works had for several years kept a low profile. But the company's competitive tactics called for an advantageous tax rate, and BIW did not hesitate to make that position clear, especially in view of the city's unavoidable postwar economic catch-up, which necessitated raising taxes steadily. In March 1950, for example, BIW Vice President J. William Schulze officially informed City Council Chairman Rodney Ross, Jr., that the future prospects for Bath's leading taxpayer were not bright and that "if we are to pull ourselves up by our boot straps, every element of cost must be reduced to its minimum . . . including taxes. Viewing the situation realistically, it is our considered opinion that this is no time for the City of Bath to increase its expenses and its taxes—it is a time to reduce them."[14] Bath's tax rate did not rise that year. Meanwhile, the onset of the Korean War had helped the company's fortunes take a decided turn for the better.

In 1950, Pete Newell relinquished day-to-day management of the Iron Works to his son John. He stayed on as Chairman of the Board until his death in 1954. Newell's death caused a virtual shutdown in Bath, during which 1,500 Iron Works employees attended a shipyard memorial service in his honor.[15] The corporate chairmanship was assumed by Archie Main.

BIW's local prestige and labor relations would never be the same after Pete Newell's passing. His son's impressive qualifications did not include his father's charisma, nor did Main's, although both were far more active in civic affairs than he had been. Times, meanwhile, had made the Iron Works a much different entity than the yard Pete Newell had brought back from the dead.

Bath's mix of businesses changed significantly in the postwar years. In June 1946, a spark from an electric motor apparently ignited a fire in the Bath Box Co. sawdust shed. The result was the most spectacular fire in Bath history. It reduced the box factory to ashes, along with a million board feet of lumber. Willie McCabe, one of Bath's future fire chiefs, recalled the conflagration: "Yes, sir, you could see it! My wife—she wasn't my wife then but we were going together—and I had gone after a bunch of plumbing supplies up to Lewiston, and come back over the hill and looked and seen that smoke in the sky, and I told her right then that 'There is only one thing that can be. That is the Bath Box shop.' We got down there to Lisbon, and the Lewiston fire truck passed us. I pulled right in behind him and we had clear sailing right straight through to Bath. Down Maine Street in Brunswick there wasn't a car in the way; they had the whole street cleared. . . . I got down there by three o'clock and we were there until nine the next morning and never left. Of course, the thing was a total loss."[16] Bath Box relocated to West Bath but fell on hard times and shut down in 1954.

Just before the Bath Box fire, canning interests in eastern Maine established a sardine cannery in the North End on the site of the old Texas Steamship Company yard. The new enterprise got off to a slow start, thanks

MAINE MARITIME MUSEUM

The Bath Box Co. goes up in smoke.

RICHARD MERRILL; MAINE MARITIME MUSEUM

Workers at Bath's new sardine cannery.

to the unpredictability of fish stocks, but took hold, providing another outlet for the local female labor pool.

In the postwar years, events such as the establishment of the Bath Canning Company or the award of a contract to BIW elicited predictably cheery editorials in the local press, along with optimistic reassurances about a resurgence in the local economy. In January 1947, Harry Webber told readers that "Bath can feel well satisfied as it faces the New Year for there are all indications that a prosperous twelve months lie ahead. Our industrial plants give promise of plenty of employment. . . . Several other industries, which have sprung up since the war, are thriving with all signs pointing to their growth and expansion. So industrially Bath has an attractive outlook. . . . "[17] The overall economic picture in the Shipbuilding City, however, was so grim that it engendered a Bath Chamber of Commerce, in which concerned businessmen organized to bring talent, resources, and influence to bear on the stagnating economy. Results were very disappointing, because Bath lacked available space and was accustomed to a high wage scale.

The economic picture further darkened as runaway inflation swept the nation. By the new year of 1948, Harry Webber admitted that Bath was on the spot: "The cold, cruel facts are that consumer prices have advanced within the last year 23 per cent. Food prices have jumped 40 per cent; clothing 18 per cent. Businesses large and small have struggled under increasing costs of wages and materials. . . . There is no denying the fact, as much as we hate to admit it, that there is a lot of inflation in a lot of places."[18]

Three state construction projects—preparation of Reid State Park in nearby Georgetown and construction of bridges in Arrowsic and Westport—eased economic pressure slightly in 1949, but state unemployment figures acknowledged that 1,700 were jobless in the Bath area, of whom 750 were city residents. (Official figures took into account those receiving unemployment assistance only, so they were below the actual figure.) The park and bridge projects were a response to the reactivated tourist trade, which had reached prewar levels by the summer of 1946. Tourism was likely to be a real growth industry because of the newly completed Maine Turnpike that ran from the state's southwestern border to Portland, about forty miles west of Bath. But Bath was still not a tourist city and not equipped to exploit the summer trade.

RESTAURANT PROPRIETOR GIVES FREE DINNER TO KIDDIES

. . . approximately 50 kiddies . . . enjoyed an excellent Christmas dinner Thursday at the Splendid restaurant on Washington Street, made possible through the generosity of the proprietor, George Kakalis who told City Marshall Frank L. Moriarty that he would give a free dinner to every kid in the city who was needy and otherwise would

TIMES RECORD

have to go without a real Christmas meal. The youngsters had all the turkey, potatoes, squash, turnip, pie and ice cream they could eat and then were guests of the Opera House management for the afternoon matinee. The list of youngsters was supplied by Major Albert Warren of the local Salvation Army corps. . . .

BATH DAILY TIMES, 27 DECEMBER 1947

HAPPY CHRISTMAS FOR FAMILIES IN OLD FOLKS HOMES

Christmas at the Old Folks Home was a joyous one this year, with everybody receiving gifts galore. The large parlor was beautifully decorated with Yuletide reds and greens, Christmas bells and a lighted tree, with candles at the windows. . . .

The day for members of the Old Ladies Home, High street, was also a very happy one. . . .

Mrs. Sadie Harnden, matron, told a representative of the Times she had never seen the Home more beautifully decorated or the ladies more generously remembered than this Christmas. . . .

Christmas noon a splendid chicken dinner was presented each of the ladies. The center piece, presented by Mrs. Fred Dean, was a large birch log, hollowed out and a forest scene built into it with ferns, flowers and candles. The effect was really lovely.

BATH INDEPENDENT, 1 JANUARY 1948

As the national labor market became more and more distressed, Washington made available federal development loans and construction assistance to areas with an official unemployment rate of 12 percent or higher. Although Bath's official figures were not nearly that high, a group of concerned downtown businessmen took extraordinary action. In January 1950, Arthur Hutchins, Bill Skelton, William Rogers (son of Pete), and ten others dispatched a wire to Senator Margaret Chase Smith, asking her to help obtain a federal employment survey of Bath so that the city might qualify as a distressed area and merit federal relief.[19]

There was no question of getting such relief; Bath was not close to being a distressed area, statistically speaking. Accordingly, the request got no attention on the Potomac. But it attracted plenty on the Kennebec, where members of the struggling Chamber of Commerce regarded it as a grandstand play. Why had self-styled "vigilantes" gone to such extremes? asked the scandalized Chamber, which had been at pains to publicize Bath as a pleasant spot for industry and tourism alike. Now the group feared that such unfavorable publicity would harm the city's credit rating, to say nothing of various businessmen's. The perpetrators replied that their admittedly hasty act had been designed to draw attention to the deteriorating economic situation in Bath.[20]

The vigilantes' request for federal relief was a tempest in a teapot that cooled rapidly, but it got the community talking about ways and means for revitalizing Bath. A dramatic example, quite a contrast to the stiff-upper-lip journalese of the *Times* or the hand-wringing apologies of the Chamber, was a letter from a dozen working females, published in the *Times* and the *Independent*, that minced no words about the need for change and challenged the acceptance of Bath's lean times as part of the normal course of events: "In the institution where we women work, there are 75% of us whose husbands are out of work. Is this normal? The wives here are the only bread winners and most of them have from 1–8 children to feed besides themselves and their husbands. Feeding these family units on their salaries alone is impossible. Is this normal?

" . . . These are not the families who are always 'on the town.' These are public spirited, hard working Americans just as you and I. If you think Bath employment is normal, ask any businessman how much money is due him.

"While the husbands are out looking for non-existent employment, who is caring for the children? The children, therefore, are not receiving proper care. . . .

"Congratulations to the young businessmen who had courage enough to bring this business out of the darkness and let the thinking citizens of Bath have a good look at it. . . . "[21]

But, after all, what were concerned citizens to do about improving the job situation in a hurry? The Chamber's resourceful efforts to attract more businesses were almost totally rebuffed, for practical reasons. Bath, in fact, was a one-industry town whose fortunes were lashed to BIW's ability to promote government contracts. Expectations had risen remarkably in the years since the Depression, and, if the opinions of vigilantes and irate women may be taken as representative, Bath was as ready as ever to let Uncle Sam take up its slack.

Uncle Sam did. When the Cold War turned hot in Korea, the Iron Works received contracts for LSTs, escort vessels, and destroyers. The resulting acceleration of business was nothing like the previous decade's, but it pulled Bath out of economic trouble once again. By 1954, the Chamber of Commerce, founded to stimulate new industries, had folded. Its failure was partly due to its entirely voluntary character, but mainly attributable to Bath's unattractiveness as a site for new businesses. How many of the city's businessmen saw that in the early fifties is hard to say. In 1954, when word of a proposed newfangled shopping center at undeveloped Cooks Corner reached Bath, downtown retailers expressed no concern about possible competition from the Brunswick area. Some pointed out that shopping centers were a passing fad.[22] Meanwhile, the Shipbuilding City was again a paying proposition.

BODY OF FIRST BATH BOY TO DIE IN KOREA IS DUE HOME FRIDAY

. . . Mr. and Mrs. Fred Hersom, Chestnut street, received word from the War Department, that the body of their son, Ronald A. Hersom was en route to New York, and is expected to arrive in Bath sometime Friday.

The late Pfc. Hersom, U. S. M. C. was wounded in action on September 15 at Inchon, and succumbed as the result of head wounds two days later aboard the hospital transport ship, the U. S. S. *Pickaway*. He was 19 years old. . . .

A strange coincidence concerns the story of two boyhood friends. Marine corporal Richard F. Black, a Bath boy, was a pal of the late Pfc. Hersom. As youngsters, they played together—they were "buddies." . . .

Black became a member of the Fifth Division, Hersom was assigned to the First Division. . . .

At the time Hersom was wounded, Black was on duty in Inchon. He was helping to transport wounded marines to the *Pickaway*.

"It was night that we did that sort of work," Black told the Hersom family where he was a recent visitor, "and it could be possible that I may have helped to take Ronnie aboard ship," he said. Continuing he said, "It was dark and there was much confusion and we had to hurry, but naturally I'll never know for sure."

The body will be accompanied from New York by Pfc. Conrad Hersom, 18, brother of the dead marine, and Corp. Black. . . .

BATH DAILY TIMES, 19 JUNE 1951

When Billy Haggett was a seventh grader at the Dike School in the North End, he and his fifth-grade pal Brud Stover received a visit from no less a personage than School Superintendent Loring R. Additon. It was a solemn occasion, for to grade schoolers, the superintendent was an awesome figure, far more imposing than teachers or even principals. Additon's purpose in visiting Dike was to put a stop to unruly student behavior there. The school had been plagued by rowdies, including one who was a foot taller and a hundred pounds heavier than the petite principal, and matters had reached a chaotic state, with unmotivated students showing their disdain by leaving class via the windows. The purpose of the superintendent's visit was to enlist Billy and Brud as lieutenants. As Haggett later recalled, "Brud was the leader in his class (he was a class or two behind me). I guess Loring thought I was the leader in my class. He took the two of us out on the front steps of the school house and lectured us on the importance of getting more decorum into the Dike School environment. . . . I'm sure that Brud and I sat there in fear and trembling!" Brud and Billy agreed to help, and their example presumably helped restore order in the school.[23]

The Dike School story is memorable on two counts. It serves as an example of the superintendent's attention to small problems and his circumspect way of handling them. (As one wag put it, "Loring liked to have all his ducks in a row.") It also illustrates the sort of problems a school system could expect with crowded classrooms and rickety facilities. Overhaul of the Bath schools was past due.

Once the question of a new city charter had been decided, Bath's stickiest municipal issue in the postwar decade was the annual battle of the schools, whose budgets moved steadily skyward. Bath schools were in a woeful state by the late forties because of wartime budgetary restraint and the overwhelming demand made upon those aging structures.

The city government had expected enrollment pressures to subside when the postwar job market constricted. As employment fell off at the Iron Works, Hyde, and elsewhere, thousands of wartime newcomers did indeed leave town, but many other families with young children continued to fill the low-rent Lambert and Hyde Park housing projects, regardless of the job situation. To general surprise, therefore, Bath schools in the postwar years became more crowded, not less so. By the end of the forties, another contributor to rising enrollments was the celebrated wartime "baby boom." Uncle Sam had underwritten construction of the now-crammed Huse School, had subsidized the enlargement of Morse High, and had paid an annual fee to the city for educational expenses. Furthermore, Lanham Act funds were extended long after V-J Day to help wartime boomtowns readjust, and Bath had reaped its share. But from the start, Bath city fathers and the Board of Education insisted, federal aid had never covered the real expense of educating so many children. That was why, they said, Bath's antiquated schools had deteriorated almost beyond repair. What to do about the crisis, and how much to spend on it, was what divided civic leaders.

Loring Additon had resolved to do more than reverse the wartime deterioration of the city's educational facilities. Additon was a forceful advocate of educational improvement, thoroughly conversant with the ways and means of securing federal assistance but determined to get from City Council every nickel he needed beyond that to accomplish his mission.

After graduating from Bates College in 1926, Additon had begun his professional career as principal of a two-teacher school 'way downeast: "This superintendent down there . . . called me . . . and hired me over the phone

MAINE MARITIME MUSEUM

Loring Additon.

to come to Columbia Falls as principal which I did at the magnificent salary of $1,500. I had one assistant. I taught half of the subjects and she taught the other half. I coached baseball and dramatics and public speaking." After several similar positions, he had become superintendent of the Calais schools before taking over Bath's system for a twenty-year stint in 1944. In Bath, Additon had driven hard bargains with mayors as far back as Pete Rogers ("a tightfisted fella if ever there was one"), and, after the war, had stretched Lanham Act subsidies for years by demonstrating that the Shipbuilding City had taken unusual wear and tear during the national emergency.[24]

As time passed, there were new federal entitlements for which Bath qualified, but one central problem persisted: There never seemed to be enough money to accomplish what Additon, Bath's teachers, and the school board thought was essential. For one thing, Uncle Sam had a way of delaying entitlement aid and then paying less than was expected because of federal budget cuts. For another, fiscal economy was the perennial watchword of the old and new city charters alike, making better schools a low priority for many city councillors. Then there was inflation, which necessitated ever-higher appropriation requests. Because the school request was by far the largest item in the city budget, its increases were conspicuous and controversial.

The school superintendent was directly accountable to an elected Board of Education that almost always saw eye to eye with him on the need for better facilities, salaries, and curricula. Additon enjoyed a particularly constructive relationship with Edward (Ned) Andrews, longtime chairman of the Board of Education. Customarily, it was Additon who took the heat during budget debates, not the school board members. "I never felt they pushed as hard as they could have and should have for budgets," he recalled. "They'd sort of complain a lot about the City Council not coming through, but they left it up to me to do the pushing."[25]

The school budget had to undergo review by the city manager (who usually recommended it be reduced) and City Council (whose pencils were often sharper than the manager's). Additon's view was that "they'd start slashing it and we'd take some big cuts, which they thought we should have every year. That continued right through to the end. I never had what I'd call a City Council who was as appreciative or interested as they should have been in the schools."[26] Debate over the annual school request could get hot and heavy, but arguments to reduce it were often ineffective. After all, better education was a motherhood issue, and what councillor knew more about educational costs than Additon, who never came before City Council without every budgetary "i" dotted and "t" crossed? In view of his airtight presentations, it is no small wonder that economy-minded councillors who crossed swords with Additon found him tough, even high-handed.

Additon and his board had an ace in the hole, however: The school department was more autonomous than other city agencies. Once a final sum was approved, the superintendent (with Board of Education approval) had discretionary powers unknown in other departments: freedom to reapportion funds within his budget wherever he saw the most need. If, for example, City Council had cut the budget request for a raise in teacher salaries, funds approved for, say, building maintenance could be diverted to that cause. This loophole prompted accusations that parts of the school budget were deliberately padded to provide discretionary funds for others. It even led to rumors of a hidden educational war chest made up of accumulated unspent monies.[27] Bud Guild, a councilman in the early 1950s, summed up Additon's tactics: "He'd ask for the world and in a good many cases he got it. . . . You just allotted them a lump sum and they did what they wanted with it. He was pretty cagey. I think he was very capable, too."[28]

Additon, in fact, did not always get what he wanted, because many items in his requests (such as teacher refresher courses or improved lighting) appeared as frills to some. But whenever he was on the spot, he went on record that a vote for cheaper education was a vote against Bath's future. In early 1950, for example, when an intransigent Council bent on keeping the tax rate where it was cut his budget by $33,000, he warned city fathers that they bore an awesome responsibility, adding that they were "working a real hardship to the children by curtailing the opportunities we are offering them."[29] The next year, fielding questions about why he had spent lighting money on teacher salary hikes, he replied that Bath teachers were "dissatisfied to the point where they are seeking employment elsewhere, and the general morale of all the teachers has been lowered" by the low salary scale. Referring to that incident, the press acknowledged that such exchanges had "widened the rift which had been increasingly apparent between the council and the Board of Education."[30]

Rift or no rift, Bath's toughest education problem was its need to replace old buildings. The education agenda was based upon a citizens' committee study completed in 1948, calling for some of the city's tottering grade schools to be closed altogether and their pupils consolidated in fewer, larger buildings. Problems of school overcrowding had become critical. By 1948, there was simply no more schoolroom space of any kind to handle the still-rising enrollments. This was a time when the Board of Education literally monitored each new birth in the city with trepidation. A trickle of federal money helped, but pressures to economize on the city budget were still strong.

A standard obstacle to new school buildings was the entrenched fear of incurring city debt. In response to such thinking, a citizens' committee circulated petitions in favor of establishing a school district. If approved by the State Legislature, the proposed district would have been empowered to raise funds through bond issues entirely independent of the city's restrictive debt limit. City Council approved the scheme, but it was rejected in a September 1950 referendum. Meanwhile, City Council made an emergency appropriation and floated a bond issue to enlarge Huse School. The ancient, shabby Center Street School—Additon's view was that it "was a disgrace in any community to call it a school building"—was closed forever, thanks to a momentary lull in enrollment pressure, but the postwar baby-boom onrush was just around the corner.

With no other choice, and with voter approval, the city began some ambitious new school construction, assisted by a $455,000 low-interest state educational loan (which did not count against its statutory debt limit) and substantial federal funding. In 1953, the Lillian B. Fisher Elementary School opened in the South End, and, a year later, the city unveiled the roomy new Bath Junior High School, "an ultra modern structure of brick and glass . . . , definitely a step forward in the progress of education for the city. . . . "[31] In the interest of economy, however, the junior high was not fully completed. Its gymnasium and auditorium were postponed, an example of short-run conservatism that proved very costly in the long run. The new building encompassed grades seven through nine, allowing the closing of another aged building and relieving Morse High of the need to accommodate the ninth grade. At the end of the 1954–55 fiscal year, Bath's bonded debt stood at $331,000. (Added to the above education debt, its total liability was about $3.2 million in 1986 dollars.)[32]

New construction gave the city a breather, and, in the postwar decade, repaired the damage of neglect. But one type of upgrading implied another. In 1956, a major standoff developed among City Council, the Board of Education, and the Bath Teachers Club. According to Additon, "Every time you increased the salaries of teachers, that was quite a figure in the budget and . . . [the Council would] say, 'Where are you going with this? Where is this going to end?' "[33] Militant teachers, disgusted with Bath's uncompetitive salary scale, threatened mass resignations unless a substantial across-the-board wage hike was approved. Nine teachers quit before a last-minute compromise defused the crisis. In the bitter aftermath, it was clear that the education wars were not over. Many Bath citizens, appalled by the spiraling rates, zeroed in on the schools' seemingly relentless hunger for more funding. On the other side, the intransigence of local tightwads and their reflexive opposition to educational "frills" seemed unconscionable. All in all, the late forties and fifties added up to a costly victory for education in Bath. But like the taxes it did so much to increase, the school board had become a permanent source of controversy.

No discussion of education in the postwar period would be complete without acknowledging that those years are remembered in American popular culture as the Golden Age of High School. Bath was no exception; beneath the surface of salary battles, overcrowding, threadbare facilities, and curriculum steeped in the basics flourished a teen culture that has become the stuff of national nostalgia. In the Shipbuilding City, one rallying point was athletics, notably basketball, at which Morse excelled. The "Shipbuilders' " home games, played in "the pit," as the Morse gymnasium was called, were packed. Sally Haggett remembered that "the excitement came in the winter when the basketball games started. The whole town would go and sit around the pit . . . and there was standing room only. It was very exciting. My parents went, my grandfather went well into his eighties. That was the excitement."[34] Bath's ardor for Morse basketball had been unleashed when, after a lackluster showing in wartime, the 1947 Shipbuilders took the Western Maine championship. That was a season when, as one team member put it, "the town just literally closed the doors and everybody went to the games. . . . "[35]

MORSE CHAMPION BASKETBALL TEAM HONORED WITH BANQUET AND GIFTS

Several hundred basketball fans gathered at Morse High school auditorium Monday evening to honor the 1946–47 Morse High school basketball team, winners of the Western Maine Tourney championship and to witness the presentation of gifts to the boys which was made possible by the generous donations of cash by citizens.

A banquet, prepared by the ladies of the

> South End P.T.A. was served in the gymnasium to members of the High school team, the Central Grammar school squad, winners of the State Grammar school title, special guests and nearly 100 supporters of the team.
>
> . . . As a tribute from the fans of Bath, the Morse boys [Paul Ouellette, Kenny Coombs, Blaine Trafton, Clarence (Squeak) Irish, Everett Parker, Charlie Andre, Burton (Bub) Smith, Knute Holmsen, Eugene (Ace) Burgess, and Fred Sturtevant] received gold chains and pen knives, individual trophies and 17 jeweled gold Hamilton wrist watches. They had previously had a trip to Boston with all expenses paid, from the same source. In addition . . . the entire squad received blue jackets, given by the athletic department of the school and gold basketballs which were awarded them in Portland at the close of the tournaments. Gold bracelets were given the cheer leaders and the assistant coaches . . . were presented bill folds as were Athletic Director Henry D. Small and Assistant Athletic Director Nathan Watson.
>
> . . . Flowers to decorate the banquet tables were presented by Kennebec Greenhouses and the tables themselves were beautifully arranged with the school colors, blue and white, predominating.
>
> *BATH INDEPENDENT*, 3 APRIL 1947

Citywide enthusiasm for athletics was one of several elements that transcended physical shortcomings to fashion a strong bond between students and Morse High. Another was MOHIBA, the Morse High Bazaar, begun in 1927 as an athletic fund-raiser. An annual event, MOHIBA expanded over the years from an evening of refreshments and decorations into a much-ballyhooed, well-attended variety show complete with a beauty queen.[36]

Such activities apparently made their mark, because Morse graduates proved to be unusually generous in later years. By the fifties, at every commencement, deserving students received dozens of awards and scholarships, a hefty portion of which were provided by members of previous graduating classes. The categories of these were endless and all-encompassing; for example, the Club "42" Award honored "the typical high school girl—one who has cooperated and been popular with her teachers and fellow students, who has participated in several extracurricular activities and who has been a sincere student."[37] Alumni support for Morse continued to build to a point where, a generation later, the school boasted that its alumni association was the largest and most active in the nation.

Another manifestation of what in the fifties was called school spirit was the steady stream of in-house publications emanating from the high school. The most substantial of these was the yearbook, which, like thousands of others in America, celebrated the nation's recent discovery that teenagers were a breed apart, but had yet to make a political issue of the matter. Morse yearbooks of the fifties provided a well-organized array of formal and humorous photographs, home-grown poetry, musings about the future, and the inevitable "most" list, which in the Golden Age covered such categories as "Most Sophisticated," "Best Dancers," "Nicest Voice," "Best Complexion," "Ideal Teeth," "Cutest and Sweetest," and that tribute to triumph over peer pressure, "Best All Round."[38]

Examined in hindsight, these interesting period pieces are windows into the ever-changing nuances of adolescent culture. Those from the fifties reveal Morse teenagers as industrious, respectful of school authority, and cliquish, although the latter phenomenon was not based on blue collar-white collar or geographical considerations.[39] The city's battles over education were apparently of scant interest to students. The widening pool of commercialism aimed at the youth market had made them extremely self-conscious about arcane matters of deportment, possessions, and personal appearance. Laura Gilliam Ridgewell, Class of '58, listed some of these: "The poodles on our skirts, the felt skirts, the socks rolled down. . . . We wore Ivy League shirts (the boys did) with buckles across the back of their pants and across the heel of their shoes, they wore white bucks, and when they really wanted to get on top they wore white shirts and dungarees and they combed their hair back and it had a little bit of curl on top and it went flapping back behind their ears! And then of course when Elvis Presley sang 'Blue Suede Shoes,' there wasn't a boy next morning in my class that didn't have blue suede shoes on."[40]

Because cars had not yet become standard equipment for high schoolers, lining up transportation to the abundant far-flung attractions became a major preoccupation. Close to home, however, there was a wide assortment of recreational activities at school, the Y, the churches, and downtown. At least one downtown joint was known to sell beer to minors, which provided a premise for any number of clandestine festivities.[41] Drugs hard and soft were unknown.[42]

Looking back on his high school days, Bill Haggett recalled that "there was a good relationship that existed between students and faculty. It was a fun time, a lot of laughs, good experience. A small percentage of the people in the class were really motivated to achieve academically. I wasn't among those. . . . It was an easy time, relativeiy low-key, a lot of fun."[43]

PROPOSAL BANNING SHORTS WIDELY DISCUSSED

The end of an era is in sight. Gone from the American scene are the horse and buggy, the Model T Ford, the steam locomotive, and, in fashions, the celluloid collar, bustles and ostrich plumed hats. Possibly the next to

TIMES RECORD

go, at least locally, will be feminine shorts. . . . Police chief Frank L. Moriarty has said he will request an ordinance banning bare midriffs and shorts that are less than knee-length. Even if adopted the proposed ordinance would not go into effect until Aug. 7, according to City Clerk Harry E. Ring, Jr. . . . So if you're a sun-worshipper, don't put your shorts away yet.

BATH DAILY TIMES, 18 JUNE 1954

WILL TAKE ACTION ON COMIC BOOKS

Magazine dealers in the city have now had ample time to remove objectionable comic books which feature crime, horror and sex from their stands, was the opinion expressed by a special committee of the City Council meeting Wednesday night in City hall. This committee was designed primarily to clean the city of this type of literature designed primarily to appeal to youngsters.

Activity of the committee resulted in all

magazine dealers in the city being invited to meet with Municipal Court Judge Gardiner R. Deering . . . for a discussion of the problem. Most of the dealers . . . were present at this meeting in which Judge Deering read state statutes regulating sale of such types of publications, and warned the dealers that, if necessary, police action would be taken against violators.

. . . Councilman Stanley R. Hunter, chairman of the committee, said Thursday morning that . . . all dealers who desire to cooperate have had plenty of time to clean their shelves. He said a further study would be made shortly and that in instances where these undesirable books were found to be available, police action would be taken against the dealer, under provision of the State statutes.

BATH INDEPENDENT, 4 NOVEMBER 1954

MISS CAROL BARTELS OF BATH WINS TITLE OF "MISS MAINE" FOR 1957 AT PORTLAND

An 18-year-old Bath girl woke up at 11 a.m. Monday after enjoying the first long sleep she's had since last Thursday. Pretty Carol Ann Bartels, selected Miss Maine of 1957 in weekend competition at Portland, still finds it hard to believe she's not in a dream. "I still can't believe it's true," the blue-gray eyed lass whispered to a Times reporter. . . .

Miss Bartels received much attention from the Maine press. Flashbulbs popped, photographers requested various poses and reporters plied her with questions as she cried with happiness over her selection. Friends of the local girl wept openly when her selection was announced. . . .

A very tired young miss returned to Bath late Sunday. . . .

Appearances of the girl are being handled by the Portland Junior Chamber of Commerce. As Miss Maine, Carol is under contract with the Portland group, sponsors of the

TIMES RECORD

Pine Tree State entrant in the Miss America Contest which will be held in Atlantic City, N.J., in September.

. . . The last Bath girl to be selected Miss Maine was Miss Iva Stewart who won the honor in the early 1930's.

BATH DAILY TIMES, 22 JULY 1957

Morse High School, which as an institution was greater than the sum of its parts, exemplified how Bath's quality of life transcended the vagaries of business and the inconsistencies of politics. A few vital institutions, in fact, existed almost entirely outside the political process, supported by endowments, local charitable trusts, United Fund drives, and deep-pocketed citizens willing to make repeated donations. Given the small size of the city and the frequency of fund drives therein, it is clear that Bath was blessed with an abundance of charitable trusts and affluent, public-spirited individuals. Foremost among the former group was the Davenport Fund, which regularly assisted local churches, civic groups, service organizations, and deserving individuals (including a bevy of Morse High School graduates moving on to college). Among the latter were members of old-money families (the city's "Silk Stocking Group," as Loring Additon put it).[44] So great were Bath's reserves of charitable wealth that they probably desensitized city politicians to the legitimate needs of public service organizations and the occasional entitlement of such organizations to municipal assistance. The Plant Memorial Home, the Bath Memorial Hospital, the Patten Free Library, and the Bath YMCA—all vital parts of the community—were largely dependent upon private charity.

The Plant Home exemplified the best in Bath philanthropy. It was a gift of Thomas Plant, a wealthy shoe manufacturer, who in 1917 underwrote its construction "to provide a comfortable home for the aged men and women of Bath who . . . have earned the right to a comfortable old age."[45]

The building was a handsome, impressively oversized Georgian structure built on the bank of the Kennebec at the extreme South End. Its operations were assisted by an endowment established by Plant, and its board was a blue ribbon assortment of Bath civic and business leaders. To be admitted, applicants were required to turn over to the home their property and assets in return for lifetime tenure. The Plant Home faced two challenges in the postwar era: the rising number of elderly citizens, and the inevitable tendency of applicants of means to distribute some of their assets among loved ones before seeking admission.

The Bath Memorial Hospital (originally known as the Bath City Hospital) had been founded in 1907 by a group of the city's most wealthy and influential citizens.[46] From its inception, it remained a special interest of Bath's old-money families, although its supporters were by no means restricted to them. A nonprofit, general care facility, Bath Memorial was overseen on a volunteer basis by a board of trustees and corporators, some members of which gave years of service and financial support. Ray Small is an example: "I didn't get interested . . . until I had my appendix out. That was in the mid-forties somewhere. Those were the days when the doctor kept you—gee, I was in there for fifteen days, and I really got settled into the hospital world life. . . . I really started getting interested in it. I had lost my mother not too long before that, and it gave me a good chance to do something, so I set up a memorial room for her. From that time on, I really got interested. . . . I went on the board . . . and from there I have been on ever since, serving in various offices, past president and so forth."[47]

The hospital's perennial problem was keeping abreast of medical advances and increasing demand for its services, and its trustees exhibited great readiness to expand accordingly. Bath Memorial's original capacity was thirty-six beds. By the end of the bonanza of World War I, that had grown to fifty. By the onset of World War II, despite hard times, the hospital had added a clinical laboratory, a maternity ward, and X-ray equipment. During the war, the federal government more than doubled its capacity by constructing a new wing, although that proved to be a mixed blessing. "I've heard it likened to a stable," recalled Ray Small. "The government built it to government specifications and they would allow no deviations. From that time on, that building was considered substandard in the eyes of bureaucrats. One argument against it, of course, is that there is a lot of wood in the building. . . . They had trouble with the piping . . . and so on. That place was a problem from there on."[48]

After the war, the hospital's physical and financial condition was so shaky that the influential Pete Newell recommended it be closed. That was out of the question, for even though other medical facilities existed in the area, Bath Memorial had become a source of local pride. Furthermore, its ever-increasing usage persuaded many that it was essential to the community's well-being. The hospital struggled on, never far from financial worries, living from year to year on donations from the community. In a pinch it could raise what it needed, thanks to its favor in the eyes of many benefactors, generous and supportive press coverage, and the efforts of its postwar president, Archie Main. With help from BIW's financial officer Sidney Eaton, Main imposed orderly accounting and administration and used his community prestige effectively. Demand for hospital services increased steadily. In 1947, Bath Memorial admitted 1,534 patients. A decade later, it treated 3,659 within the same facilities, although that sometimes required bedding patients in the halls.[49] Bath Memorial was at a crossroads: enlarge or close or, possibly, merge.

There had been some murmurings during the fifties about merging Bath's and Brunswick's medical facilities in a spot between the two towns so as to avoid redundancy and, as a single unit, acquire a larger share of governmental assistance. Bill Mussenden, a board member, described the climate of opinion at Bath Memorial on a merger: "They had some dear, sweet-old-ladies-with-the-tennis-shoes up there on the board. I'm not going to name them. They were lovely people. But my God, running a place like that, they were lost. Everything was emotion, you know: 'My babies were all born up here and we're not going to have a hospital out to West Bath.' You know, typical small town stuff."[50] Feelings that Bath was the regional pacesetter and that Brunswick was a slightly jerkwater follower were a time-honored tradition in the Shipbuilding City. Besides, a merger would mean starting from scratch.

It was not to be. In 1958, after an architectural review, the hospital board launched a $400,000 fund drive for a thirty-two-bed wing. Bath Iron Works played a key role in the drive. Its cochairmen were Mr. and Mrs. Baer Connard; Connard was a BIW executive and a Water District trustee. The company pledged to give a dollar for every two raised privately, imparting tremendous momentum to the drive. The trustees, however, determined to double the size of the originally conceived project, expecting to receive governmental and foundation assistance. Amounts forthcoming from such sources were less than anticipated, necessitating a long, nail-biting campaign. Construction proceeded, and the new wing was dedicated in October 1960, but all its bills were not paid until early 1965. Ray Small, meanwhile, had assumed leadership of the Bath Memorial board following Archie Main's death in 1960. Five years later, when the hospital was financially out of the woods, he acknowledged publicly that it was "a great relief to all of us."[51]

A. M. MAIN, NONAGENARIAN, RECEIVES CERTIFICATE OF MERIT FROM BATH C. OF C.

The coming 90th birthday party of A. M. Main, honorary chairman of the Board of the Bath Iron Works, was remembered Friday afternoon with the awarding of a lifetime membership by the Bath Area Chamber of Commerce.

Chamber President Marc N. King made the award for the "many wonderful things you have done for the community." He joined dignitaries from all over Maine in honoring Main, who became a nonagenarian Sunday. . . .

King said, "These awards are in recognition of the numerous contributions you have made over the years in the business, civic, social and charitable affairs of our Bath area community.

"The role you played in the growth and success of the Bath Iron Works Corporation, your work on behalf of Memorial hospital and the YMCA, the efforts you put forth as a member of the Recreation Commission, to mention but a few of the many wonderful things you have done for the community, have meant much to us all." . . .

Main, a BIW vice president for many years, became chairman of the board in 1954, following Newell's death. He was re-elected honorary chairman last Monday.

He has been president of the Directors of the Bath YMCA, and Board of Trustees of Memorial hospital since 1947, and served as a member of the Municipal Recreation Commission from the time of its inception in 1945 until he retired last year.

Other posts include a directorship in the New Meadows Yacht club, president of the Board . . . [and] a director of the Pine Tree Society for Crippled Children and Adults. . . .

BATH DAILY TIMES, 22 APRIL 1960

MAINE MARITIME MUSEUM

The Patten Free Library in the city park.

Like Bath Memorial Hospital, the Patten Free Library, ensconced picturesquely in the city park between Washington and Front streets, owed its existence to the unceasing efforts of public-spirited citizens. But historically, it had chosen to live cautiously and within its immediate means, thus becoming the most used, least publicized facility in the city.

Named for George and John Patten, prominent Bath shipbuilders and shipowners who founded the institution with a group of subscribers in 1847, the library continued throughout the nineteenth century to receive the vast majority of its funding from private benefactors, although the city, in recognition of its contribution to Bath's cultural affairs, awarded it nominal support.[52] In 1891, thanks to a gift from Galen C. Moses, a local banker and investor who also built the nearby YMCA, the library opened to the public in a well-appointed and professionally staffed building. Use of the facilities was free to citizens of Bath and nearby communities, and, for generations thereafter, hundreds would share the ambience of the library's elegant reading room, with its carpeted floor, wood paneling, wing chairs, and ticking case clock.

By the end of World War II, the Patten Free Library housed more than 40,000 volumes.[53] Books were chosen by a committee of staff and volunteers that screened suggested titles to prevent redundancy and ensure acceptability. (According to an account from the late fifties, if "certain books do not come up to standards—a chance that there will be objections to any books, then they are removed from the list.")[54] The library always maintained a strong selection of juvenalia.

To meet its expenses, the Patten Free Library relied largely upon gifts, trusts, Davenport Fund grants, and occasional fund drives. During the Depression, it had received support from the city in the form of tax abatements on its property; later municipal assistance was at times determined by the size of the Davenport annual grant. Unlike the hospital, the library avoided growth. Despite increased usage, Patten's physical plant therefore did not change much until 1960, when Mildred C. Wright donated $150,000 for construction of a new wing housing a children's room, a youth room, a lobby, and a lecture hall. The Davenport Fund donated money for a new level of stacks, thereby doubling the number of bookshelves. Mrs. Wright's gift, roughly equivalent to $550,000 in 1986 dollars, was one of the greatest in the distinguished history of Bath philanthropy. The new wing, constructed in a style harmonious with that of the original building, did promote more use of the library after its opening in 1962. Its lecture hall became a frequent site of talks and exhibits on art and literature, the more commodious stacks and more visible displays increased circulation of books, and the "youth room" invited students to congregate for study (and of course for socializing under watchful librarian eyes) in record numbers. A subsequent bequest by Mrs. Wright afforded the library enough investment income for its trustees to consider enlarging their institutional mission for the sixties.

Meanwhile, another of the library's quiet public contributions was its fulfillment of the need for local historical study. It was strange but true that the Shipbuilding City, its colorful past and distinguished citizens notwithstanding, was about the only Maine community of any size without a local historical society. The library's growing collection of maritime, regional, and genealogical history materials, therefore, would become by default the center for local historical research.

By 1962, when the new wing was completed, anyone pausing on the Patten Free Library's front steps would almost certainly have been pleased by the scene, which included two important symbols of Bath's civic pride. Facing the city park from the corner of Washington and Winter streets was the soaring steeple of Winter Street Church, one of Bath's most conspicuous antique landmarks. In the corner of the park just opposite the big white church was a new landmark: William Zorach's bronze statue and fountain, "Spirit of the Sea." Erection of that monument contributed an odd chapter to the annals of Bath philanthropy, one that revealed much about civic ways and means in the city.

In 1948, the Bath Garden Club, lately inactive, had been revived. Its civic purpose was the betterment of the community through landscaping and beautification of public sites. A decade later, with a membership of about fifty, the club undertook to replace the city park's toppled fountain, whose ruined condition seemed to indicate a slippage of municipal pride. The club's Community Betterment Committee went straight to the top for this project: William Zorach, the region's most celebrated sculptor. Zorach agreed to help.

Opinions vary about the importance of William Zorach's sculpture, but by any definition he was an artist of international note, so winning his participation in the park fountain project was something of a coup for the Garden Club. Zorach, born in the Imperial Russian province of Lithuania in 1887, had come to the United States as a small boy. His training had included study at the Cleveland School of Art and the National Academy of Design, as well as informal study in Paris, where, before World War I, he became acquainted with modernist styles and Bohemian intellectual circles. Zorach and his wife, painter Marguerite Thompson, whom he had met in Paris, had settled a few miles from Bath at Robinhood Cove, Georgetown, in 1923.[55] Over subsequent years, Zorach's painting had given way to granite sculpture of refined simplicity, by which he earned his substantial reputation.

Zorach told the Garden Club that he would design and create a new fountain as his gift to the City of Bath. The club assumed responsibility for raising funds to cover casting Zorach's model in bronze, paying for an appropriate base for it, and having the work installed.[56]

Instrumental in seeing the project along were Barbara Sargent, wife of Winter Street Church's Congregational minister; Laura (Mrs. Arthur) Sewall; and Adelaide Bowker, who chaired the club's Community Betterment Committee. It took two years to raise the $15,000 sufficient for the task. "That summer," Bowker remembered, "we had a big auction out to the [Sewall home at] Stone House Farm, and the next summer we had another one. At Christmastime, we had Christmas coffees with things for sale." The club raised $8,000 of the needed money. The remainder was provided through donations from private clubs and benefactors. According to Bowker, Zorach "did some of the enlarging himself, at his own expense, so really he contributed tremendously."[57] City Council, having approved the project, agreed to cover the costs of site preparation. Left to his own devices, Zorach conceived "Spirit of the Sea," a kneeling female figure with arms uplifted, which would rest upon a base of black granite.

Early in 1960, however, the story took a distressing and novelistic turn: A local schoolteacher noticed in a back number of the Congressional Record a reference to Zorach as a communist sympathizer. There was nothing to the report (politics were of scant interest to Zorach), as garden clubbers looking into the allegations soon determined. "We tried to keep this thing as small as possible," Bowker recalled.[58] But it would not stay small. A rumor began to make the rounds in Bath describing the artist as a leftist whose work was inappropriate for public display.

Prominent citizens, notably John Newell, expressed concern. The club members, having stuck their necks out financially, were not about to be intimidated by rumors or pressure, and they accordingly voted to continue the project. The rumor, however, would not go away, and in May 1960, City Council decided to meet with the women to discuss the fountain's "suitability."

Zorach, meanwhile, had not stood still. Surprised by the innuendo, he

R.L. SNOW

William Zorach's controversial "Spirit of the Sea."

threatened to sue its alleged perpetrators.[59] Then he wrote a lengthy and forceful denial of the rumor to the *Bath Daily Times* that appeared the day of City Council's hearing on the matter. By the time of the hearing, councillors apparently had decided to let the matter blow over, for, as Bowker recalled, the discussion concentrated on the style of the fountain, not the rumor that had engendered the controversy: "The council members refused to be drawn into any discussion of the true issue. 'Suitability' was the only angle pursued."[60] Having gone through the motions, City Council dignified the occasion by drawing up a lofty resolution that the fountain would surely be a credit to Bath: "We, the Bath City Council therefore commend the Bath Garden Club and William Zorach for this project and wish them success in its speedy completion."[61] Bowker's later summation was less lofty: "Small town stuff, you know; panic."[62]

The statue, once placed upon its base, was kept carefully draped until its unveiling in August 1962.

TOUCH OF FLORENCE ADDED WITH FOUNTAIN UNVEILING

. . . Bath has done something in the tradition of Florence and Athens, Professor Philip Beam, head of fine arts at Bowdoin College, Sunday afternoon told the estimated 800 persons on hand for the dedication of the new City Park fountain.

Speaking at the ceremonies marking the

completion of the three-year Zorach Fountain project of the Bath Garden Club, Professor Beam called the installation of the major piece of sculpture "most extraordinary" and said it brings credit not only on the coastal communities . . . but "the entire state of Maine."

The sculptor William Zorach, who presented the gift to the city, said that of all his public monuments including . . . work in more than 60 museums . . . "it is this monument, the Spirit of the Sea which had provided my greatest pleasures."

Sunny skies greeted the dedication ceremonies, despite an overcast morning that at times threatened rain.

Bath Daily Times, 6 August 1962

During the 1950s, Bath's city government grappled with a few large issues and many small ones. Concurrent with the battle of the schools, and related to the teachers' salary issue, was a concerted drive to upgrade municipal salaries. In 1951, under pressure from inflation, and the police and fire departments, City Council approved an across-the-board raise for all city employees. The tax rate continued its climb.

Another important question was how or whether to take political action to ease Bath's acute postwar shortage of low-cost housing, which hung on regardless of economic conditions. There was almost no private construction undertaken in the city during the postwar decade. Stewart Day remembered how difficult it was for him and his wife to get settled in 1950: "Boy, there were a lot of bad-looking houses. . . . I don't think they'd built a new house in Bath for years. . . . I gave up. I couldn't find anything I wanted. It was just old stuff that had thousands of dollars worth of work on it. I built a new house."[63] In 1948, Uncle Sam had proposed that Bath take over the Lambert Park and Hyde Park projects, a plan that City Council rejected on Ralph Mittendorf's advice. But the Korean War further aggravated the local housing shortage, prompting the federal government to propose during 1952 that a housing project for Navy personnel be built in Bath. Based on the experience of World War II, city fathers held out for the stiffest possible terms, inducing Uncle Sam to shop elsewhere. The project went up in the Cooks Corner section of Brunswick, a controversial turn of events that would grow in importance with passing years as patterns of development gravitated toward Brunswick.

In 1955, City Council again considered taking over the Hyde Park and Lambert Park projects, which the federal government was very eager to dispose of. That proposal did not pass. Instead, some of those properties were sold to private parties; the rest were taken by an out-of-town realty company.

Residential expansion continued to stagnate in Bath because available lots were not serviced by city utilities. The tax base thus vegetated as the tax rate rose.[64]

In the many interviews conducted for this book, a common view was that Bath was in the doldrums during the 1950s: stable at best, stagnating at worst, preoccupied with problems that were trivial compared to those of earlier and later years. With the notable exception of the schools, Bath's municipal accomplishments seem in hindsight to have been overshadowed by its robust civic activities. Evidence from the period does indeed suggest that, after its initial honeymoon, the city government had not made good on the auspicious council-manager system, and that infighting and second-guessing plagued the conduct of municipal business. The condition looked to many like a decline in talent, and even the local press took note.

CITY COUNCIL CANDIDATES APPEAR BEFORE P. T. A. GROUP

Most of Those Seeking Election February 13 Are Non-Committal in Their Answers To Questions Asked

Members of the P. T. A. Council and a few interested citizens met Monday evening at the City Hall auditorium to interview members and candidates for the City Council. . . .

City Council Chairman Rodney E. Ross, Jr., introduced the speakers. None of the speakers were committal to any great extent.

First speaker was Arthur E. Hutchins, Jr. . . . After being asked to give his views on schools Mr. Hutchins replied that he had rather be asked questions. In response to a query from the floor as to whether or not he favored the School District bill he stated that he was not, at this time, prepared to say.

When asked the same question . . . , Andrew M. Butterfield, the next speaker, said: "We want better everything. . . . The School District is well and good if you can pay for it." The speaker went on to say that "these are hard times and we can get nothing for nothing."

Arthur E. Sturtevant . . . was the next

speaker. He said he would look into both sides of the issue if elected but did not know at this time which way he would vote.

. . . Mrs. Emma F. Leonard . . . said that we "can't go further into debt." She said she disapproved of the Topsham students coming to Morse High school and also mentioned that the U. S. Senators were getting too much money. She said that she was a friend of all the schoolchildren.

H. Joseph Madden . . . told of his interest for children and said that he would do everything possible to help.

Several candidates were unable to attend due to illness and business reasons.

BATH INDEPENDENT, 1 FEBRUARY 1950

More than ever, it seemed, city government indulged in the kind of petty squabbles the council-manager system had been designed to correct. BIW's corporate influence had ceased to be a bone of contention. Council debates, comic and otherwise, were sparked by disagreements about spending priorities, mistrust of the new managerial system (which some saw as a creation of Bath's elite), and conflict of personalities. Looking back, Bud Guild attributed the situation to the city's class system: "It was something you could feel. Anything that was brought up by somebody from the North End wards, some of the people in the South End immediately took exception to it. They figured all these wealthy guys, white-collar workers . . . wanted something for themselves, and so they just automatically would be against it. Then, there was always somebody in the background pulling the strings, namely Red McMann."[65] Harold Rubin, city solicitor during the fifties, recalled that many councillors "had had no experience in dealing with people from a standpoint of representing governmental authority. I think their ego carried them away, because this was the only time that they had any presence other than the ordinary resident of Bath and shipyard worker. I'm not a psychologist, but I always felt that a good many of the people who served on the City Council through the period . . . were ill-prepared and ill-suited for that kind of work."[66]

City Hall's vague records of municipal business and the press's oblique coverage thereof have left only skeletal traces of the postwar decade's mini-controversies. A few brief examples must therefore suffice to provide a sense of the period's preoccupations. During 1949, after City Manager Ralph Mittendorf had promoted a police patrolman to a vacant sergeant's position, members of City Council objected, saying the spot should have gone to onetime marshal Percy Kingsbury. One councillor even called for an investigation of the force, notwithstanding the facts that the promotion had been made through proper channels and that City Council was prohibited by the new charter from kibitzing about civil service appointments. Mittendorf prevailed.[67]

Big news during 1951 was the matter of new fire equipment. According to then-councillor Bud Guild, a son-in-law of Pete Newell, "my father-in-law . . . was a director of Mack Trucks. He was quite interested in getting a Mack Truck in here, and he told the powers that be down at Mack Trucks that they had better match the price or better so that there was no way we could pick something other than a Mack truck. And that's the way it turned out. There was no funny business involved. The price was right and it had all the specifications that the fire department wanted. The chief . . . was a big follower of Seagrave. . . . I think he was a little disappointed when they bought the Mack."[68]

Fire Chief Richard (Benny) Frates, meanwhile, sought a motor vehicle more befitting his office than the small departmental truck he was stuck with. The request seemed reasonable to some. How would it look when Bath's chief firefighter alighted from a truck at a professional convention?[69] Then Bud Guild introduced a controversial stipulation: "I think I got up and said I went along with it so long as it was painted red, since that would prevent him from running around on personal tours with it. I don't know whether I ever got the credit or the blame for it!"[70] Frates countered that red was passe for a fire chief's car because the color faded. More controversy. The chief settled for a red car.

CHIEF GETS NEW CAR—
EVERYBODY SHOULD
BE HAPPY NOW

TIMES RECORD

Above is shown Bath's fire chief, Richard Frates, receiving the keys to the new Chevrolet chief's car from E. Rodney Brooke, proprietor of Brooke Chevrolet, Inc., of Bath. . . . Smiles are the order of the day. Chief Frates is happy over getting the new

> car; Mr. Brooke is happy in selling the automobile, and City Manager Ralph Mittendorf, on the left, must have found something to be happy about as he's smiling too. The fact that the car is a bright and shiny red, brilliant enough to be seen a country mile, and the fact that the chief has on a uniform will probably make some others happy, also. The question of the color of the car and the matter of having the chief provided with a uniform have been the topics of considerable discussion at city council meetings. The car is sufficiently red to even satisfy "Uncle Joe" in Moscow. . . .
>
> *BATH DAILY TIMES*, 30 JUNE 1951

In 1953, the recreation department drew fire. Despite the dogged efforts of department director Red McMann—and in part because of them—recreation was a perennial Cinderella. In May 1953, City Council investigated the department after it was learned that McMann had let a sizable contract without taking competitive bids. The matter blew over when Council noted that the city manager and clerk had both authorized the contract, which presumably diluted accountability to an acceptable degree. Another minor crisis occurred when one councillor admitted having taken a load of city gravel for his private use. Discussion of the matter unraveled as city fathers tried to affix, diffuse, or excuse responsibility.

In January 1952, city fathers were surprised by the resignation of Ralph Mittendorf. A major stockholder in a family savings and loan company in Ironton, Ohio, Mittendorf said he was returning to his hometown to oversee that business. (The next year, he reportedly turned down an offer to serve as Cincinnati's manager at almost five times his former Bath salary.)[71] Mittendorf's departure was a major setback for the Shipbuilding City, because none of his successors for the rest of the decade possessed his years of experience. Harry E. Ring, Jr., city clerk, stood in as manager until June 1952, when Nathan C. White, a thirty-year-old assistant manager from Windsor, Connecticut, took office. White left for greener pastures early in 1955 and was replaced by Stanley W. Judkins, twenty-six.

Meanwhile, the matter of political pettifogging had gone public with a bang. In January 1954, Harry Webber published a long letter from John Newell, president of the Iron Works and past chairman of Bath's Common Council. The letter was important because, in addition to alleging that Bath's quality of leadership had seriously eroded, it marked Newell's reemergence as an active, influential player in the municipal forum.

Running Bath, Newell's letter stated, was like running a million-dollar business. "It requires good management by people who know something about management. It requires team work. It requires sound policy decisions. It requires a Council which will support the City Manager and leave the operating details to him, but will exercise over-all control in line with policy.

"No business would be a success if its manager were consistently harassed by a board of directors which questions minute details and in doing so pulls down his morale. . . .

"That seems to be the condition in our city council. It is time that the taxpayers take notice. What is needed is a body of men . . . who, in addition to being worthwhile citizens personally, have an understanding of what it takes to make an organization function efficiently, men who know the difference between establishing a policy and encroaching on a manager's job.

"We have many capable men in our city who are competent but under existing conditions they cannot be blamed for reluctance to become involved in the endless bickering that is typical of council meetings.

"Such men could be induced to serve, I believe, if groups of interested taxpayers in each ward would undertake a concerted effort to see that the council is made up of qualified men. The present practice of signing nomination petitions of candidates largely because they are friends and neighbors . . . is not good for the city. I, for one, would pledge all the assistance I could render if an effort were made such as this.

"Our people voted for the Council-Manager form of local government in 1947. . . . It is a great improvement over the old City Government in which I spent several years. Things get done efficiently and with a minimum of effort and expense—that is, when the Manager is not hamstrung by the Council.

"We had a fine City Manager in Ralph F. Mittendorf. He left town—'fed up' with the Council and their harassing. We have another Manager in Nathan C. White. . . . Let us not lose White for lack of support by an intelligent, progressive Council." Newell called upon interested citizens to organize to elect "a city council of which we could all be proud."[72]

Newell was speaking both as Bath's most influential businessman and as a private citizen whose subsequent activities would prove he practiced what he preached. His willingness to speak out so openly contrasted starkly with his father's more subtle and indirect style. It achieved one important and immediate result: public endorsement by Harry Webber, who broke his rule about not publicizing civic discord and furthermore called for support of the council-manager system. Webber's conversion to the new system had been further strengthened by a close relationship with the now-departed Mittendorf. Speaking to the current situation, he wrote that "Bath should not have a council so divided that one group is ready to oppose practically any proposition which an opposing group has to offer. . . .

"There is no good reason why a man should be elected to the council

MAINE MARITIME MUSEUM

John Newell.

simply because he wants to be. Instead the citizens should study the ability and qualifications which a man possesses . . . rather than whether he is a personal friend or just a 'good fellow' who wants the office."[73] For Webber, this was an astonishingly candid statement. Together with Newell's remarks, it constituted a powerful admission by two of Bath's most authoritative insiders that things had to change. One can but wonder whether or not Webber reflected upon the part the local press had played in supporting the conditions he now decried.

Stanley Hunter, City Council chairman, promptly rebutted Newell and Webber, expressing surprise and distress that councillors were perceived as

MAINE MARITIME MUSEUM

Stanley Hunter.

bickering snipers and denying that they were out to get the city manager. As for the old cry that councilmen should be businesslike, he continued, he himself had tried to interest managerial professionals in city government, "but they all say they are too busy. In fact, not long ago I urged Mr. Newell and Rodney Ross, Jr., to return to the council. It's hard to get businessmen to serve on boards and commissions these days."[74]

However unintended, such a comment was a restatement of the problem that John Newell had denounced. (One of Hunter's fellow councillors, affirming that there had indeed been bickering, facetiously suggested to the press that " 'all Council meetings be tape-recorded from now on' but thought the cost of recording tape would be prohibitive.")[75]

The guarded public remarks of managers Mittendorf and White tended to corroborate Newell's characterization of City Council. At Webber's request, Mittendorf responded from distant Ironton, saying that during his Bath service he noted more intramural bickering among councillors than opposition to himself. Had such bickering driven Mittendorf off? "In all probability, I said to Mr. Newell, in discussing city affairs, that I was 'fed-up' with the actions of the council. That situation, although not serious, did carry a lot of weight, when I had to make a final decision to leave Bath to return to private business. . . . "[76] And did it still obstruct the work of the city manager? One year later, after abruptly resigning, Nathan White recommended to the people of Bath that "when my successor is appointed, I feel that you should help him to become familiar with all aspects of the City as rapidly as possible, listen to and critically analyze his recommendations, many of which are bound to have considerable merit, and try to take advantage of his new prospective [sic] and thinking when establishing overall policy. With such cooperation on your part, I am sure that he will be able to do a better job with you and for you."[77]

When a man like John Newell sneezed, all of Bath could catch cold. Predictably, citizens' committees were formed to commence a systematic search for meritorious candidates. The next year brought a few upsets, most notable of which was the defeat of a six-year incumbent by a twenty-four-year-old Bowdoin College sophomore. But there were more ways to change city government than beating the bushes for the dutifully competent, as subsequent events revealed. A successful effort got underway to reduce the number of serving councillors and with it the propensity for debate. During 1954, a proposal to reduce representation from two to one per ward (seven in all) was rejected by the incumbent city fathers. Motivated Bath citizens strenuously objected to such peremptory action, calling for a referendum.

Early in 1955, State Representative Rodney Ross, Jr., who as former City Council chairman had weathered many municipal controversies, won approval in Augusta for a Bath charter revision. His proposal called for a nine-person Council elected at large rather than by wards, so voters could make their choices on a citywide basis. Each councillor was to be paid $250 per year, a recognition of professionalism. The proposal generated stormy debate and heated personal exchanges in City Council, where opponents argued it would undermine the democratic committee system, end neighborhood representation, and concentrate power in the hands of too few. (Stanley Hunter, for example, reportedly stated his belief that members should be added to the Council, not subtracted from it.)[78] But approval of the proposal squeaked through the Council by a six-to-five vote in March 1955. Six months later, Bath voters passed it by referendum.

Reducing the size of City Council was not the only far-reaching measure approved in the 1955 referendum. Voters also authorized the appointment of a three-man Bath Parking District, empowered to issue bonds independent of the city government for the purpose of acquiring downtown properties, razing structures thereon, and converting the cleared land into off-street metered parking lots. The district was expected to fund itself through meter revenues. Capably chaired by Frederick Drake, a popular and influential businessman, it soon became a very important component in city government. Downtown parking, of course, had been a serious and hotly debated issue for years, and the district met the problem head on. Over its twelve-year existence, it zeroed in on the Commercial Street waterfront and Water Street (which ran behind Front). Besides easing the parking crunch for downtown shoppers, the district substantially altered the look of downtown Bath by tearing down several quaint but shabby landmarks and many more budget-priced eyesores. In addition, critics of City Council's bickering could take satisfaction in the fact that the district was helping defuse one of Bath's sorest issues.

The Parking District was a creative step in maintaining the viability of the downtown shopping area and, in turn, the tax base that those properties provided. So was the creation of the Planning Board in 1956. Bath had been in need of a master plan for development for half a generation at least, and John Newell deflated financial arguments against its establishment by providing a BIW grant of $5,000 to get things moving. Like the Parking District, the Planning Board attracted and utilized the talents of individuals burned out by the rigors of City Council service or disinclined to involve themselves with it. Likewise, by bringing expertise to bear on details that had paralyzed City Council, they effectively segregated them from the pernicious bickering and delay that had stifled decisive action in the past. By the late fifties, it was becoming imperative for Bath to establish its priorities and somehow widen its tax base through creative development. Perhaps the revised city charter, the involvement of more citizens in the mechanics of government, and the strengthened civic infrastructure would bring the city out of the doldrums.

Stanley W. Judkins, who became city manager in March 1955, made substantial contributions to the refinement of Bath's city government. Judkins labored under the disadvantage of tender years, and he was a large and somewhat ponderous man whose eccentricities made him a comical target for detractors. But his college training had been in civil engineering and town management, and he lately had served as manager of Warren, Maine. It probably did not hurt that he was a born-and-bred downeaster.

Judkins took over in Bath at a propitious time, when opposition to his two predecessors' efforts was a public issue and citizens seemed determined to make the city's charter function effectively. He backed the creation of the Planning Board and successfully pushed for resurrecting the defunct Chamber of Commerce. He soon made a name for himself as a defender of the interests of the city departments.

Judkins's favorite city agency was the fire department, because he was a dedicated fire buff. He liked nothing better than tooling through town with Benny Frates in the chief's car, or attending the occasional heavy suppers to which firefighters were devoted. His frequent absences from his City Hall office in favor of the ambience of a fire hall got him into hot water with watchful councillors, but he followed through on his predilection to the point of spearheading, with help from Councilman Stanley Hunter, capital improvements in the fire department. Most notable of these was the Central Fire Station, financed through a bond issue and built during 1957 on High Street near Morse High.

How the city was motivated to build the new station is an interesting tale: The old one was condemned as a fire hazard. Before 1957, Bath's downtown fire station had been located in a sagging brick structure on Water Street, amid the rickety buildings targeted for demolition by the Parking District. Norman Kenney, a firefighter and future chief, recalled that "they had originally built it for horses and wagons, and they had to put . . . bolts through the walls with plates on the outside of the wall with a turnbuckle in the center. The building had started to bow so that the floor joists were pulling out. . . . Still the city wouldn't do anything. That old thing would creak and groan in the night in the wind. The whole building would move! The wiring was bad. So the guys got together one day and they called up the fire marshal's office in Augusta and said they would like to have an inspection. The fire marshal's office came down and inspected the place and put a red tag on the meter and said, 'Don't use it.' Then the city had to do something!"[79] Under Judkins's management, the city's fire budget increased faster than that of all other departments.

Judkins's love affair with the fire department created a major uproar during 1959 that cost him his job briefly. Because Bath's firefighting equipment was predominant in the area, the city had contractual arrangements to answer alarms in adjoining towns. For this, Woolwich, Arrowsic, Georgetown, West Bath, and Phippsburg paid a nominal fee. The fee was too nominal for the city manager, however, who arbitrarily jumped the rate by an order of magnitude. When the surrounding towns protested, Judkins told them to take it or leave it. Leaving it, of course, meant forgoing adequate fire protection. The town governments protested to the Bath City Council, and there were threats of a business boycott. The Chamber of Commerce, which had become distinctly regional in its membership, also applied pressure, voting no confidence in Judkins. Meanwhile, the matter had become a political issue in the 1959 municipal election. Two candidates, Arthur Hutchins and John F. Leonard, who openly opposed the city's position on fire aid, were elected. Leonard became Council chairman. At the same time, Judkins's proposed 1959–60 budget threatened to raise the tax rate an astounding 15 mills in one fell swoop, which of course mobilized the enemies of high taxes. Especially controversial was Judkins's costly upgrading of city salaries and equipment. The matter of so young a man making so high a salary was also an issue. Given the relative degree of budgetary and supervisory responsibility, some asked why the manager's pay should exceed that of the school superintendent, or, for that matter, a high school principal.

Bath backed down on the fire aid issue, settling with the towns for a 10 percent increase in the old rate, and angry taxpayers forced trimming of the budget to a 10 mill increase for 1959–60. The city's budget now stood at almost $1.5 million, and there was growing alarm that Bath's lackluster growth rate was being outdistanced by its capital needs. In May 1959, after having received a no-confidence vote by his City Council opponents, and having aroused a similar sentiment on the part of "at least one community industrial leader," as a *Times* reporter coyly put it, Judkins was prevailed upon to resign.[80]

Judkins's forced departure strongly smacked of a sellout, and the community was distinctly divided over the matter. Many councillors and civic leaders were convinced that the manager had become the latest whipping boy for opponents of the manager system and Council's inability to take responsibility for budgetary restraint and/or the tax-rate problem. Accordingly, supporters of Judkins staged a gala farewell banquet in his honor. In attendance was an impressively numerous array of past and current friends. (Absentees included Loring Additon, Chamber of Commerce brass, and one community industrial leader.) During the long round of testimonials, Arthur Gediman, a longtime councillor and dedicated foe of fiscal extravagance, praised Judkins's diligence and pointed out that "the lot of the manager is a hard and difficult one. If he accomplishes something, he gets no credit. If he fails, he is condemned." Even former mayor Donald Small put in a few good words about Judkins: "He has been a very patient man. He has taken criticism beautifully, and that probably goes with being a good public servant. At his age, considering what he has done here, he'll make good wherever he goes."[81]

As things turned out, Judkins did not have to go far to make good, at least for a while. In the wake of that crowded testimonial dinner, the same City Council that had obtained his resignation mysteriously reversed itself and asked him to return. Why? Apparently as a backlash against the outside influence that had brought on the decision to dump Judkins. At that time, recalled Jim Temple, who had returned to city government, "John Newell sent us a letter. . . . That had a strong influence on it. . . . We agreed we ought to ask him to leave." Later, however, councillors changed their minds, because "then the anti-BIW theory started to take effect and [the feeling] that John Newell shouldn't tell us what to do. . . . So then, they reversed it. . . . " Judkins accepted the offer to return and stayed in office until September 1961. Temple, who had been a supporter of Judkins during the 1959 flipflop, gave up on City Council: "I didn't run again. I'd had enough of that."[82]

During the fifteen years after World War II, Bath had accomplished a major overhaul of its political process, municipal services, and civic infrastructure. To a large extent, this effort was repair work: replacing the creaky facilities of the thirties and forties, and designing a new political system capable of moving with the times.

Much of the discord, bickering, and unprofessional conduct bemoaned by John Newell, Harry Webber, Jim Temple, and others was an inescapable function of the process of change. The war had effaced the controversy about BIW's influence over municipal matters. But when, in the postwar years, BIW's business slackened, the question of alternative development for Bath again arose, a knotty problem for a city so specialized and geographically constricted. Meanwhile, the new city charter had erased the old partisan character from municipal politics, substituting in the name of efficiency a structure that seemed increasingly removed from popular democracy. Hindsight makes clear that the council-manager format was salutary. But the tremendous cost of repairing years of neglect necessitated big budgets and spiraling taxes, not the professional economy that many obviously expected. At the end of the fifties, Bath's debt stood at close to $550,000 (about $1.95 million in 1986 dollars, of which fully 77 percent was attributable to education).[83] The once-sacred policies of tax discipline and debt reduction had fallen along with the old city charter.

But taxes were still very much an issue in the Shipbuilding City. Bath citizens' expectations had risen along with those of the rest of the nation. Thus, the city would have to continue its momentum of postwar improvements. How was it to do so? There had been almost no new commercial or residential development in the Shipbuilding City for years, and by 1960 the tax base was severely strained. As always, Bath's largest single taxpayer was determined to keep its taxes under control, and the outspoken John Newell was on public record to that effect. Somehow, the city had to find new sources of revenue.

GUIDED MISSILE DESTROYER THE USS CHARLES F. ADAMS IS LAUNCHED HERE TUESDAY

BY ROBERT C. CUMMINGS

"No community in America has a longer or more distinguished history in shipbuilding than this section of Maine," Fred A. Bentz, undersecretary of the Navy, said Tuesday afternoon on the occasion of the launching of the Navy's newest guided missile destroyer at the Bath Iron Works Corp.

The launching of the sleek and deadly U.S.S. Charles F. Adams, "a frontrunner among an entirely new generation of destroyers," required three blows of the traditional champagne bottle before it broke only a fraction of a second before the bow slid out of the reach of the 80-year-old sponsor, Mrs. Robert Homans.

Mrs. Homans, sister of the late secretary of the Navy for whom the vessel is named, shared the launching platform with many distinguished guests. . . .

The 3,370-ton warship slid down the ways at 5:45, just as the sun was sinking behind the huge sign on the structural assembly building proclaiming the "Bath Iron Works, Shipbuilders."

BATH IRON WORKS

. . . Equipped with the Tartar missile, two five-inch 54 rapid fire guns and the latest anti-submarine weapons, the ship's complement will be 24 officers and 330 enlisted men. . . .

Bentz reminded the many persons on hand . . . that the "great American shipbuilding industry got its very start on the shores of the Kennebec river. That beginning—over 352 years ago—was the little Virginia—a very small and well built sailing craft about 50 feet in length. . . .

"The launching of the Adams will mark the 132nd destroyer to be delivered to the Navy by the Bath Iron Works."

BATH INDEPENDENT, 10 SEPTEMBER 1959

RAILROAD STATION SALE TO BIW IS COMPLETED

The Bath Maine Central Railroad passenger terminal has been formally sold to the Bath Iron Works Corp.

. . . G. Baer Connard, assistant to the president, confirmed reports that one of the possible uses to which the building may be put is to house the BIW Recreational Assn. activities.

When the negotiations were first announced several weeks ago it was pointed out that acquisition of the building was part of a long range program to purchase for future protection property near the Iron Works as it becomes available.

The terminal has not been used for passenger uses since railway passenger service on the Brunswick to Rockland branch of the MCRR was halted last spring.

BATH INDEPENDENT, 8 OCTOBER 1959

John Newell's outspokenness on taxes, politics, and other municipal matters exemplified another important trend: Like the old city charter, the old guard of leadership had given way. Pete Newell's passing has already been mentioned; his son had assumed his mantle. What John lacked in charisma he compensated for in zeal.

John Newell resembled his celebrated father in few ways, but one noteworthy similarity between the two was their belief that the interests of the city of Bath and the Iron Works were congruent. The younger Newell was altogether committed to bettering Bath, and he backed up his actions by buying and improving properties, giving generously of his time for civic causes, and, significantly, overtly using his influence to further his business and civic agendas. His high public profile showed great integrity but underestimated Bath's growing resistance to bigshots throwing their weight around.

Newell's 1954 denunciation of City Council was by no means his only public statement. In 1957, for example, he made it clear that as Bath's largest single taxpayer, the Iron Works could ill-afford an increase in its valuation. Raising the company's overhead could jeopardize contracts, and that might mean layoffs. Newell offered to swap a supplementary payment to the city in return for holding the line on valuation.[84] The city did not oblige. That incident, taken with the backlash against his positions on tenure and the Zorach statue's suitability, indicated that Newell's open activism might be counterproductive.

Another member of the old guard, the venerable Harry Webber, died in 1955. His publisher, the even more venerable Frank Nichols, died in 1960. Webber's passing precipitated another important change in the style of the city's daily transactions. His place was taken by Ivan (Ace) Trueworthy, a longtime *Times* employee who had mastered the complex technical skills of getting out a small daily. Under Trueworthy, the *Times* continued to chronicle the social notes that were its traditional mainstay, but otherwise the paper changed noticeably. It lost the old-fashioned style and the classy editorials that had been Webber's trademarks, relying more and more on syndicated novelties, cheesecake items, and canned AP editorials. The newspaper did, however, continue a trend begun during Webber's last years: more detailed coverage of municipal affairs, warts and all. Blind and bylined items alike contained implicit criticism by seasoned reporters, and any interested reader could thus gain a close-up view of municipal transactions. The paper remained aloof from backing specific candidates, however. Editorials on local issues all but vanished. Circulation fell. In 1961, the weekly *Independent* ceased publication.

Although in decline, the *Times* played a vital role in shaping public perceptions of city affairs. Shedding its traditional screen of bland approval and generalities may even have increased its influence among civic-minded citizens.

Another interesting example of the dismantling of the old power base, albeit a largely symbolic one, occurred in 1960, when the bank so long associated with the late Rupert Baxter disappeared in a merger. The Bath Trust Company's strength had for years rested upon the stock and securities it had acquired under Baxter's shrewd, conservative management more than its restrained investment in the community. Harold Rubin, Bath Trust's attorney at the time, put it this way: "They weren't running a bank, really.

They were running a sort of mutual fund . . . because the bank was living off the dividend income from the securities."[85] The value of the bank's holdings, carried on the books at their purchase price, had soared along with the stock market to a point where cashing them in was irresistible to the stockholders, especially when considered in light of the Internal Revenue code's sweet terms for such transactions. The stockholders took the plunge. Bath Trust was then merged with the First Portland Bank (along with the First National Bank of Bath, of which Donald Small was president and John Morse, Jr., vice president). The disappearance of Bath Trust and First National presaged the trend wherein local financial institutions would be acquired by regional ones that, in turn, would eventually be absorbed by interstate conglomerates.

By the early sixties, Bath's population had dropped back to its prewar level, but the city was a world apart from the war years. More than a decade of strenuous effort had fashioned the civic facilities and organizational wherewithal to plan and implement future priorities. Necessity, aided by new procedural methods and new talent, had emasculated the power of its traditional fiscal conservatism. But, ironically, the city's future problems were the same as those of the past. By what means could a close-knit, static, geographically circumscribed, highly specialized community fulfill its increasing needs and expectations? What were its economic options? How far was Bath prepared to stretch to ensure future prosperity and stability? The city could now face these old questions with such new devices as its tortuously refined council-manager system, its dedicated school and planning boards, its autonomous Parking District, and a revitalized Chamber of Commerce.

Creative management of Bath's future depended upon harmonizing its traditions and strong sense of community with these new institutions. In view of the controversies of the fifties, was consensus possible?

NOTES

1. Dominique J. Tardif, Interview, West Bath, April 1987.
2. Ibid.
3. Ibid.
4. Ibid.
5. BI, 7 March 1946.
6. Tardif, Inaugural Speech, Bath, March 1946, in *City of Bath Annual Report*, 1946–1947.

7. Eastham Guild, Jr., Interview, Bath, February 1987.
8. BI, 5 June 1947.
9. Harry E. Ring, Jr., Interview, Bath, June 1987.
10. Ibid.
11. Ralph F. Mittendorf to BDT, Ironton, OH, February 1954, quoted in BI, 11 February 1954.
12. Snow, p. 415.
13. *A Legacy of Pride . . . A Future of Promise: The First Hundred Years of Bath Iron Works* ([Bath]: Bath Iron Works, n.d.).
14. J. William Schulze to Rodney E. Ross, Jr., Bath, 8 March 1950, quoted in BI, 23 March 1950.
15. Bob Niss, *Faces of Maine* (Portland, ME: Guy Gannett Publishing Co., 1981), p. 29.
16. McCabe interview.
17. Editorial, BI, 2 January 1947.
18. Ibid., 8 January 1948.
19. BI, 19 January 1950.
20. Ibid., 26 January 1950.
21. Ethel Tourtelotte, Mabel J. Taber, et al. to BDT, Bath, January 1950, published in ibid., 26 January 1950.
22. BDT, 16 December 1954.
23. William E. Haggett, Interview, Bath, August 1987.
24. Loring R. Additon, Interview, Sabattus, ME, August 1987.
25. Ibid.
26. Ibid.
27. Sally T. Haggett, Interview, Bath, May 1987.
28. Guild interview.
29. Additon, quoted in BI, 30 March 1950.
30. BI, 17 May 1951.
31. Ibid., 9 September 1954.
32. *City of Bath Annual Report*, 1954–1955.
33. Additon interview.
34. S. Haggett interview.
35. Blaine Trafton, quoted in Aldridge, p. 58.
36. Aldridge, pp. 53, 91.
37. Notebook of Morse High School Activities and Awards, 1927–1964 (Alumni Room, Morse High School, Bath).
38. The *Clipper* (Morse High School yearbook), 1953, 1955.
39. Donald A. Spear, Interview, Bath, June 1987; W. Haggett interview.
40. Laura G. Ridgewell, quoted in Aldridge, p. 66.
41. Burden interview.
42. Ibid.; W. Haggett interview.
43. Ibid.
44. Additon interview.
45. Owen, p. 338.
46. Ibid., pp. 316–17.
47. R. Small interview.

48. Ibid.
49. BI, 19 August 1958.
50. Mussenden interview.
51. R. Small, quoted in BDT, 15 February 1965.
52. Owen, pp. 222–25; *Patten Free Library, 1847–1952* (Bath: Patten Free Library, 1952), pp. 18–19.
53. Kendall.
54. BI, 16 August 1959.
55. Zorach discusses his artistic evolution in his *Art is My Life: The Autobiography of William Zorach* (Cleveland: World Publishing Co., 1967); see also Gertrud A. Mellon and Elizabeth F. Wilder, eds., *Maine and Its Role in American Art* (New York: Viking Press, 1963), pp. 121–22.
56. Zorach, pp. 174–75; Adelaide S. Bowker, Interview, Bath, July 1987.
57. Bowker interview.
58. Ibid.
59. Zorach, p. 176.
60. Bowker interview.
61. BI, 12 May 1960.
62. Bowker interview.
63. Day interview.
64. *City of Bath Annual Report*, 1956–1957.
65. Guild interview.
66. Harold J. Rubin, Interview, Bath, June 1987.
67. BI, 14 July 1951.
68. Guild interview.
69. BI, 26 April 1951.
70. Guild interview.
71. BI, 18 February 1954.
72. J. Newell to Webber, Bath, 27 January 1954, published in ibid., 28 January 1954.
73. Editorial, ibid.
74. S. Hunter, quoted in ibid., 4 February 1954.
75. Harry Cooke, quoted in ibid.
76. Mittendorf to Harry Webber, Ironton, OH, February 1954, published in ibid., 11 February 1954.
77. Nathan White to Citizens of Bath, Bath, 7 February 1955, published in ibid., 10 February 1955.
78. S. Hunter, quoted in BI, 31 March 1955.
79. Norman C. and Virginia Kenney, Interview, Bath, August 1987.
80. Robert C. Cummings, "Bath Sees Changes and Controversy . . . in 1959," BI, 7 January 1960.
81. Arthur Gediman and D. Small, quoted in BI, 18 June 1959.
82. J. Temple interview.
83. *City of Bath Annual Report*, 1959–1960.
84. BDT, 20 April 1957.
85. Rubin interview.

4

"A Shot in the Arm"

Laura Ridgewell would someday lose interest in downtown Bath, but during the late fifties, that spot was a weekend mecca for her and hundreds of other shoppers and socializers: "The first thing I heard when I came into Bath would be the Salvation Army . . . right on the corner [of Center and Water streets at] the old Sears store. . . . You would have goose bumps because the music was *there*; they were actually playing the horns and drums and you could actually touch the people if you wanted to. People used to gather around and ask them to play certain hymns and put the money into their baskets. Senter's [on Front Street] . . . used to smell of Tweed perfume. . . . They sold it and had the bottles open so you could try a little bit if you wanted to. Now that was an elite store, Senter's. That was like Bergdorf Goodman now, or Altman's. . . . The awning was a little bit special: it was green and white with *Senter's* written on the front of it. And there was always a bakery. . . . The fish market was there too, and there was a meat market. . . . You knew where you were by the smell. On Water Street there was a place called the American House. That place was bad. Bad. The American House was taboo. You just didn't go near that place, ever, but in front of the American House . . . there was a candy shop where they made candy—right there. You could stand there and wait for them to dip what you wanted. And, of course, Mikelsky's [furniture store] was there forever. . . . These shops were all flourishing. It wasn't a bunch of those mall things all mushed together. It was every little shop, and you could smell every distinct odor from every shop. . . . It was great!"[1]

The view from City Hall was a bit different. Instead of the unpretentious, enticing shopping district described above, city fathers saw a warren of small-time retail shops plagued with critical parking problems, outmoded buildings, lackluster merchandising, and increasing failure. The smell was not of fresh fish or perfume but commercial decay. As Planning Board member Roger Luke put it, "Stores began to close and weeds started to grow in vacant lots in downtown Bath," a condition that had led to the creation of the Planning Board in 1956.[2]

By 1960, the board had armed itself with a scheme to revitalize the commercial district that was nothing less than startling. Imagine: Future shoppers in the downtown would have no vehicular traffic to contend with because both Front and Center streets would be pedestrian malls accented with greenery and park benches. Cars would be conveniently parked in extensive landscaped lots nearby. Gone would be the blocks of Federal and Victorian buildings with their old-fashioned tradesmen; in their place, as 1959 planning sketches revealed, would be functional, modernist buildings adorned with the textured panels, glass expanses, and graphic signs dear to the hearts of postwar architects. A few of the purposeful figures that invariably populate such drawings are paused on an "auditorium plaza" overlooking Commercial Street, enjoying a view of a tree-shaded waterfront that sports a marina, a boatel-motel, and a maritime museum.[3]

A pipe dream? Not exactly. The concept was the painstaking product of professional city planners, and a sizable chunk of Bath leadership saw this plan as a prerequisite for the city's survival, for it would revitalize business, raise property values, and thereby refinance the city's needs. The best part of the package was that Uncle Sam might pick up three-fourths of the tab. By 1960, Bath, like hundreds of other communities across the nation, teetered on the edge of a major urban renewal program. Few in the Shipbuilding City suspected how volatile a proposal it would prove to be, or how the pros and cons of rebuilding the downtown would split the community's new leadership into two hostile camps. Urban renewal became THE issue in Bath from 1960 to 1965.

The federal government's massive urban renewal program was firmly in place long before it attracted attention in Bath. As long ago as the Depression, Congress had recognized the need for federal leadership in slum clearance and public housing. And, as Bath had already witnessed, Uncle Sam by World War II had become a seasoned, expeditious builder of emergency housing under the Lanham Act. In 1949, a new federal housing act, passed with bipartisan support, enlarged upon previous approaches to urban rehabilitation. Recognizing that in the crumbling inner cities of America, real estate had been divided into parcels too minuscule and numerous to attract large-scale developers, Congress authorized funds with which cities might acquire small urban properties and amalgamate their plots into parcels of sufficient size to interest private builders.

Although the primary purpose of the housing act was residential improvement, the federal government soon bowed to the arguments of planners that a cityscape was more than housing, and that needs for rehabilitation existed in cities and towns throughout the nation, not merely in the largest metropolitan centers.[4] By the mid-fifties, therefore, federal funding was available for rehabilitating commercial properties. Furthermore, Uncle Sam had extended coverage to "blighted areas": neighborhoods that were not outright slums but presumably were headed that way.

Urban renewal funds were administered by the Housing and Home Finance Agency (HHFA), later the Department of Housing and Urban Development (HUD). Their purpose was to permit needy communities to purchase properties, using eminent domain if necessary, compensate displaced householders and businesses, clear sites, improve municipal facilities thereon, and sell or lease the upgraded and/or enlarged parcels to private developers. To sweeten the deal for developers, financing for private construction on such parcels was made available through the Federal National Mortgage Association. Urban renewal thus did not involve Uncle Sam directly in downtown construction.

A community interested in qualifying for urban renewal assistance was required to develop and submit a "workable program"—a detailed plan of action tailored to its specific needs and objectives. If HHFA approved such a program, a community could usually expect the lion's share of its costs to be borne by Washington. The community's share of the cost was expected to be recovered through higher property taxes once redevelopment had run its course.

Urban renewal, then, proceeded under several innovative but controversial assumptions: that reversing the decline of "blighted" downtown areas was a good long-term investment for the nation; that achieving that goal necessitated wholesale removal of existing structures and the repackaging of property into larger parcels; and that the painstaking details of a funded project were the responsibility of community officials, not federal bureaucrats. (That last point was an important rebuttal to arguments that urban renewal was a conspiracy of big government to undermine local authority.) By the end of the fifties, the program's rationale had persuaded hundreds of American cities and towns to prepare and submit workable programs.[5]

All of this had been duly noted in Bath. During the late fifties, a homegrown variety of urban renewal had begun in the Shipbuilding City, propelled by the Chamber of Commerce, the Parking District, and the Planning Board. Ramshackle structures on Water Street were coming down, and it was just a matter of time before the big bad American House followed them. Several sagging waterfront buildings, woebegone relics of the age of sail, were scheduled for future demolition. Over on Front Street, a 120-year-old brick landmark, the Ledyard Block, succumbed to the need for better traffic flow. Front Street merchants resolutely parked their cars in front of

MAINE MARITIME MUSEUM

The beginning of a trend: The Ledyard Block comes down.

their establishments, heedless of the consequences for their businesses. This practice created an intolerable bottleneck just north of City Hall near the *Times* office, where the Ledyard Block and its sidewalk protruded into the street. In 1959, Bill Mussenden assembled a consortium including John Newell, John Morse, Jr., and BIW executive William Niss to buy the block. It was demolished and its protruding strip sold to the city for street widening.[6]

Meanwhile, the Planning Board, thanks to seed money from BIW via the Chamber of Commerce, had received enough state and federal assistance to undertake a detailed analysis of Bath's options and devise a redevelopment scheme for the city. A Boston planning firm, Atwood, Blackwell and Young, was hired for this purpose.

All of which would suggest that the downtown was keeping up with the times. Evidence gathered during 1957–58, however, suggested otherwise. Two surveys, one each by the Chamber of Commerce and the city planners, identified what the latter called "The Case of the Disappearing Dollars": "An absolute decline of some $750,000 in sales tax items alone was experienced [in Bath] from 1956 through 1958. This occurred during a period of inflation, rising sales elsewhere and greatly expanded personal and family income. More than 7 million resident Bath shopping dollars went elsewhere for retail purchases in 1957 alone. The reasons for this seem mainly centered about the shabby Downtown appearance, also Bath merchandising practices."[7]

Identifying problems and curing them was what planning was all about. But for Bath, the magnitude of the cure approached that of the disease. Reporting to the Planning Board in February 1958, consultant John Blackwell made it clear that the Shipbuilding City simply did not have the land or labor pool to attract additional large industry. In addition, Sagadahoc County's consumer index (the ratio of spending to income) was the lowest in Maine. That meant that extraordinary efforts would be necessary to improve business. Bath, said Blackwell, had two options. One was to ally itself with nearby Brunswick to develop the extensive land between the two communities, allowing economies of scale to work for mutual benefit. In view of the strong parochialism of both communities, that recommendation had little chance of success. Blackwell's other suggestion was that Bath exploit its "distinguished characteristics"—historic architecture, colorful past, and extensive river frontage—to attract shoppers, tourists, and small retail businesses.[8] Doing so would necessitate major beautification of the waterfront, creation of ample parking and parks to open up the downtown, and the renovation of the shopping district's old-fashioned stores—all in all, a big order.

In published summaries of their findings, Atwood, Blackwell and Young did not paint rosy pictures for Bath citizens. They reiterated that the city's topographical limitations were a discouragement to future industry and a restriction upon growth. Bath should take her planning cues from these peculiarities and turn them to advantage. For example, future residential construction should be slow and judiciously confined mostly to the fringes of the built-up area where utilities were already in place. The city should take pains to protect its rural greenbelt, which the planners deemed one of the region's most attractive assets. (How that must have surprised boosters of industrial development!)

Protecting and marketing Bath's attractiveness, the planners maintained, was the city's best shot at a brighter future. Atwood, Blackwell and Young were particularly sensitive to the recent state and federal highway bonanza and its inevitable consequence for a city that lay athwart such routes of expansion. Since 1947, when Route One's traffic to and from the Carlton Bridge had been smoothed out by a new Leeman Highway that passed under High Street and avoided the Center Street snarl altogether, Bath's traffic picture had been changing. In 1959, as the Maine Central Railroad discontinued passenger service to Bath, Leeman Highway was connected directly to the bridge by a limited-access viaduct. The car was now king. Through traffic no longer had to cope with downtown drivers; but the blessing of the viaduct could be a curse to business, because it invited travelers and sightseers to keep moving past Bath's crowded downtown. In 1961, construction was to start on still another incarnation of Route One, a four-lane superhighway that would, by the latter sixties, connect Brunswick to Bath's Leeman Highway: another boon to through traffic and vacationers headed for destinations beyond the Kennebec. Obviously, in the future, any commercial district worth its salt must equip itself—rebuild itself, if need be—for the comfort, care, and convenience of the almighty motorcar.

The planners met this issue head-on: "As Bath enters the last half of the

MAINE MARITIME MUSEUM

The shape of things to come? Bath's model for urban renewal. Note the waterfront treatment.

20th Century, the city faces a new complex of factors unlike any in its history. New regional limited-access highway will soon reach the city, making downtown Bath only one hour from the great, almost solidly built-up urban pattern extending from north of Portland to south of Washington, D.C. . . .

"Opportunities as well as problems will result from this new relationship. Increased leisure time and ease of travel will give to Bath a splendid opportunity to cash in on its geographic location as a gateway to Maine's growing downeast recreation area. The city may find itself limited by topography.

"Community growth hitherto has been dependent almost entirely upon employment in Bath's ocean-oriented industries, which have a bright future. However, additional growth may come to depend more and more upon Bath community attractiveness and way of life within the region than upon purely local employment. It may well be that future Bath residents may commute over good roads to work locations elsewhere.

"Bath has a great opportunity to develop its Downtown and the downtown Kennebec Riverfront as first steps toward making itself one of New England's most attractive and unique cities. Bath's treasure of old houses, colonial streets and scenic riverbank site need to be complemented by an equally attractive downtown center if the community is to grow and prosper."[9] The planners thus contended that revitalizing the downtown was crucial to Bath's survival.

The Blackwell Report's emphasis upon aesthetics and tourism instead of industry was a substantial departure from previous discussions of revitalization of the city. It called for major changes in strategic priorities and major surgery on the city's commercial district. The plan might have gone no further except for the fact that it had the makings of a workable program to attract federal urban renewal funds. Planning proceeded.

In November 1959, Bath dignitaries assembled in City Hall for a formal presentation of the long-awaited planning report. Also on hand were reporters, photographers, and movie cameramen from the state's Department of Economic Development, who recorded the occasion in the hope that Bath's renewal might become a model for other Maine communities. The *Times* gave the event favorable coverage.

How much of a model Bath would become was a matter of federal funding. Although a published outline of the Blackwell Report stipulated that "little hope is extended for any federal urban renewal funds . . . for downtown redevelopment purposes in the next few years,"[10] consultant John Atwood told the city fathers and assembled media personnel that if Bath followed the appropriate guidelines, federal assistance would probably be forthcoming.[11] There is little doubt that the implied promise of such assistance persuaded VIPs to give the plan a try.

Bath's plan was a long-term one; completing it might run twenty years. It owed much of its appeal to the careful integration of its components, and was therefore not to be undertaken in half measures. Besides the elements already noted, it called for a circular traffic flow around the fringe of the downtown, with new streets and widened old ones to improve access to the shopping district, and the eventual conversion of the intersecting blocks of Front and Center streets into car-free pedestrian malls. (Closing off that area to vehicles would abet the proposed circular traffic flow.) The plan also stressed the need to raze empty and/or unproductive structures to make way for larger, more enterprising replacements. None of these elements seemed to dampen general enthusiasm for the report.

Should Bath undertake urban renewal? To do so, the city would have to create an urban renewal authority to apply for assistance, maintain liaison with HHFA, refine the Blackwell Report into a workable program, and

MAINE MARITIME MUSEUM

Room for improvement: waterfront buildings on Commercial Street in 1959. The Kennebec riverbank lies just to the right of the picture.

control the prodigious red tape the project would certainly generate. Most important and difficult of its responsibilities would be to determine systematically, with the assistance of consultants, which properties would be acquired and demolished in order to effect the downtown renaissance.

In February 1960, Bath voters turned out heavily to endorse the creation of the Urban Renewal Authority (URA). In March, City Council appointed five citizens to the new URA: John Newell (who became URA chairman); Thatcher Pinkham, an ex-BIW employee and current factotum for Newell (who became vice chairman); Rodney Ross, Jr. (who became treasurer); Louis Silverman, manager of Mikelsky's; and William Boyle, a cashier at the Bath National Bank. With funds advanced by HHFA, the authority set up shop in the former Maine Central Railroad station, now owned by the Iron Works but leased to the new organization. Ex-Congressman Charles Nelson was hired as the first URA executive director. City Council formally approved the Blackwell Report as its basis for urban renewal and authorized URA to proceed. Some councillors had to swallow hard to characterize their downtown as "blighted," a prerequisite for further negotiations.

In June 1961, city fathers made the final payment on the antique Knox & Lincoln debt. For years, that obligation had symbolized the pitfalls of municipal indebtedness, although such symbolism had lost most of its punch since the war. Nonetheless, former mayor Donald Small, speaking at the inevitable ceremony marking the K&L payoff, warned Bath citizens against falling into the same trap in the future. Was his comment possibly a reference to urban renewal responsibilities? No amount of sermonizing, however, could mar the symbolic value of Bath's escape from its financial past, and city leaders, meanwhile, were primed for downtown renewal.

FINAL KNOX & LINCOLN BOND IS BURNED THURSDAY NIGHT

Bath celebrated the end of an era Thursday evening, as several hundred persons clustered about the City Hall plaza to honor the paying off of a 92-year debt to the Knox and Lincoln railroad.

The "match"—a cigarette lighter held by Council Chairman Arthur E. Hutchins, assisted by City Treasurer Eva Kingsbury—touched off the final $5,000 bond on the debt that according to estimates cost the Shipbuilding City at least $2 million in capital and interest costs.

The burning climaxed the 45 minute

ceremonies that featured a review of the history of Bath's excursion into the deficit side of the railroad business, by former Mayor Donald M. Small.

On hand for the celebration were the Elks Band, the Buccaneer Drum and Bugle Corps and a bevy of former chairmen—including Dominique Tardiff [sic], former mayor of Bath in the days immediately following World War II, who made a special trip from Lewiston for the occasion . . . .

Small drew a moral from 92 years of railroad indebtedness. Though pinpointing no blame . . . Small said he hoped that in the future Bath people will look at their Knox and Lincoln experience when they face the prospect of a major debt.

But Council Chairman Hutchins saw a possible different conclusion. He suggested that without Bath's railroad investment the city might never have had an Iron Works or a Hyde Windlass . . . .

BATH DAILY TIMES, 2 JUNE 1961

PAUL REVERE BELL IN BATH'S CITY HALL TO RING TOMORROW

BY ROBERT C. CUMMINGS

Bath's Paul Revere Bell, cast in Boston's North end foundry of Paul Revere and Son, back in 1802, and one of the relatively few still in existence is going to be rung Thursday for the first time since Bath's centennial celebration 15 years ago.

The bell, one of the oldest known and one of the few remaining that was probably cast by Paul Revere himself, will be rung "by hand" by city Messenger and City Hall custodian Theodore Burns at 1 o'clock as part of the "Bells Across the Nation" observance being sponsored on Patriot's Day by the National American Legion.

The City Hall bell has been largely inactive since the 1930's, but is scheduled to be used more frequently in the future. An engineering inspection last summer revealed no cracks or other structural defects in the 160

> year old bell itself, but seriously decayed wooden supports. . . .
>
> A new welded aluminum stand has been donated by the Bath Iron Works to hold the bell, estimated to be worth in excess of $25,000.
>
> *BATH DAILY TIMES*, 18 APRIL 1962

Other recent events had heightened the need to renovate the downtown. The city's never-ending need for capital improvements and increased municipal wages made a higher tax base absolutely essential. So, probably, did the state's passage of a bill mandating a fifteen-year cleanup of the Kennebec, which would require installation of a sewage treatment plant in Bath. Meanwhile, the local business mix that constituted the tax base was also changing. In October 1961, Rodney Ross, Jr., announced the sale of hard-pressed Hyde Windlass to the Bath Iron Works, which would continue to operate Hyde as a corporate division. Ross assured the public that as a discrete company, Hyde had reached a dead end, but that the BIW deal would guarantee that local jobs stayed local.[12] Three months later, Torrey Roller Bushing, down to twenty employees, called it quits. By way of contrast, BIW's concurrent announcement of another hefty Navy contract made it clear that, more than ever, Bath's economic eggs were in one basket. As for downtown trade, it continued to nosedive, despite wage increases at BIW.

On the other hand, early signs were that Bath's downtown had a good chance of achieving its sought-after vitality. Construction was under way for a new "Early American" A&P supermarket on Front Street; the large, old Columbia Hotel and another structure came down to provide the site. Up the street, adjacent to City Hall, the 1894 business block that was home

HERBERT DOUGLAS; MAINE MARITIME MUSEUM

Old and new "Early American" on Front Street in the early sixties.

MAINE MARITIME MUSEUM

A block on Front Street, built in 1894
and home to the *Times*, shortly before demolition.

to the *Times* went under the wrecking ball. In its place rose a determinedly Georgian structure to house Bath's branch of the First National Bank of Portland. The change permitted further widening of Front Street. The *Times* moved into a nondescript, efficient, modern building nearby. Another conspicuous change occurred when URA Director Charles Nelson persuaded Senator Margaret Chase Smith to pull the necessary strings to get the post office, a grimy but handsome ex-customs house between City Hall and the Carlton Bridge, sandblasted to spiffy presentability. Reportedly, Nelson had told Smith that the sooty post office was "right in the middle of the area we plan to improve and beautify" through urban renewal, and it was therefore "too bad to have the federal government spending money to renew and reconstruct municipalities and leaving one of their own buildings the only remaining eyesore."[13] That did the trick. But in 1962, the truth was that the post office sat among buildings that, pending urban renewal decisions, constituted an array of eyesores. The eyesore problem was going to get worse in the downtown, because it was pointless for property owners to improve structures whose days might be numbered. When and where, owners and occupants wondered, would demolition take place? Bath citizens, it turned out, were not prepared for long time lags and malingering uncertainty as urban renewal's red tape unwound.

To conform to Uncle Sam's elaborate prerequisites for urban renewal assistance, City Council had passed a housing code; and to smooth out the hundreds of planning rough spots, the URA had retained another consulting firm, yet managing the ongoing details of Bath's renewal proved tedious and time-consuming. More time was lost before a permanent director was

HERBERT DOUGLAS; MAINE MARITIME MUSEUM

An eyesore on Water Street holds out against municipal demolition.

in place. Charles Nelson, in poor health, resigned that position and was replaced briefly by local attorney Donald Spear, whose other commitments forced his resignation early in 1962. Spear was replaced by former City Council Chairman Arthur Hutchins, an exceptionally hard-working public servant. Hutchins's experience made him an apt choice for the URA spot. He ran a kitchen design and construction firm in Bath's downtown, so he knew the area's problems intimately. He had been one of those concerned "vigilantes" who, in 1950, had raised the touchy issue of Bath's being a distressed economic area. More recently, he had been active in the revitalized Chamber of Commerce and had been a member of the original Planning Board. As a city councillor, he was an outspoken opponent of Manager Stanley Judkins after the fire-aid controversy. Hutchins resigned his Council seat to take on the Urban Renewal Authority's directorship. Bath now had a blueprint for its future, a fighting chance at funding to accomplish its goals (once all the administrative and bureaucratic details were covered), and the manpower to see the plan through.

But the plan did not go through expeditiously. Instead, Hutchins, like his predecessors, found himself beset by delays because of Uncle Sam's voracious appetite for detail. Zone boundaries had to be established and revised. Planning maps had to be redrawn. Mistakes in wording had to be rectified. Bath's workable program consequently underwent a series of delays. The lost time was more than inconvenient; it was a disaster for the URA.

During the lull in 1962, as the novelty of Bath's urban renewal plan wore off, its stern realities loomed larger. Urban renewal, after all, was primarily a program of site preparation, the dirty work of which was the purchase and demolition of existing structures and the relocation of businesses and occupants to other sites. In any renewal plan, such matters could be touchy, because inherently they stepped on many toes and pitted agencies against individuals who were hard-put to oppose bureaucratic power. By 1962, dozens of American communities had learned that the whole process could drag on for years while local and federal authorities calibrated the fine points of a program.[14] The wait could be agonizing. And some communities that proceeded were finding the toll of human suffering and destruction of small businesses was unacceptable.[15] To combat a crescendo of opposition, Uncle Sam mounted a substantial public relations campaign, but critics of urban renewal were having a field day. Criticism ran the gamut from right-wing accusations that the program was a communist conspiracy to subvert private ownership, through arguments that it was a massive boondoggle for planners, lawyers, and sharp developers, to fears that it was a technocratic process that choked the life out of neighborhoods and gratuitously displaced the little guy in the name of some grand design.[16] All of these opinions were widely read, circulated, and discussed in Bath as the long wait continued. Rumors began to fly and misgivings about the program mounted in the Shipbuilding City.

John Newell and Arthur Hutchins, Urban Renewal Authority chairman and director, respectively, were firm believers in their cause. Although the program conflicted with his rock-ribbed distaste for big, liberal government, Newell had become so dedicated to the program that wisecrackers dubbed him Urban R. Newell.[17] But despite their dedication and willingness to plough through mountains of strategic detail, neither Newell nor Hutchins proved adept at public relations. One problem was the public profile of Newell himself. As a businessman, he presumably swung a great deal of weight around town, but his civic power had become more apparent than real by the sixties. The decade since his dramatic denunciation of city politics had seen the old power structure crumble in Bath, and Newell, by his very name, was a holdover from the old days. Meanwhile, BIW had grown beyond the virtuoso operation it had been during its early years under Pete Newell. John Newell's well-motivated concern for the city was offset by his solitary lifestyle, his candid displays of opinion, and, no doubt, irrelevant comparisons between himself and his father. Such matters are clearer in hindsight than they were in 1962. "One of the interesting things about Bath that nobody really recognized," recalled Robert Cummings, a *Times* reporter assigned to cover urban renewal, "was that John Newell had no influence in the community, which is amazing, since he was president of the Bath Iron Works. But he had no real influence with the Council or the public. . . . Simply because John Newell said urban renewal was good had almost no impact, or perhaps a negative impact."[18] In view of his corporate position, Newell's URA role looked peculiar to some and obnoxious to others: If urban renewal's purpose was to widen Bath's options beyond one big local industry, why was that industry's chief executive overseeing the program?

In March 1962, at City Hall auditorium, a packed house heard Newell apologize for the six-month delay, which he attributed to the URA's personnel changes and its inexperience with red tape. To allay fears about the program's cost to Bath taxpayers, Newell assured citizens that Uncle Sam would pay about 75 percent of the final tab and that, in the meantime, funding the program would not sidetrack the city's planned school construction and other capital improvements. Newell knew that local businessmen were anxious to learn whether or not their establishments were scheduled for demolition, a matter that consultants had under confidential review. Newell, however, could not be specific about such plans, although he stipulated that every effort would be made to spare local business: "The fewer people we have to relocate, the better we will like it."[19]

Persistent public fears about the cost of urban renewal probably influenced a crucial decision by the URA to postpone indefinitely the rehabilitation of the waterfront. That phase of the plan was a real stumbling block; it was hard to visualize a beautified waterfront, much less create one, when Commercial Street was home to railroad tracks, hopper cars, and the decidedly unscenic Coal Pocket. Could the URA afford to acquire a going business of that magnitude in order to rehabilitate the waterfront? If Bath had to forgo part of the Blackwell Report in the interest of economy, that was the part. Accordingly, in August, Newell announced that waterfront renovation had been deferred, "not forgotten."[20] The benefit to Bath, he said, was lower project costs to the city. But, as critics pointed out, the rest of the program was now in jeopardy because a beautified waterfront was crucial to the Blackwell concept's overall success. How attractive would Bath be to developers if cleared lots overlooked a grimy industrial site obscuring the Kennebec?

Arthur Hutchins, meanwhile, had been busy squelching rumors about the blitz urban renewal was sure to unleash on downtown businessmen. He had little ammunition, however, because the confidential survey and appraisal of properties was not yet complete and he was therefore unable to get down to cases with jittery individuals. In May 1962, the best he could do was to circulate an unapologetic letter advising businessmen to sit tight and keep an open mind: " . . . there are reports and rumors circulating that are not only misleading but in some cases completely false. Because reports of this nature can be very disturbing to those involved, the Authority is requesting that you ignore any reports except those released by this office."[21] Hutchins also made the rounds to civic group meetings, denouncing the dissemination of right-wing, anti-urban renewal, political propaganda by an anonymous "Save Bath Committee," whose tactics he characterized as "negative, selfish," illegitimate, and controlled by out-of-town interests.[22]

It was late July before the URA completed its application for urban renewal assistance. The stack of necessary forms, documents, maps, and supporting materials stood a foot and a half high on Hutchins's desk. Before sending the packet to the HHFA, Hutchins submitted it for City Council's review. At last the public got a look at its details.

What the public saw was a proposal based upon the Blackwell Report but pared down financially so that Bath could continue municipal business as usual without exceeding its debt limit. To accomplish the necessary reduction, the URA had suspended the waterfront phase except for some street widening and provision for a small grassy area on Parking District land. It had also dropped the idea of pedestrian malls on Front and Center streets, which, like the waterfront concept, had been one of the Blackwell Report's most intriguing elements.

But most conspicuous was the program's approach to downtown demolition. In the downtown project area, which encompassed 187 buildings of all types, half of that number were slated for destruction and fourteen others for rehabilitation. Most were clustered in the inner core of the business district, the area from the bridge north to the city park at Summer Street, and from the river west to Middle Street. Thirty-eight establishments were targeted for removal on Front and Center streets alone. It began to sink in that to consolidate parcels for reconstruction, the URA would have to condemn sound buildings as well as dilapidated ones. A great many citizens were surprised by that fact.

Hutchins estimated the total cost of Bath's urban renewal program at $2.298 million, of which $398,000 might be recouped through land sales to developers, leaving a net of $1.9 million (close to $7 million in 1986 dollars). Bath's share of the costs would be between $226,000 and $326,000, depending on whether or not Uncle Sam would credit the city for the value of such in-kind contributions as the Zorach fountain, the new library wing, and the YMCA's new swimming pool.[23] Such credits were unlikely.

Smoldering doubts and uncertainties quickly gave way to outright opposition to the scheme. In City Council, Arthur Gediman and William Rogers, both of whose businesses occupied buildings on the URA demolition list, tried unsuccessfully to submit the plan to the voters in another referendum. But Bath had committed itself to legally prescribed urban renewal procedures, so the voters would not get a chance to rule on the package until the federal government had approved it. Accordingly, the workable program went to the HHFA in August, much to the anger of a few politicians and a large number of downtown businessmen who thought the voters had been given a fast shuffle. Many insisted they had not understood the finality of setting up an agency whose interim activities were beyond review.

Bath's urban renewal now faced two problems. Its basic plan had been emasculated in the interests of short-term economy (penny wisdom was an old story in the Shipbuilding City), and its administrators had failed to win the critical cooperation of downtown merchants, whose district was the program's ground zero. The latter problem was the product of a deliberate strategy of the URA board, recalled Bob Cummings. As a *Times* reporter, Cummings, who favored urban renewal, attended URA board meetings: "At the first meeting, they made it a policy of not being open with the public. Their theory was that they would develop a plan and then they would sell the plan. I protested vigorously. The word came over from Brunswick and Cam [Campbell Niven, grandson of the late Frank Nichols and publisher of the *Times*] that we would cooperate 100 percent with the Urban Renewal Authority. I told Cam and the Urban Renewal Authority that if you were not selling this project as you went along, it didn't have a chance in the world because a lot of little storekeepers were going to be hurt, and they met with hundreds of people in the course of a week, and they would be the key unless you built up a strong base of support. They never did." According to Cummings, the URA board kept its distance in the name of ultimate salesmanship: "I remember [Louis] Silverman saying, 'I'm a businessman, and I know the way to sell something is to come up and make a big splash, and you can sell anything. A lot of little splashes doesn't do anything.' "[24] But when the URA unveiled its program, its biggest splash was the controversy over demolition. This was the time for painstaking diplomacy.

In the fall of 1962, while the HHFA's verdict on Bath's program was still pending, owners of downtown property received a form letter from Hutchins: "This is to advise you that certain property you now own will be acquired under the plan now developed for the renewal of downtown Bath.

"This program was undertaken, as you know, because of the decline in the downtown area. It was designed to reverse that decline with the object of improving the economic base. . . .

"The program offers many opportunities to the investors in downtown real estate. Modern store and office facilities, wider streets with an improved circulation pattern, free off-street parking . . . , good sidewalks, and better street lighting are among the improvements that will create a much more attractive downtown environment. Land use controls will be imposed. . . . Other codes and regulations will add quality to the investments which we do not now have. It might interest you to know that highly competent real estate appraisers have found that approximately 22% economic obsolescence exists now in our downtown area.

"It is now timely for you to start giving serious consideration to your future plans. Such questions as re-investment of proceeds of sale for tax purposes, organization of real estate corporations, space requirements for your own business operation, and many others should receive your immediate attention.

"This is also to advise you that premature action in regard to relocation may prevent you from obtaining the full benefits available under this program."[25] A similar letter was sent to tenants of buildings scheduled for removal.

Hutchins's letter was probably good news to a few large property owners in the downtown—John Morse, Jr., for instance: " . . . [my] buildings that were slated for demolition were some that were not all that great anyhow. I had planned . . . to buy some of the developable property and build some new buildings."[26] But to small owner-occupiers and tenants, the notice was impersonal and provocative, especially because the URA was still unprepared to divulge the prices it intended to pay for properties.[27] Hutchins's letter touched off a revolt.

Charles A. (Bud) Shepard, Jr., was one local businessman who had few complaints about the downtown. Growing up in Bath, he pursued musical and artistic inclinations and, after graduating from Morse High, had a fling with art achool in Boston before settling down at the University of Maine: "I studied art at Maine. I didn't study business. I never studied business, actually, until I got out. I then started taking courses in marketing and buying and all those sorts of things." Shepard came back to his father's Front Street shoe store and soon branched into men's clothing. "We were really doing well at that point in time, in the fifties. And when I took over in the sixties, I did better every year than the year before. When the *Bath Times* was showing photographs of grass growing up in the cracks of the sidewalks, my business had reached a very satisfying level. A lot of times my customers would come in and say, 'How can you be doing well when the downtown is falling around your head?' It wasn't true. The town wasn't falling down."[28] Shepard was as unimpressed by the surveys outlining economic atrophy, which he regarded as statistical sleight-of-hand, as he was by the unflattering *Times* pictures of the business district.

The Shepard store was a regular stop for anyone who liked to shoot the breeze, and urban renewal had become the hot topic of the day for people "who were concerned, Charlie MacDonald, for one. I'd known Charlie for a long time. And then the Burgesses, Charlie Burgess and his wife. Local people like that. . . . [Urban renewal] was not a big deal in the beginning because the information regarding it was not out. I would talk with Charlie MacDonald, and he would tell me what was discussed the night before at the Council meeting. It was not terribly alarming. He was alarmed, but I wasn't . . . , and as I recall there were not many people on the street alarmed until it really began to gather momentum and more things came out about it."[29]

Shortly after the Hutchins letter, Shepard, whose store was slated for demolition, cofounded an organization calling itself the Renewal Review Association (RRA). Its purpose was to protect its members from what they regarded as "the wholesale destruction of perfectly good, sound, good-

MAINE MARITIME MUSEUM

Bud Shepard's store, one of many downtown properties slated for demolition under Bath's urban renewal plan.

looking business properties."[30] Charter members included Paul Bagdikian, a chiropractor who had reversed his once-favorable view of urban renewal after beholding its impact on other cities he visited; Theodore Kaknes, a downtown optometrist, and William Rogers, both of whom would lose their business sites. The organization quickly attracted other members politically or personally opposed to urban renewal. By January 1963, the RRA had about thirty members.

The RRA's public statements at first projected an image of bewildered citizens in search of a hearing, people who had never dreamed that by setting up the Urban Renewal Authority they were forfeiting further participation in a workable program: "We met with the Urban Renewal Director, we met with the planning board, we met with the Citizens Advisory Group, we met with anyone who wanted to talk urban renewal. . . .

" . . . as time went on and our information grew, we noted a great lack of flexibility in whatever plans the urban renewal men were forming. Our questions and suggestions were always met with a pleasant but firm negative response."[31] Beneath the bewilderment, however, was a core of political savvy. Fully appreciating the *Times*'s interest in urban renewal and the role the press would play in determining the final outcome, the RRA made good use of publicity. Nor was the group hapless about legalities. It retained an attorney, Orville T. Ranger of Brunswick, an outspoken, irresistibly quotable, and conservative political activist in that town.

Much of the Renewal Review Association's displeasure had a gut-level democratic appeal. As Shepard put it, "I started in because I don't like being pushed around." Furthermore, it appealed to Bath's blue-collar population, many of whom saw urban renewal as an elitist conceit designed by outsiders and tailored to the tastes and needs of big government, professional consultants, and local bigshots. There were many lions' tails to be twisted.

Finally, there was the matter of the town's high expectations versus its structured tax base, and the argument that the downtown was not paying its share of the tax burden. Looking back, Shepard gave his and the RRA's rebuttal: "Whose fault is that? . . . That's the City of Bath's problem, and the people who own the buildings. We don't have to tear down the whole downtown because three or four [big] landlords aren't paying enough taxes."[32]

The RRA meant business. It intended to run candidates for City Council who would kill urban renewal.

GO ON RECORD AS OPPOSED TO PRESENT URA PROPOSALS

Nearly 30 Bath merchants and interested persons attended a meeting of the Urban Renewal Review Association held at Nick's Coffee Shop on Front street Wednesday night, and publicly went on record as being opposed to the current urban renewal project proposed for Bath's downtown business section.

At the conclusion of the meeting, the group released the results of a survey conducted among 175 citizens who work or own property in the affected area. . . .

Results of the survey, released by Charles A. Shepard, Jr., who presided at the meeting, indicated that 85 per cent of the persons polled feel they do not understand urban renewal thoroughly. . . .

95 per cent understood that URA's project was to remove only dilapidated buildings;

90 per cent understood that URA's project was to be a survey and not a reality;

90 per cent understood that the people would have another vote in the affair;

95 per cent are not in favor of urban renewal as it is now explained.

Shepard told the group that URA's project would result in "getting rid of all the little

> fellows." It would call for the removal of 77 of the 102 stores in the clearance area, he said, with no provisions for renovations.
>
> *BATH DAILY TIMES*, 18 APRIL 1963

Charlie Burden's first conspicuous civic activity was his work in support of urban renewal. Ever since his wartime days of antiparatroop patrols and paper drives, Burden seemed earmarked for local prominence. A model student and leader at Morse High, he had graduated from Yale and the Harvard Medical School, married a Bath beauty queen, and purchased a stately, historic house on North Street that had been the residence of the late Frank Nichols, for whom he had worked summers as a youngster. Burden hung out his physician's shingle about the same time as Bath's urban renewal controversy was heating up.

An inspired, workaholic pediatrician, Burden possessed a gentle, teddy-bearish charm; a classy, resonant voice; and a boyish enthusiasm for both his profession and his chosen avocations. These qualities made him an effective leader of the embattled Citizens Advisory Committee in its attempts to restore support for urban renewal. Burden's personal advocacy was not based upon his familiarity with cities undergoing major urban renewal: "I was not prejudiced for or against urban renewal because of Boston or New Haven. I do remember large areas of New Haven being torn down near the New Haven Hospital, but I never really associated it with the Bath urban renewal cause." Nor had he a vested interest in upgrading downtown properties. "No, I was just concerned with the business district

TIMES RECORD

Charlie Burden, a staunch advocate of urban renewal.

in Bath, Maine, being unattractive; not the sort of town I would be proud to live in or the sort of town that I would like to have people come and visit."[33]

The widening debate about Bath's plan, and the rise of the Renewal Review Association, played itself out in media battles and public debates, in which Burden often occupied the rhetorical spotlight and hotseat. His quotable defenses of the program made him a more effective pundit than John Newell or Arthur Hutchins, who would have been verbally outgunned by the likes of Orville Ranger and Bud Shepard. Witness Burden's performance at a public meeting attended by friends and foes at City Hall in February 1963. As reported in the *Times*, "Chairman Newell admitted the authority had spent a great deal of time pondering the problem of the older buildings in the [downtown] section, but finally came to the conclusion that they had to go in the interests of widening the street and in establishing salable resale parcels.

" . . . Newell said the major problem facing the city is preserving and improving its downtown section. He predicted that Bath will 'suffer a very sharp loss of trade in the next 10 years' if improvements aren't made."[34]

Burden, however, was willing to tackle some of the deeper issues that were polarizing the community. Assuring the assembled parties that the program represented "very little risk in terms of both money and human values," he added that "Bath's dumpy business district" had repelled new industry. As for the conservative fear of involving big government in a small city's future, Burden, himself a conservative, "discounted what he called the 'bogey man' of federal intervention which has raised opposition to the renewal plans." Bath citizens, he said, "will be paying for urban renewal projects from Bangor to Little Rock, Arkansas," and he suggested that Bath get its share.

"He added that he had no fear of federal money," Cummings reported, "noting that it's such money that keeps the town's principal industry prosperous.

"Dr. Burden expressed some surprise at the many rules designed to protect the individual from being hurt . . . , declaring the government 'is really watching out for the little guy.'

"In answer to charges that the city will be putting power in the hands of the authority, Dr. Burden called the trustees 'five decent people,' chosen by City Council to carry out a project approved by the citizens. . . . "[35]

Those were effective words, but the war of words kept intensifying in 1963. Both sides recognized the average citizen's apparent failure to understand either the spirit or the letter of urban renewal and, over subsequent months, both sides (especially Burden and Shepard) grew adept at milking publicity for all it was worth.[36] But the opposition leaders, with very specific, material things at stake, were the more highly motivated. The RRA, in fact, was making political hay out of the controversy.

Two hundred people crowded into City Hall auditorium one night in May to hear the RRA counterattack. Shepard rose to the occasion by reportedly stating that "urban renewal will strike forever the small businessman from his rightful place on Maine [sic] Street, USA, and more particularly, Front street, Bath, Maine." Shepard granted that the downtown had its weak and seedy spots, but he warned against playing into the hands of professional planners. "I believe in the necessity of having a modern, progressive business structure . . . , but I also believe in the individual's freedom to achieve that echelon of commercial perfection in his own way, with his own initiative and at his own pace." Redevelopment? "A plan that sacrifices a poor businessman for a rich one is contrary to our American way of life."[37]

The rebuttal to that argument was that Bath merchants, left to pursue commercial perfection in their own way, had largely treaded water. Since the days of World War II, when, as John Dos Passos noted, they could sell almost anything without trying, downtown merchants had not kept pace with changing consumer tastes and still seemed oblivious to the nationwide trend toward out-of-town shopping centers. Realizing that urban renewal was at least a program for change, Shepard offered an RRA alternative whereby citizens would unite, repeal the plan that exchanged little birds in hand for a big one in the bush, demolish only dilapidated buildings, and, somehow, collect enough funds to revitalize the downtown without Uncle Sam's involvement. This was more a manifesto than a plan; but, getting more specific, the RRA formally proposed that the Urban Renewal Authority reduce its project area to "one or two blocks" so as to sample accurately how much developer interest actually existed in the contested space. The RRA also called for a promise to demolish only unsound buildings, keep the public precisely informed, and submit any plan to citywide referendum. These proposals were at odds with federal procedures. Newell politely rejected them.[38]

As the 1963 city elections drew near, the RRA promoted a slate of Council candidates for the five available seats. They were a mixed bag: Arthur Gediman, with years of municipal service; Charles MacDonald, a well-informed conservative opposed to federal programs in general and Bath's in particular and an enemy of further municipal debt; C. Lloyd Hooker, a mail carrier, local political buff, and long-time member of the Board of Education; Red McMann, who had reservations about Bath's plan but was undecided about it; and Edward Berkery, a newcomer to the city who was similarly uncommitted. All of these candidates could be characterized as "little guys"; they did not represent BIW's senior management, the upper Washington Street carriage trade, or the city's growing medical and legal cadre (most of which, incidentally, favored urban renewal). But Gediman, MacDonald, Hooker, and McMann were seasoned at the political game and knew where and how to get votes. They were opposed by Donald Perry and Edward Atkinson of BIW; Oscar Marsh of Hyde; and Hayward Newcomb, proprietor of a commercial cleaning service, all of whom supported urban renewal.

September 1963 witnessed a storm of debate and advertisements in the *Times* and over local radio station WJTO (whose owner, Winslow Porter, was a staunch urban renewal advocate). The outcome of this electioneering was uncertain until, just before the election, a letter appeared in the *Times*, firmly exhorting voters to elect urban renewal's proponents and reject the obstructionism of its detractors. The signatories were John Newell, now speaking as president of the Iron Works, and Omar King, BIW's works manager. Here was the heavy artillery, rolled out to save urban renewal. The upcoming election, wrote Newell and King, was one of the most critical in Bath's history: "The area is losing more and more business to adjacent communities. . . . Several important present stores are awaiting a chance to rebuild if urban renewal is approved. If it dies, these stores probably will leave Bath, thus greatly diminishing local trade and tax revenues.

"On several occasions in recent times the Bath Iron Works and Hyde Windlass Company have been unable to attract badly needed technical and managerial personnel . . . because of the poor impression Bath—especially the downtown area—makes on a newcomer looking over the town for the first time. It is important to the future of these companies that they be able to employ the best talent available if they are to survive in a highly competitive business climate. The calibre of a company's personnel determines its success and its future more than anything else. Bath must retain the industry it has and also try to attract new ones in the years ahead.

"Federally subsidized Urban Renewal programs have been proven to be the only practical way to revitalize blighted, decayed, rundown areas. . . . The communities alone can not do it. They have neither the authority nor the funds to carry out such projects. . . .

"The Bath Iron Works and Hyde Windlass Company pay over 30% of the local taxes directly. The employees of these companies also pay local taxes . . . so that the great majority of all local taxes can be traced to the payrolls of these two industries. As substantial taxpayers, we realize that there is a price tag for Urban Renewal. It is an investment, however, that the community can not afford to turn down. . . . A progressive economy will not move to or remain in a backward community.

"The forward looking candidates who believe in Urban Renewal should be elected to the City Council next Monday."[39]

Was Newell saying that BIW might move if urban renewal didn't stick? Whatever the case, the letter was a tactical blunder that opened a window of opportunity for the RRA. Shepard dove through it: " . . . this association finally has come to realize how insignificant we are to the welfare and continuance of the City of Bath. We now are able to see, what must have been obvious to everyone else, that this city is supported by, and responsible to, the Bath Iron Works.

"We believe that the merchants of Bath owe an apology to one of our larger industries for holding back its progress all these past years. If we had only known how our lack of progressiveness and withering appearance has affected said industry we surely would have tried much harder to be successful.

"Well, folks, the cat is out of the bag. Through use of this newpaper the B.I.W. top officials publicly stated their opposition to our association. The multimillion dollar industry, along with its high level executive officers, is pitted against a group of apparently ill-informed merchants and approximately 2,000 common citizens.

" . . . A progressive business district needs the help and support of all its citizens, but it does not require the interference of the Federal Government or anyone else. We cordially welcome their suggestions but strongly oppose their demands."[40]

On 21 September 1963, 3,095 voters—more even than turned out for the 1946 Tardif-Rogers contest—went to the polls. By a two-to-one margin, they elected the RRA slate in a clean sweep. All Bath was surprised by the size of this apparent reversal of public opinion on urban renewal. It was now likely that City Council would stop the plan in its tracks.

Three weeks after the election, Charlie Burden attended a seminar in Augusta at which Charles Horan, HHFA's regional urban renewal director, warned that projects everywhere were under mounting danger from opposition groups gunning for the federal government while program proponents "stuck quietly to our knitting and tried to get the best possible job done."[41] Horan had undoubtedly heard of Bath's flipflop. In the Shipbuilding City, the urban renewal war was not over, but defeat of the program looked imminent. Bath's Planning Board chairman, George Carey II, resigned in the light of the recent election, telling colleagues that the "spirit of progress in Bath has gone into eclipse."[42] A few months later, after a "very interesting" tour of duty, Rodney Ross, Jr., left the Urban Renewal Authority. Could matters get worse for supporters of the plan? Yes. Late in 1963, the HHFA told the URA that it would have to do more planning homework because the city had not projected enough parking spaces to meet the formulized quota for such a district. The HHFA pointed out other omissions and oversights of Bath's plan, making it clear, as John Newell later admitted, that the URA had itself to blame for many of the delays that were now wearing down even Uncle Sam's patience.[43] Federal authorities now wondered whether or not Bath was serious about urban renewal. The city exchanged consultants another time.

The one bright spot in the darkening picture was the possibility that since fewer new buildings could be mandated, more old ones might be saved, thus mitigating the "Hiroshima effect" that was uglifying so many American cities and making local businessmen see red. Meanwhile, however, signs of accelerating "blight" were increasing. The venerable Bath Department Store, an important magnet for shoppers, closed its doors, and several smaller firms either shut down or moved away. The city's rising tax rate went a notch higher to cover the losses.

DEPARTURE MARKS THE END OF AN ERA

BY ROBERT C. CUMMINGS

The last vestiges of the era of Bath as the "Shipping City" ended this morning as the coal collier *Berwindvale* headed down the Kennebec river for what is expected to be the last time. The *Berwindvale* pulled out of its berth at the Kennebec Wharf and Coal Company under tow by two tugs shortly after 9 o'clock, heading for Norfolk, Virginia. . . .

The *Berwindvale* has plied the coastal route between Bath and the southern coal ports for the last 15 years, carrying some 10,000 tons of coal each trip.

. . . The final shipment of coal to the Kennebec Wharf and Coal Company was last winter and since that time the thousands of tons of coal normally stored in Bath have been cleaned up until now it is all gone.

Local company officials and those from the parent firm—the Atlantic Coal Company of Boston—have declined comment on the future status of the business.

But the sale of the *Berwindvale* along with

MAINE MARITIME MUSEUM

the depletion of the local stocks of coal appears to indicate the local firm is about to close up shop. . . .

The Kennebec Wharf and Coal Company was the last regular user of the port facilities in Bath for regular coastal shipping activities. . . . The demise of the local coal trade followed the recent conversion to oil of two of the firm's largest customers, the Pejepscot Paper Company of Topsham and the Oxford Paper Company of Rumford.

BATH DAILY TIMES, 1 NOVEMBER 1963

KENNEBEC WHARF & COAL CO. PROPERTY SOLD TO ME. FIRM

Maine Minerals, Inc. Will Use The Facilities To Store And Handle Salt For Use On The Highways

. . . David F. Mahoney of North Hampton, N.H., confirmed today that he has purchased the property from Blair's Realty Corporation of Boston and Portland—the company that took over the land and buildings following the demise of the long time Bath coal concern.

Mahoney, president and treasurer of Maine minerals, Incorporated, said the property will be used as a terminal and storage area for bulk road salt. . . .

BATH DAILY TIMES, 25 AUGUST 1964

BATH RETURNING TO NORMALCY AFTER RECENT TRAGIC EVENTS

Monday Is Observed As A Day Of Mourning With Interfaith Memorial Service In The Evening

BY PAUL FOURNIER

The Shipbuilding City began taking up the everyday problems of business and living today, still numbed by the shocking series of events precipitated by the assassin's bullet that felled President Kennedy at Dallas, Texas, Friday afternoon.

Schools, stores and municipal offices reopened this morning, after most had been closed all day Monday [25 November] in accordance with President Lyndon Johnson's proclamation of a national day of mourning. . . .

City Manager Harry E. Ring said at noon that City Hall was quiet this forenoon, with all municipal offices open and operating at normal. . . . But while the city was again bustling, there were still reminders of the weekend's tragedy.

Flags in the Shipbuilding City were flying at half-mast, and would continue for the official 30-day mourning period for President Kennedy.

The A. G. Page Company on Front street displayed a memorial to the President in its north window. A picture of John F. Kennedy was flanked by American flags, and on the left of the picture was a flower arrangement of red, white and blue carnations. In the background was a candelabra with six white candles. . . .

Bath paid its tribute to President Kennedy Monday night as a capacity crowd filled the Bath Armory for an interfaith memorial service.

Led by a Buccaneers Drum and Bugle Corps color guard with drums muffled, a long line of marchers joined in a solemn procession from Bath Junior High School to the Armory. . . .

BATH DAILY TIMES, 26 NOVEMBER 1963

During early 1964, urban renewal staged a startling comeback in Bath, despite the fact that City Council was now populated by opponents of the program. The tide may have turned when Arthur Hutchins somehow persuaded Council to request an extension of planning from the HHFA and thus keep the pipeline open. Some display of interest was necessary, Hutchins said, or the government would take its cue from the recent election. Council complied. The Chamber of Commerce likewise came forward, formally endorsing Bath's plan. Meanwhile, still another organization, the Citizens For Progress Committee, had been formed by proponents determined to fight the RRA on its own terms.

Members of the RRA had decided to go for a kill by petitioning City Council to abolish the Urban Renewal Authority by ordinance. On April Fools' Day 1964, another crowd filled City Hall to hear Harold Rubin, city solicitor, rule against such a move. (It was not legal, Rubin said, because the URA had not been created by ordinance.) The meeting featured considerable public debate. Burden presented the advocates' usual argument that most people simply did not understand urban renewal, otherwise they surely would be for it, to which an opponent replied that more than 2,000 people had understood the issue well enough to elect its enemies to public office. Wasn't that clear? To dramatize the full measure of opposition, Orville Ranger called for a poll of the assembled crowd. But the Citizens For Progress had apparently seen that coming. To the Council's amazement, supporters vastly outnumbered the attending opponents in the room. Urban renewal had weathered another challenge.

The most important reason for the plan's endurance, though, was that the newly constituted Council proved willing to let the matter ride as long as it did not cost the city anything. Furthermore, Councillors McMann and Berkery had warmed to the whole concept since coming to office. Objections by the RRA to Berkery's growing sympathy to urban renewal outraged the councillor, who insisted his conscience did not belong to the RRA. He had, he said, made no deals before his election.[44] Furious over RRA pressure, Berkery became a sworn enemy of that group.

In May, when the time had come to formally request another HHFA planning grant, John Newell won an important moral victory: He told the councillors not to string matters along by asking for more money, but to forgo the grant request if they intended later to disapprove the plan. In other words, a vote for more federal money should constitute Council's implied determination to stick with the program. The resolution passed. Only Gediman, MacDonald, and Hooker voted no.

Thus, as of mid-1964, to the outrage of the Renewal Review Association, City Council was still tacitly behind urban renewal, owing to McMann's and Berkery's unexpected support. Later that year, when the four other City Council seats became vacant, the RRA and urban renewal's heartened proponents squared off for another showdown. The resultant municipal campaign, intensively publicized, was the bitterest in Bath history. Some of its rhetorical extremes, undoubtedly, were exacerbated by the national trauma over the assassination of President Kennedy a few months earlier. Others echoed the polarized presidential campaigns of Lyndon Johnson and Barry Goldwater, which were now in full swing.

This time, the RRA took no chances, backing unequivocal foes of urban renewal. Hobby-shop proprietor Bradford Belanger, for example, came down hard on big government, which he believed wanted to "reach down into municipal governments and control them from Washington."[45] Another candidate, Ernest Brown, a BIW worker, attacked urban renewal as insensitive elitism: "There are college professors and all kinds of experts with lots of diplomas and degrees who have come to Bath to build beautiful air castles for us.

"These experts who work in absolute security, who never have to get their hands dirty, and who never had to meet a payroll seem to know more about business than the businessmen themselves.

"What I am afraid is going to happen if they succeed in shoving urban renewal down our throats is that most of our businessmen are going to move to the outskirts and set up a shopping center. If they do, you won't be able to give away what is now productive business property in downtown Bath."[46]

But business was already fleeing from Bath, with terrible consequences for the tax base, and in turn, for taxpayers who would have to take up the slack. Charlie Burden brought this point home when he told a meeting of the Citizens Advisory Committee that fifty-nine downtown businesses had called it quits in eight years, and another twenty were expected to vacate over the next five or six.[47] In view of that, what did Bath have to lose? Wasn't urban renewal at least a game plan to hold business and beat the tax trap? Was there, after all, a practical alternative? Never in memory had there been so perplexing and divisive an issue in Bath.

Meanwhile, the nationwide progress of urban renewal had passed its painful adolescence. By 1964, about 85 percent of the land cleared for redevelopment was either under construction or had been optioned for same.[48] In addition, Washington had added provisions entitling displaced individuals and businesses to increased monetary benefits to cover such "intangible" factors as inconvenience, relocation expenses, and earnings lost during movement to a new site. Changing times were thus improving the program's attractiveness in Bath by August, when the city's workable program, dutifully revised and zoned to federal specifications, was formally approved by the Planning Board and City Council and handed in to the HHFA. The program's basic concept was unchanged. But, as revised, it would condemn fewer buildings. Excluding sheds and ancillary structures, the plan now earmarked about fifty-four discrete buildings. The recent, distressing decline of downtown business also eased the plan's future impact, inasmuch as there were now fewer to displace: about two dozen going firms. The Center Street mall idea was included to improve circular, one-way traffic flow around the downtown core. The financial news, however, was bad. The HHFA declined to credit Bath for its recent in-kind investments. Furthermore, clearing less property meant less money recouped in future property sales. According to the 1964 estimate, Bath would have to cover its share of urban renewal costs by a bond issue of $625,000, the consequences of which would be a dangerously high debt level (although opinions differed on this point), a higher mill rate or valuation, or both. Each side was now righteously convinced that its objective, philosophically and practically speaking, was the only appropriate one for Bath.

Growing up in the Shipbuilding City, where his father was a BIW worker, Bill Haggett had been uncertain about his future: "I guess I never thought a great deal about what I was going to do the rest of my life . . . and that was never troublesome to me. I always knew something would happen. I went through high school taking a college preparatory program because it was a broad program . . . , went to a liberal arts school [with assistance from the Davenport Fund] because I really didn't know what I wanted to do. I graduated from Colby and then started thinking about a career. . . . Working at Bath Iron Works was the last thing in my mind. . . . I never expected to work there and I never expected to hold a senior management position in the company. I thought if I could ever reach the point in life where I had a job that paid me $10,000 a year, I would be the happiest person that ever lived and lead a very comfortable life. Those were awfully high sights to shoot for, but I wasn't certain I would ever get there." Haggett, who had taken ROTC at Colby, spent three years in the Air Force after graduation. Then, in 1960, he and his wife, Sally, also a Bath native, returned to their hometown, where Bill got a middle-management job at BIW. "The city really needed a shot in the arm in a lot of different areas in the late 1950s. I can remember coming back and getting actively involved in Winter Street Church, . . . and the observation that was made by the older people in the church was that Sally and I were about the only young people—by that I mean people in their mid-twenties—who were actively involved in the church. Young people were growing up in Bath, moving away from Bath . . . , and there was not much of an infusion of new blood into the community. It had been stable for a long period of time and it needed a shake-up, in my view."[49]

Haggett was attracted by the city's urban renewal proposal. In 1964, he and a few kindred spirits decided to take action. "Brud Stover was one of them; he had moved back to Bath at the time. George Sarkis [an incumbent councillor] was another one who had been actively involved in this community for a long period of time. Eddie Cummings was the fourth. . . . The four of us, not collectively but one at a time, made a decision to run for City Council. . . . I think we shared a common interest in giving the city an uplift. . . . We ran for office at a point when there was a huge debate going on on the issue of urban renewal."[50] Haggett, Stover, Sarkis, and Cummings made public their intentions to keep an open mind on the plan's merits until further discussion was possible.

Haggett and Stover, old school pals, were well known around town and enjoyed fair-haired-boy status, but they had an uphill fight in the bitter campaign of 1964. "We talked to groups," recalled Haggett, "talked to people, went door to door, and did the kinds of things which, prior to the sixties, just didn't have a place in Bath politics (and they haven't been done very much since that time). We actually sought the job. We didn't spend a lot of money—and didn't have any money, really—but went out and actively campaigned for the jobs: telephoned people, organized on a ward-by-ward basis a get-out-the-voter kind of thing, tried to identify where our support was and get our support to the polls. In my particular case, I predicted within twenty-five of the votes that I would get."[51]

The campaign, a possible showdown for urban renewal, was meticulously covered by the *Times*. When the RRA candidates declined to meet Haggett, Stover, Sarkis, and Cummings in public debate, it eased the way for their challengers.[52] According to Stover, "We were going nowhere, but the other guys ran an atrocious campaign. They refused to come out and speak at a public meeting. . . . They felt they had the right side of the issue, and maybe they didn't feel comfortable speaking publicly. But they didn't campaign. They defeated themselves."[53]

The RRA, which had enjoyed a clean sweep in 1963, saw not one of its candidates elected. Haggett, Stover, Sarkis, and Cummings swept the field in another record-breaking election in which almost 4,000 voters turned out. Although the victorious councillors had been formally noncommittal, it was apparent by the end of 1964 that City Council possessed a five-to-four majority of urban renewal sympathizers. In January 1965, the HHFA gave its informal approval of Bath's plan. Inside of a year, the tide had turned again.

During early 1965, the Renewal Review Association and its friends in City Council continued to search for a legal means to terminate the Urban Renewal Authority, taking the fight as far as the State Legislature. Such efforts failed to achieve anything other than provoking the URA's defenders. The fate of the program would be decided when the voters said yes or no to the bond issue by which it would be financed locally. No bond issue, no urban renewal; it was as simple as that. The propaganda mills for both sides went into high gear.[54] Accusations and bitterness grew by the week.

After the completion of Bath's revised plan, John Newell had left the chairmanship of the Urban Renewal Authority. He was replaced by William Skelton, formerly of Bath Trust, now a vice president of the First National Bank of Portland and an active civic leader.

Now that the details and financial obligations had reached final form, Bath citizens could concentrate upon the plan's inherent merit. It is surprising that critics made little of the fact that, having sidelined waterfront rehabilitation, the Urban Renewal Authority had undermined the Blackwell Report's original premise. The plan now stood or fell on its ability to inject life into the everyday commerce of the city.

The plight of the downtown had worsened considerably. Business after business vanished. Most of these establishments were, however, not the "magnet" or "anchor" stores that were crucial to downtown commerce. The city might survive the loss of coffee shops and notions stores, but who would shop in Bath if Sears, Newberry's, Senter's, or W. T. Grant's departed? One key virtue of urban renewal was that reparceled land would allow large stores to expand if necessary. But since urban renewal was a clearing operation, not a building program, its success in Bath depended upon the certainty that large stores would indeed replace small ones.

It is important to note that none of the buildings occupied by the city's biggest stores were slated for demolition under urban renewal, but every one of Bath's magnet stores was cramped in its current site. Aside from downtown Bath, local department stores had one other possible option for expansion: a proposed shopping center to be erected at Cooks Corner, between Brunswick and Bath. The impact of such construction upon Bath's downtown commerce was, oddly, a minuscule part of the debate over urban renewal.

Of all the downtown stores, the Bath branch of Sears, Roebuck and Co. was correctly viewed as exponential to any revival plan. Sears's current building stood on the northwest corner of Center and Washington streets. "It was a good store," recalled Harry Ring, city manager during the urban renewal struggle. "The money was coming into Bath then, with the Iron Works employees and others. . . . People came over the bridge, of course, and even from Brunswick. It was a very good store, but a bad location. . . . very little parking in back, and that's all they had. To do anything that would have been appropriate, they would have had to move out and build on their own."[55]

Urban renewal offered Sears the option of staying downtown, as long as the company could find a more desirable site.[56] Recollections of Bath kingpins vary widely on the details, but all agree that Sears had made it clear to city fathers that it urgently needed larger, more accessible quarters.[57]

As far back as 1963, while flexing BIW's muscles, John Newell had stated publicly that "several important present stores are awaiting a chance to rebuild if urban renewal is approved. If it dies, these stores will probably leave Bath."[58] The oblique reference to "important present stores" was probably a diplomatic necessity at the time, but it is likely that the group included Sears, Grant's, and Newberry's. The local managers of those stores personally favored urban renewal, but did that bespeak the sentiments of their home offices? It was unfortunate that the specific intentions of such key stores were not made clearer to Bath voters.

Regarding Sears and the other magnet stores, therefore, there was enough vagueness to allow the public to draw its own conclusions. For example, as Bill Haggett put it, "The people in Bath were saying, 'Okay. We still don't want to tear down some of the old buildings, and Sears is going to stay anyway. It doesn't make any difference whether we go ahead with urban renewal; we're not going to lose Sears.' Sears was committing to go with a new building . . . , but those [large] businesses were not threatening to leave. Don't misunderstand what I'm saying. I don't have any recollection of Sears, Grant's, Newberry's, or Senter's, or anyone else saying, 'If this [plan] doesn't happen we're going to leave.' There was a very clear impression in my mind that that would happen, also a clear recollection that they were committing to stay, in new facilities, if the plan went ahead. . . . "[59]

On the other hand, some believed that keeping stores such as Sears downtown was hopeless in any event and therefore irrelevant to the urban renewal argument. One was Bud Shepard: "You learn these things from reading business magazines; that's where I found most of this stuff. . . . What was happening [nationwide] with the major chains was the fact that they were expanding into a new type of retailing. Now, a simple thing like when Sears went into automotive. Bath would never have been able to accommodate a Sears store with an automotive department. Where would we put a store with a five-bay garage? That's what they were building. They weren't building little stores. And that class of store that Sears had here, that Woolworth's had here, was just totally wiped out." That was why, Shepard believed, urban renewal was a lost cause for saving the largest downtown stores. Looking back, twenty years later, Shepard was convinced he had been correct about this: "Is there any Sears, Roebuck in downtown Brunswick? Downtown Lewiston? Downtown Portland? Is there any major department store in any small community that you know about? No. There hasn't been for a long, long time, and there won't be again. . . . I've had people come up to me as lately as the last sixty days and say, 'Boy, . . . we could have had Sears, Roebuck here.' Who the hell are they fooling?" During the height of the controversy, Shepard had contacted the Sears home offices in Chicago about the company's long-term strategy, from which he concluded that there was no chance Bath's store would stay in the crowded downtown. He did his research "for my own edification, you might say. I never told anybody. Well, I told some people, but I would not say it publicly. I wouldn't come right out and say it because that wasn't the way they told me. You know, shopping centers were new at the time; the idea of having all that inexpensive, flat land that every major chain in the United States was going for. They're not going to come to a place where the land costs a whole lot of money when they can buy acres and acres . . . out there at Cooks Corner."[60]

By early 1965, the critical factor of keeping magnet stores in the downtown was cloudy at best in the public mind, another case of how the Urban Renewal Authority could not maintain close touch with the people. At a public meeting in April, parties who had expressed interest in redeveloped land were listed. All were local retailers or landlords.[61]

In May, City Council met to decide whether or not to approve the

TIMES RECORD

The embattled City Council: Charlie MacDonald makes a point while Red McMann and Bill Haggett listen.

$625,000 bond ordinance and submit it to voter referendum. In the discussions about the approved plan, Council split four-to-four over several last-minute amendment proposals and on the matter of the bond endorsement itself. Each time, Council Chairman Bill Haggett cast the tie-breaking vote. The four opponents (Gediman, MacDonald, Hooker, and McMann) tried unsuccessfully to amend the plan to save two downtown structures and scuttle altogether the concept for a Center Street mall. Were the opponents now so defensive that they would settle for such compromises? Were they possibly afraid of a referendum? Their tactics were denounced by Berkery, who reportedly charged "that the urban renewal opponents have sought to delay the final . . . decision for the past 18 months and declared that in his opinion the series of amendments at the final session were similar to delaying tactics."[62] The four pro-renewal councillors (Stover, Sarkis, Cummings, and Berkery) were then able to get the plan officially endorsed for a bond ordinance after Haggett broke the deadlock with his favorable vote.

On that evening of the final City Council decision, each councillor had the opportunity to speak for the record. Haggett's remarks were perhaps the most statesmanlike. As reported by Bob Cummings, "Chairman Haggett admitted what he called 'justifiable concern over the slow development of Urban Renewal in Bath and the unfortunate mistakes which were made in early planning.'

"He declared, however, 'If we as Councilmen allow our thinking to be biased by errors made three years ago, we will be doing a great injustice to the majority of Bath's citizens and our city will pay the penalty in the years to come.

" 'The present plan preserves the best features of downtown Bath, allows us to retain the basic characteristic of a small New England city and yet eliminate conditions that have stifled growth for many years.

" 'A large percentage of the structures programmed to be removed are already empty, with owners unable to rent space that has been available for months.'

" . . . He noted a proposed shopping center at Cooks Corner, which will further reduce Bath's downtown business section if something is not done. . . . "[63]

In a rare show of unanimity on 17 May, City Council members set 7 June as the date of the bond ordinance referendum.

Meanwhile, the media war was reaching a very noisy climax. Wildly exaggerated figures on costs and demolition were being bandied about in an RRA flyer, prompting an angry rebuttal by the *Times*. Awash in published letters pro and con, the newspaper formally declared itself behind urban renewal (although its position had always been quite clear). Citizens were barraged with appeals to patriotism, grim reminders of the Knox & Lincoln fiasco, contradictory financial estimates, ominous images of a future ghost town, alarums about threats to private enterprise, and case histories of how urban renewal had proven a blessing or a curse in other communities.

Despite forceful statements from both sides, there remained in Bath a soft core of uncertainty about the whole scheme. Could the city attend to other capital needs if urban renewal was added to its bonded debt? Who would pay for it all, with businesses folding and more scheduled for relocation? How would land be redeveloped? By whom? Was there any choice but to take federal aid? Worst of all was the question of how a city so bitterly divided would be able to cope constructively with either of its options.

Suddenly, it was all over but the referendum. Sixty percent of Bath's eligible voters turned out: 3,273 Bath citizens rejected urban renewal by almost two to one.

The lopsided upset defied precise explanation. It was especially surprising in view of the growing defensiveness of the RRA and its erstwhile attempts to set aside the plan before it could reach the voters. The whys and wherefores would never be settled satisfactorily; but, in the puzzled aftermath, the *Times* dutifully rose to the occasion. One critical factor, it said, had been an eleventh-hour burst of "grass roots politicking" by the RRA: "Over the final weekend the Renewal Review flooded the city with last-minute literature attacking the proposals and conducted an intensive telephone and personal contact campaign. On election day the Association covered the city with workers bringing voters to the polls.

"Though supporters organized a last minute crew of poll workers and drivers, it failed even to cover all seven wards.

"Opponents laid the ground work for the defeat with a massive campaign aimed at convincing voters that urban renewal threatened their homes and would result in higher taxes and obnoxious governmental controls."[64]

Another tactical reason for the defeat was the recent distraction of Charlie Burden, whose tireless advocacy had been decisive during 1964. Lately, Burden had involved himself in spearheading development of the new Bath Marine Museum, causing him to wind down his efforts for urban renewal.[65] No one had filled the gap.

Another reason, certainly, for the program's rejection was the Urban Renewal Authority's unapproachability, inability to provide details on demand, and agonizing delays in getting its plan validated by the federal government. A further tactical blunder had been the repeated assertions by the plan's white-collar proponents that if people truly understood the concept they would be for it. That position may have been valid, but it sounded condescending. It also exacerbated popular suspicions that managers, doctors, lawyers, and assorted bigshots—few of whom had businesses in the downtown—were giving the little guy a raw deal. Along that line: URA Chairman Newell's public disparagement of the "decayed" downtown as aesthetically distasteful to BIW hirees, and his farfetched implication that the company's loyalties to Bath had limits was a major psychological miscalculation. In Bud Shepard's view, such actions had exposed urban renewal advocates' chronic self-deception: "They could taste it. . . . They thought they could do anything they pleased at that time and it would work. I don't believe that particular group ever had a feel for this community."[66]

Possibly. But the entire program labored also under inescapable, historic drawbacks. Urban renewal had been conceived as a slum-clearance program whose objective was the stimulation of better housing. Renewal of commercial zones, a rider to that objective, had opened the way for communities such as Bath, with problems altogether different from slum-ridden inner cities, to declare themselves "blighted" and pursue funds for commercial rehabilitation. Small wonder the Urban Renewal Authority was hard-put to present applicable housing and zoning codes, parking density programs, and the like. In Bath's case, federal urban renewal was a very large square peg for a very small round hole. Furthermore, the city plan had shrunk from its original, waterfront-based rationale, and its scheme for downtown revitalization was illogical to the small retailers it would have uprooted.

By the time Bath's plan came to referendum, there were almost 1,600 urban renewal projects underway across the nation,[67] which provided local businessmen with disturbing examples of the loss rate among small businesses. Despite growing government assistance, many displaced cigar stores, lunch counters, meat markets, bakeries, filling stations, and barbershops were not reopening after displacement.[68] Stopping urban renewal was seen as simple self-preservation in many cases. Finally, there remained the oversimplified but potent argument that federal and local bureaucrats should not have the impersonal power to evict a taxpaying, productive individual for any reason.

BATH URBAN RENEWAL REPORTS BEING BURNED; FURNITURE SOLD

The downtown Bath Urban Renewal Project, killed by vote of Bath citizens two months ago, is in the process of being burned, buried and sold this week.

. . . Most of the records compiled by the URA trustees . . . have been hauled to the municipal dump or burned; bids for the sale of office machines and furniture will be opened today and the URA headquarters in the former railroad terminal on Commercial Street will be officially closed on Friday. . . .

Burned yesterday afternoon were remaining copies of the two key urban renewal documents—the appraisals of downtown property, developed at a cost of $30,000 and the nearly $5,000 marketability and reuse study conducted by William H. Ballard company of Boston. . . .

The burning took place in the security incinerator at the Bath Iron Works and came at the suggestion of the Housing and Home Finance Agency (HHFA) in New York and by vote of the URA trustees. . . .

Bath Daily Times, 18 August 1965

BATH WAS 1 OF 4 TO REJECT URBAN RENEWAL

Although Bath voters turned down a bond issue last June . . . elsewhere in Maine urban renewal is burgeoning, according to the annual report on urban renewal activity in Maine, released this month.

> The report . . . , reveals that one Maine urban renewal project has been completed, five projects are in the process . . . , 17 others are in various stages.
>
> . . . Only four cities and towns have rejected urban renewal.
>
> . . . The other communities, Rumford, Calais, and Pittsfield, have turned down creation of urban renewal authorities in referendums.
>
> All but three of the Maine projects underway or being planned are of the "downtown" commercial type as was rejected in Bath. . . .
>
> *BATH DAILY TIMES*, 28 JANUARY 1966

Even though it was not implemented, urban renewal was one of the most important episodes in the history of Bath, because it forced citizens to face facts and take sides about their city's future. It also effected the emergence of a new leadership group. It would take a very long time, however, for that new, crisis-oriented leadership to put the divisive issue to rest. As Harry Ring recalled, the wounds were especially severe to those who thought Bath had turned its back on close to $2 million in federal assistance and would now have to fund its own salvage operation: "It hurt. . . . There were a lot of feelings, in Council and out, for a long time. You could feel the undercurrent even in some of the Council meetings, I'd say for as long as a year after that. It was a shame because we had plenty to do."[69]

Immediately following the bond referendum, a few urban renewal zealots circulated petitions asking for another vote on the project, hoping somehow to keep it alive. Bath City Council and the URA both spurned the effort, and there was scant public support for it. The petition drive did, however, stir one of Bath's thoughtful and respected citizens to speak out. Published in the *Times*, Jim Temple's words were a forthright epitaph for the whole episode: "I am a patient man and slow to anger but the events of the past few days will not permit me in good conscience to remain silent.

"Prior to the recent election I refrained from expressing publicly any opinion on the pros and cons of Urban Renewal in Bath, as I felt each citizen should consider the information available . . . , and in the solemn sanctuary of the voting booth there to vote, without fear of pressure, in accordance with his conscience as God gives him to see the right.

"This is the traditional 'American Way' to settle such public issues. Now all should accept the vote as the will of the majority, and anyone in public office who can not or will not . . . should step aside and allow others who do, to take up the tasks that need to be done. . . .

"It should also be obvious to members of City Council that the secret ballot is a much more accurate reflection of voter opinion than such a petition. . . .

"Now is the time for all good men to join together in acceptance of the voters' decision and permanently remove the threat of confiscation by eminent domain of down town properties and to allow the natural progress of free enterprise, with public guidance and planning, to resume the sound growth that many other communities are enjoying without outside domination."[70]

Federal urban renewal performed astronomically expensive and radical surgery on scores of American cities with very mixed results. Accordingly, the program's effectiveness would be a source of heated regional and national controversy for at least a generation. Bath was no exception. More than twenty years after its rejection by city voters, Bill Haggett, now president of BIW, was as ardent an advocate as ever: "It was absolutely the right thing to do. Everything that has happened since then has just reinforced that. The City of Bath would be a different place today. This whole region would be very different today if urban renewal had passed."[71] Charlie Burden had changed his position only slightly: "I really think Bath could have profited by urban renewal, although I am now a preservationist. I love the old buildings downtown, but I think the town is still very weak."[72] John Morse, Jr., whose realty company owned much of the downtown and who hoped to redevelop under urban renewal, had changed his mind: "A lot of the demolition that was scheduled to be accomplished by urban renewal has happened in bits and pieces subsequently without any great flap because somebody has bought the property and torn down whatever was there. It's fine to chastise John Newell or myself and the others that did at the time support urban renewal, and I'm not excusing myself from making a wrong-headed decision. Now, I'm very glad it didn't happen."[73] Bob Cummings, whose reportorial coverage of the issue had made him a believer, changed his tune in the aftermath: "It was a totally blank check that they were gambling. People felt that . . . they could create a store like Sears. But in retrospect we were all dreaming. It would have destroyed the town. Eventually, it might have come back—Bangor is coming back twenty years later—but it simply would have wiped out downtown Bath. My guess is that nothing would have come in." The result in such a case? "We'd have solved the BIW parking problem!"[74]

As feared, fallout from the rejection descended quickly. By the end of August 1965, Sears, Grant's, and Newberry's all announced that they were leaving downtown Bath. Sears and Grant's also made it known that they were "seeking a shopping center environment"; Grant's had already opted for space at Cooks Corner.[75] Bath, it seemed, was finished as a regional shopping site, and that was twice bad news for city taxpayers. How the new leadership would reverse the downtown's deterioration and accomplish Bath's spiraling municipal programs was anybody's guess in the fall of 1965.

NEWBERRY'S BATH STORE CLOSES

There was a lot of activity behind the locked doors of the J. J. Newberry Store at the corner of Front and Center Streets today as employes cleared the counters and picked up the goods. The store, which had a week-long clearance sale, as window banners still proclaim, closed last week and is leaving Bath. . . .

BATH DAILY TIMES, 3 JANUARY 1966

SHOPPING CENTER OPENING MOBBED

"It's impossible to estimate how many people visited our store for our opening day—but we were filled to capacity almost all day. The response was wonderful and we're very pleased."

Thus Clayton Stalker, manager of the new W. T. Grant Store at the Cooks Corner Shopping Plaza, summed up his observation of the opening of the first major department store at what is slated to be the region's major center of shopping.

Also officially opened there yesterday afternoon at a ribbon cutting ceremony was the 22nd branch office of the Canal National Bank. . . . The next store to open in the shopping complex will be a Shaw's Supermarket opening next Wednesday. A Singer Sewing Center and a men's and women's clothing specialty shop . . . will open next month. . . .

With the opening of a new specialty shop compound and Sears Store next year, this will be the largest plaza in Maine.

BATH DAILY TIMES, 13 MAY 1966

Charlie Burden remained sensitive about urban renewal for years. ("Some people forgive easier than I do.") It was appropriate, therefore, that he fired what was probably the last shot for a lost cause: "It was long after urban renewal had died. Arthur Berry . . . was one of the active [opponents of urban renewal], probably more than Gediman and some of the others. Arthur Berry had an oil company [on the waterfront]. . . . Arthur Berry,

I, and Bill Haggett were bitter enemies, I'm sure. There was this big sail loft next to his property that was going to be torn down for parking . . . and Bill Haggett and I decided that we should take the [antique] sign off the sail loft for the museum. So we went down with a big ladder one day and . . . put it up to take the sign off. Arthur Berry came out and said that we were on his property and that we ought to get off. He said he knew who we were. He called me a *snake doctor*! . . . We obeyed his commands and pulled down the ladder and got the fire department to . . . get the sign. The museum has it today. (Bill was the one on the ladder. Bill was never afraid to go on heights.)

"Berry had in front of his store a sign against urban renewal—a great big one, probably six by ten feet or something like that—[stating] all sorts of terrible things about urban renewal, sitting in front of his place where he ran his oil company. Even a year and a half after urban renewal had gone kerplunk, it was still there. So, one night, Bill Haggett, Red Mulligan, and I were having a party at my house, and we decided that we couldn't tolerate that anymore. We got in my Scout, backed down the driveway, and drove down to Commercial Street, knocked it over with the truck first, and then took it down and threw it in the Kennebec River!"[76]

NOTES

1. Ridgewell interview.
2. R. Luke, quoted in BI, 14 August 1960.
3. [John Atwood, John T. Blackwell, and Leo Young], *1959 Bath Downtown Plan* ([Bath]: Bath Planning Board, 1959, hereafter cited as Blackwell I).
4. Ashley A. Foard and Hilbert Fefferman, "Federal Urban Renewal Legislation," in James Q. Wilson, ed., *Urban Renewal: The Record and the Controversy* (Cambridge: M.I.T. Press, 1966), pp. 96–97, 104–5, 109.
5. James Q. Wilson, "Planning and Politics: Citizen Participation in Urban Renewal," in ibid., p. 407; Martin Anderson, *The Federal Bulldozer: A Critical Analysis of Urban Renewal*, 1949–1962 (Cambridge: M.I.T. Press, 1964), pp. 42–43.
6. Mussenden interview; BI, 25 June 1959.
7. Blackwell I.
8. BI, 27 February 1958.
9. [Atwood, Blackwell, and Young], *City of Bath, Maine: 1959 Citywide Planning Guide Summary* ([Bath]: Bath Planning Board, 1959), p. 1.
10. Blackwell I.
11. BI, 12 November 1969.

12. BDT, 2 October 1961.
13. Charles Nelson, quoted in ibid., 20 May 1962.
14. Anderson, pp. 76–77; Martin Mayer, *The Builders: Houses, Neighborhoods, Governments, Money* (New York: W. W. Norton, 1978), pp. 121–22.
15. Marc Fried, "Grieving for a Lost Home: Psychological Costs of Relocation," in Wilson, pp. 359–79; Basil Zimmer, "The Small Businessman and Relocation," in ibid., pp. 380–403.
16. For examples, see Urban Renewal: *A Socialist Scheme to Confiscate Private Property* ([brochure], New Orleans: The Independent American, 1959); John C. Sparks, "The Urban Renewal Fallacy," *The Freeman*, 3 March 1962, pp. 147–49. See also Jane Jacobs's classic *The Life and Death of Great American Cities* (New York: Random House, 1961). These and other publications are known to have circulated in Bath (Norman W. Howard, comp., Personal File on Bath Urban Renewal [PFL]).
17. Guild interview.
18. Robert C. Cummings, Interview, Bath, September 1987.
19. J. Newell, quoted in BDT, 31 March 1962.
20. Ibid., 15 August 1962.
21. Arthur E. Hutchins to Norman Howard, Bath, undated [May 1962] (Howard file).
22. Hutchins, quoted in BDT, 6 June 1962.
23. BDT, 27 July 1962.
24. Cummings interview.
25. Hutchins to Bath Property Owners, Bath, undated [October 1962] (Charles E. Burden, M.D., comp., Personal File on Bath Urban Renewal).
26. Morse interview.
27. BDT, 6 November 1962.
28. Charles A. Shepard, Jr., Interview, Bath, April-May 1987.
29. Ibid.
30. Orville T. Ranger, quoted in Robert C. Cummings, "Newly Formed Organization Expresses Concern . . . ," BDT, 11 January 1963.
31. Shepard and Theodore Kaknes to the *Bath Daily Times*, Bath, September 1963, published in ibid., 16 September 1963.
32. Shepard interview.
33. Burden interview.
34. BDT, 27 February 1963.
35. Burden, quoted in ibid.
36. Burden and Shepard interviews.
37. Shepard, quoted in BDT, 2 May 1963.
38. BDT, 10 May 1963.
39. J. Newell and Omar N. King to the *Bath Daily Times*, Bath, September 1963, published in ibid., 16 September 1963.
40. Shepard (for the Renewal Review Association) to Bath Citizens, Bath, September 1963, published in ibid., 19 September 1963.
41. Charles J. Horan, "Public Information" (mimeographed transcript of a speech delivered at Urban Renewal Workshop, Augusta, ME, 15 October 1963; Augusta: Maine Department of Economic Development, 1963), pp. 1–2.

42. George F. Carey II, quoted in BDT, 25 September 1963.
43. BDT, 25 March 1964.
44. Ibid., 15 May 1964.
45. Bradford P. Belanger, quoted in ibid.
46. Ernest Brown, quoted in ibid., 2 September 1964.
47. Ibid., 10 September 1964.
48. Robert C. Weaver, "Urban Renewal Is Dispossessing Its Critics," *Washington Post*, 5 April 1964.
49. W. Haggett interview.
50. Ibid.
51. Ibid.
52. BDT, 22, 23, 29 September 1964.
53. Elford A. Stover, Jr., Interview, Bath, July 1987.
54. A favorite tactic was the planting of letters to the editor of the *Times* by influential citizens. Many such letters were written for the signatories by vested interests (Burden and Shepard interviews; Burden to Richard Cahill, Bath, 19 September 1964 [Burden File]). For other references to this practice, see James C. Steen to the *Bath Daily Times* and R. Luke to ibid., Bath, September 1964 (BDT, 18 September 1964).
55. Ring interview.
56. W. Haggett, Morse, and Ring interviews.
57. Ibid.; Shepard interview.
58. J. Newell and King to the *Bath Daily Times*.
59. W. Haggett interview.
60. Shepard interview.
61. BDT, 12 April 1965.
62. Robert C. Cummings, "City Council Approves Urban Renewal," ibid., 6 May 1965.
63. Ibid.
64. BDT, 8 June 1965.
65. Ibid., Burden interview.
66. Shepard interview.
67. William L. Slayton, "Achievements of the Urban Renewal Program," in Wilson, p. 203.
68. Basil Zimmer, "The Small Businessman and Relocation," in ibid., pp. 119–21; Flyer of the Save Bath Committee, Bath, undated (Howard file).
69. Ring interview.
70. J. Temple to the *Bath Daily Times*, Bath, 24 June 1965, published in ibid., 24 June 1965.
71. W. Haggett interview.
72. Burden interview.
73. Morse interview.
74. Cummings interview.
75. BDT, 31 August 1965.
76. Burden interview.

5

"An Intimate Seaport"

Bartlett (Pete) Van Note came to Bath in 1965 to direct the Chamber of Commerce and serve as the United Fund's executive secretary. A Maine native and a graduate of Maine Maritime Academy, Van Note was determined to remain in his home state. Four years in Aroostook County, however, had convinced him that he needed to stay close to salt water, and Bath struck him as "the saltiest town in Maine." When Van Note arrived, the Shipbuilding City was struggling to find an identity and a consensus in the aftermath of its urban renewal debacle. "The whole community was so down on itself," he recalled. "I don't think I've ever walked into a situation where there was the kind of mental and spiritual depression that the community had right at that time. I remember some out-of-town people shaking their heads, saying, 'Why would anybody want to go to Bath at this point in time?' And I remember people welcoming me here, saying, 'At least there's one thing for sure: There is no place you go from here but up.' They felt that down about the whole thing."[1] One of the jokes making the rounds those days was that the new superhighway linking Bath with Cooks Corner and Brunswick was a real blessing because it made escape that much easier.

Van Note got busy, and his efforts soon made a difference in people's attitudes: "One of the very first things I did when I got tired of listening to all this negative talk initially was that I decided to adopt the motto, 'It Can Be Done.' I went over to Russ Hatch's print shop and I had him run off cards that said in three-inch letters, 'IT CAN BE DONE,' and down in the corner in fine print, 'Bath Area Chamber of Commerce.' I started handing them out all over town, and for quite a while they were in evidence. I kind of felt that . . . that's the way you've got to start thinking." In his search for positive thinkers, Van Note was particularly taken with those activists determined to push Bath toward modernization despite the death of urban renewal. "Red Mulligan had just been president of the Chamber. I remember that Red Mulligan, Brud Stover, Bill Haggett, Dick Redlon—this was the little group of reasonably young native sons who were actively trying to kick Bath up out of its doldrums. The city manager at the time was Harry Ring, and my feeling was that Harry was constantly being enmeshed in these guys' dreams and plans. . . . I was present at a good many of the coffee klatches where the brainstorming was going on, and I loved it. There wasn't anything that they dreamed up that they couldn't turn into a real possibility inside of an hour. No matter how off-the-wall it seemed to be, they could think of ways that this could be done. . . . That kind of thinking was what the community sorely needed at that time."[2]

Several months after Van Note had settled in, Peter Cox came to town to edit the *Bath Daily Times*. Cox was another newcomer who would make an important difference in Bath's self-perception. At twenty-seven, he was a boyishly animated yet experienced newspaperman, a passionate devotee of the state of Maine, and an admirer of John Cole, the crusading, environmentalist editor of the *Times*'s sister publication, the *Brunswick Record*. In some ways those two newspapers reflected the communities they served. The weekly *Record* was growing and prospering along with Brunswick's widening commercial importance. The daily *Times*'s circulation showed no sign of improvement (although, at almost 3,000, it reached a very high per-

TIMES RECORD

New blood on the *Times:* Editor Peter Cox.

centage of households in its constituency). Few in the Shipbuilding City realized it, but publisher Campbell Niven had a long-range plan to merge the two newspapers into a single regional daily.[3] Peter Cox was part of that strategy: "I met Cam in 1960 when I was working for Frank Coffin, who was running for governor, and we got along. Then I worked for the Biddeford-Saco *Journal*, and I was offered the editorship of a daily paper over in the Adirondacks. . . . I had the experience that Cam wanted. I was ready to leave there . . . and I said, 'When can I come?' He said, 'We'll wait until the urban renewal battle is over.' It ended and I came."[4]

At least two surprises awaited Cox upon his arrival in 1966. The first was that no one had told Ace Trueworthy, incumbent editor of the *Times*, that a new editor was on the way. When Cox arrived in the *Times* office, "Ace said, 'What are you going to do?' I said, 'Well, I'm going to assign the stories, I am going to lay out the paper, I am going to write the headlines, I'm going to write the editorials.' Ace looked at me and said, 'Okay.' And he never showed up for work again. Collected his paycheck for several years but never came into the office again, for which I can't blame him. I think he had a very equitable solution."[5]

Cox's other surprise was how quickly he grew to love Bath. Being a whippersnapper "from away" did not deter him in the least from editorializing on matters ranging from the wisdom of American involvement in Vietnam, which he did not take for granted, to the intrinsic interest of downtown Bath's aging, controversial architecture, which he likewise did not take for granted. Cox plunged in with ingenuously critical yet tailwaggingly upbeat opinions on everything, and, somehow, he got away with it (although the transformed newspaper was occasionally referred to as the *Hanoi Times*). What Cox liked best was the straightforwardness of the people he met: "Bud Shepard, who was a leading sort of opponent of urban renewal and would have seen me as probably on the other side except that I happened to be very much for historic preservation, too, and really saw Front Street as a wonderful place. He took me around the city. He took me by boat up and down the waterfront to show me everything. It was that kind of openness. We still had Petlock's Market. . . . They used to run these one-inch ads, and they had put in, 'New Veal Today,' so I went and asked him if I could have the kidneys. Nobody had ever asked for kidneys before. He sold them to me for a dime. Right next to him was Gilmore's [seafood market]. Gilmore's, in those days, still had sawdust on the floor. We moved to a little house on Weeks Street . . . and our neighbors were just lovely people. Eunice was pregnant when we moved there . . . and Mrs. True brought over a new apple pie for Eunice when she got out of the hospital. . . . The whole town was like that." Nor did Cox have to guess about how his opinions were being received: "I must have written an editorial suggesting that they replace the street signs in Bath, because there was a street sign and then you'd go eight blocks and not have another street sign. To which I was told, 'That's really a stupid idea. What are you worried about? Everybody in Bath knows the names of all the streets. What do you need street signs for?' And then, shortly after that, I wrote an editorial suggesting that they have a sign ordinance. . . . Wilson's Drug Store had a beautiful gold-lettering-on-black sign in those days, and I suggested they be like that. Well, within fifteen minutes of the paper coming out, a group of merchants marched on the office and told me what a stupid idea that was. But that was great! I mean, that's the kind of town it was."[6]

Under Cox, the *Times* converted from the old hot lead to offset printing, and once again hit the streets in time for the afternoon BIW shift change. Although its days were numbered, the newspaper was more than ever a vital part of the community. When its staff moved to Brunswick to work on the new *Times Record*, which appeared in February 1967, Bath lost an important clearinghouse for big ideas and small chitchat. Despite the stated intentions of the publisher and editor, the new paper's coverage of the Shipbuilding City was necessarily thin. Ironically, the *Bath Daily Times* was declared the best small daily in New England by the New England Press Association in January 1967, scant weeks before it was merged with the *Record*.

In its last year of life, the *Times* was finding and discussing issues head-on and at length. And, between Cox's tireless commentary and the bitterness overhanging the city, there was plenty of dialogue.

After the death of urban renewal, Bath city councillors were touchy and divided. A public hearing on a proposed 1965 bond ordinance to fund the city's purchase of heavy equipment showed that there was still substantial emotional hangover. It was also clear that councillors opposed to that program—Gediman, Hooker, and MacDonald—were similarly hostile to other municipal expenditures that would raise taxes. Subsequent annual elections brought gradual changes in Council membership but did little to heal the division. More than a year after urban renewal had, in Charlie Burden's words, "gone kerplunk," personal animosities on City Council provoked the exasperated *Times* to comment that men such as Haggett, Stover, Sarkis, Hooker, and MacDonald constituted one of the strongest bodies since the council-manager system was inaugurated in 1948, yet "the bickering and suspicion has overshadowed its accomplishments and threatens to make rational discussion of the perplexing matters facing the city impossible."[7]

The role of a city councillor in Bath was unenviable in the late 1960s. The city was faced with serious problems of public finance and morale, because the defeat of urban renewal had neither curbed spiraling taxes nor provided a consensus about planning alternatives. Under the circumstances, and appearances to the contrary, Bath did remarkably well.

Consider the tax picture: Before the 1965 watershed, property taxes had increased relentlessly, probably alienating many from the proposed urban renewal bond issue. In 1962, the tax rate had reached 90 mills. That figure was based on the 1947 valuation of 60 percent. As of 1963, taxes were computed on a 100 percent valuation, so that year's rate of 57 mills constituted another increase. Nor did the rate move up by inches. In 1964, it jumped to 61 mills, in 1965 it was 63, in 1966 it made 69, and in 1967 it reached 77. In twenty years, Bath property taxes had increased more than 70 percent in constant dollars.

Where did the money go? Mostly for education and the upgrading of the city's public works department, a single agency created in 1961 by merging the old highway-sewer and cemetery-parks facilities. Manager Harry Ring, who replaced Stanley Judkins late in 1961, wanted Bath to have the capability to perform its own excavation, paving, pipe-laying, and other heavy tasks. With his promotion from city clerk to manager, Ring's former position was merged with the managership, and a new position, city engineer, was created. The rationale behind upgrading Bath's public works capability was long-range economy: time saved on repairs, independence from outside general contractors, and the power to expedite development by providing city services in new areas. This was an ambitious and costly program, but Ring had what it took to sell it. A local boy who had been known around City Hall for years, he suffered from none of the outsider pangs that beset his three managerial predecessors. Moreover, his maturity and integrity were beyond question, and he was tactful to a fault. Although he supported urban renewal, Ring was somehow able to keep enough distance from the issue to avoid going down with it or being inseparably linked with its champions. From the start of his tenure as manager, he and City Council placed a high priority on street repair and massive improvements to Bath's quirky system of storm drains.[8] Work also commenced on an extension of North Street and a new road, Congress Avenue, that would connect the extension to Center, thus opening up a sizable tract of developable land on the city's western outskirts. Although this project was compatible with the Blackwell Report, it proceeded independent of urban renewal considerations.

In 1963, City Council had approved another major bond issue for a highway garage and substantial new school construction. There had been some public concern over increasing the city's bonded debt, but the 100 percent valuation in 1963 had likewise raised the city's debt limit.

As the question of urban renewal came down to the wire, some of its opponents expressed concern about its tax consequences, which certainly helped torpedo the program. But City Council's new blood was determined to spruce up Bath one way or another, and, as Van Note explained above, was self-consciously committed to offsetting the slump in community spirit that gripped Bath. Only three months after urban renewal's rejection, and despite considerable public opposition, Council voted five-to-three to authorize $250,000 in new bonds for buying heavy equipment with which Bath could make repairs on downtown streets and sidewalks. (Gediman, MacDonald, and Hooker voted against the measure.) Work began on crumbly pavement and sidewalks on Front, Center, and Commercial streets. Late in 1967, Council authorized yet another bond ordinance, this one for additions to Morse High.

Public opinion about municipal finance was hard to fathom. Although voters had trounced the bond issue for urban renewal, and notwithstanding rumblings about Council's fixation on the downtown, there was not enough outcry against bond issues (and resultant higher taxes) to deter Council from pushing ahead. "Bath has become a city of voters in turmoil," wrote Peter Cox in September 1967. "They are not satisfied to just let things drift along any more. They want a turn in events. . . . "[9] Perhaps. But the voters, who had killed urban renewal, seemed willing to live with Council's ambitious budgeting. And in the 1967 elections, Gediman and Hooker were voted out. The former contradiction perhaps revealed a philosophical repugnance toward federal assistance; the latter was inexplicable, unless councillors were elected more on personality than issues.

In any case, rising costs and taxes were an event that recurred with painful regularity. During 1967, property revaluation took place. The next year, taxes took a 10 percent jump. By then, had not outside events interceded to brighten the picture, Bath would have been in danger of a major taxpayer revolt. The city's total debt now stood at $2.109 million (about $5.7 million in 1986 dollars).[10]

It took courage—in the face of rising taxes, an uncertain tax base, and no coherent plan—to persevere with municipal improvements. Nonetheless, the city did so in the late sixties. Voter willingness to fund capital improvements and better schools was a sign that Bath might be outgrowing its pinchpenny, here-and-now approach to major responsibilities. So was Council's prudence regarding the burgeoning issue of water pollution control, which loomed as a potential future nightmare. In a dramatic departure from tradition, Council voted to borrow money at low municipal rates and reinvest it at higher rates to accumulate a fund for water treatment in the years to come. Other improvements over past policies were the installation of a cone burner at the city dump and the purchase of scenic, undeveloped land along Merrymeeting Bay for future recreational use.

The search continued for a way to the future. Haggett stumped for community action, warning local civic groups that, having spurned federal development, the city would die unless it generated growth on its own. An Industrial Development Commission, chaired by Hooker, had been created in 1964. After urban renewal died, the city added a Commercial Development Coordinating Committee, consisting of Haggett, Hooker, Ring, Fred Drake of the Parking District, John Leonard of the Planning Board, Leonard (Red) Mulligan (an oil retailer and burgeoning developer), and Jack Stelling (outgoing executive director of the Chamber of Commerce). The committee's objective was to broaden the tax base, not just by attracting industry but also by encouraging residential development. That, in turn, implied an obligation to make Bath a more interesting, as well as more lucrative, spot. Almost immediately after the committee's formation, Mulligan, the chairman, announced the imminent establishment of a private preparatory school, to be situated at the spacious Hyde Estate on High Street. Hyde School was to a large extent the work of Mulligan, who had an uncanny knack for assembling packages of like-minded people and funding sources. Hyde School was operating under the tutelage of Headmaster Joseph W. Gauld by June of 1966.

It was becoming obvious that Blackwell had been right: Bath's economic future lay elsewhere than in cultivation of outside industry. Overtures were made to housing developers. With its well-equipped public works department, the city now offered to provide rough roads and sewer lines to developable land. Early in 1969, Bath established its own housing authority. Meanwhile, it absorbed the obligations of the Parking District, removing downtown meters that, some said, discouraged shoppers.

City fathers' steps to keep Bath alive authenticated the new leadership's determination to salvage something positive from the planning experience of the late fifties and early sixties. The steps taken at that time must have been difficult to achieve, given the state of public and political morale. They are all the more impressive when viewed in the light of the Vietnam controversy, the sexual revolution, the much-ballyhooed problems of what was then called the generation gap, and the uncertain business climate of the late sixties.

Long after urban renewal had gone kerplunk, the major issue confronting Bath continued to be the business picture in general and the downtown in particular, where too many staring or boarded-up storefronts faced dwindling numbers of shoppers. Even some going concerns had a dilapidated look because, pending the decision on urban renewal, they had received no upkeep or improvements. Not even the most diehard member of the erstwhile RRA would call Bath attractive; in fact, Bud Shepard and other downtown retailers had reorganized to see what could be done about the deteriorating situation.

One positive step was stricter enforcement of the tax law. City fathers, who had practiced salutary neglect of delinquent accounts, committed themselves to auction delinquent properties after a statutory eighteen-month waiting period. Another positive move would have been firm enforcement of the building code, which would have condemned numerous substandard properties. Some enforced demolition did take place, but, perhaps because of the stigma still attached to urban renewal, Council was reluctant to blow the whistle on such buildings, with the result that the downtown retained its bedraggled appearance.

OLD TORREY ROLLER PLANT POSES PROBLEMS FOR CITY

What do you do with a huge complex of downtown buildings that cannot be removed and cannot be occupied? This is something of the problem that faces Bath with vacant Torrey Roller Bushing Works. . . .

A building inspection has shown that the buildings are structurally sound and cannot be ordered taken down under the state run-down building statute. The owners are not prepared to enter the expensive proposition of tearing them down themselves, and there are no buyers who would do so on the horizon. . . .

The century-old complex of buildings . . . has been unused since the firm closed its doors five years ago. . . .

The building complex has been the subject of concern for a number of years. The 1959 Blackwell planning study of downtown Bath urged its removal as one of the keys to development of the downtown . . . and the waterfront and similar recommendations were included in the defeated urban renewal proposals.

BATH DAILY TIMES, 5 NOVEMBER 1965

COMING DOWN SLOWLY

Work is continuing on the razing of a portion of the former Torrey Roller Bushing Company building on Commercial Street. . . [One] portion of the building. . . under present plans will be remodeled into a new home for the Bath Elks, while . . . sections . . . are being razed for salvage and to provide space for parking and other lodge activities. A portion of the land may also be sold for commercial development according to tentative plan. The Elks purchased the complex of buildings last fall and hope to remodel the southernmost wing.

BATH DAILY TIMES, 29 NOVEMBER 1966

THEY SAY SHOP IN BATH

Dear Sir:

Wednesday, I was finishing some curtains for my kitchen and I ran out of white rick-rack. I only needed a small amount, so I decided to drive to our "well stocked downtown district" and buy a nineteen cent card of white, regular rick-rack.

If you have shopped downtown lately you know the rest. I didn't find any. I find this usual, of late, of most any item. . . . My advice is don't waste your time in Bath.

Merchants want Bath folk to shop in their stores, well, merchants, if you only stocked regular items, we women might patronize your stores more often.

. . . I am only one woman out of many who feel this way. You think our city is sick, well you are right.

You can't sit still and let other communities grow, in leaps and bounds and not do something to keep up with progress.

Until some folks realize this is 1966 and most of us women can drive, we will go out of town to well-stocked stores and more alert help.

Mrs. Virginia Kenney

BATH DAILY TIMES, 28 JANUARY 1966

Was it possible, as the RRA had maintained, for Bath citizens to renovate the business district on their own? If prosperity depended upon the presence of a large downtown department store, where would they find the financial resources to offset the loss of stores such as Sears? Such necessity, in 1966, was the mother of real invention: Bath businessmen considered erecting a cooperative department store. The incident was a revealing indicator of how far people were now prepared to go to save the downtown.

In November 1965, at John Atwood's behest, Stephen Hopkins, another Boston planner, came to town. After meeting with Haggett, Ring, and Mulligan, he was retained by the Chamber of Commerce to find a major retailer interested in locating in Bath. Hopkins had no luck with that assignment. Instead, early in 1966, he proposed that Bath citizens subscribe to a cooperative stock venture to raise money for a 50,000-square-foot department store. Local merchants could operate dozens of various concessions within such a store, which of course would fulfill the purpose of a large, competitive draw for the downtown while harmonizing with the needs of small businessmen. Getting the project started would entail the sale of $375,000 worth of stock. The entire concept, Hopkins told City Council, would closely follow that of the celebrated Harvard Coop located on Harvard Square in Cambridge, "the most successful department store in New England." Hopkins, undaunted at the recent history of Bath's business, admonished city fathers not to give up hope because three major retailers had vacated the downtown, adding that "you people will be ridiculous to let all the money earned in Bath be spent in a neighboring town."[11] Councillors, businessmen, and consumers all responded positively.

Promoting the Bath Cooperative Department Store became one of Pete Van Note's first assignments when he came to the Chamber of Commerce. "I wasn't asked," he recalled. "I was told: This was something we were going to try to do. It was a real pie in the sky. But a major effort was made. That came down to public solicitation because, in order to make it work, people in the community had to pledge that they would buy shares in this co-op. And, believe it or not, enough people did."[12]

The proposed store's design interested John Morse, Jr. It would embrace existing structures on Front (the now-vacated Senter's store) and Center (the empty W. T. Grant building), connecting these with a new diagonal wing to their rear that would share landscaped parking facilities on Water Street. The overall design was functionally modern, multilevel, and parklike. Morse agreed to put up the necessary construction and renovation money, expecting to make it back on higher rent. Here was private urban renewal, Bath style.

After sufficient pledges had been gathered, the search began for a Maine company to sign a managerial contract. None would. According to Van Note, "We approached most of them, including the likes of Benoit's and . . . the people who ran Porteous, anybody who had a Maine leaning in retailing was approached. Hannaford Bros. even was approached. I did most of the approaching, so I know that it did happen. There were a lot of long conversations and, in the final analysis, even though it was largely risk-free . . . , we couldn't find a retailer to do it." It wasn't the plan's unconventionalism that did it in, Van Note remembered. "The outside image of Bath was carrying so many negatives at the time that they just didn't want to make a commitment. It's not only that. . . . Nothing like this had ever been put together. The guy that dreamed up the idea was a developer out of Boston. While we didn't take him with us when we went calling on people, that probably hurt a little bit. Boston developers in those days didn't get listened to."[13] The plan collapsed.

Reviewing the project, Morse later concluded that, like the dream of keeping Sears as a downtown anchor, such an ambitious venture was probably foredoomed. "It had even less likelihood of success, because by that time . . . the Cooks Corner shopping center would have been drawing heavily out of the people that should have formed the basis for success of a cooperative store."[14]

Bath did get a downtown department store—for a few years. In April 1967, two out-of-town businessmen leased from Morse the Front Street space vacated by Senter's that would have been part of the proposed cooperative store and undertook impressive renovations. The new department store, called Barden's, opened in August to great fanfare. To some it was a sign that Bath was not finished as a shopping district. But it, too, proved uncompetitive and closed after a few years. Cooks Corner, by way of contrast, was booming.

MILITARY BURIAL FOR DWIGHT PRICE

BATH—Funeral services were held Friday afternoon for Pfc. Dwight A. Price, a casualty of the Vietnam War, at the Seventh Day Adventist Church on High Street. Price, 22, was killed during the prolonged battle for the Marine outpost at Khe Sanh and is believed to be the first Bath resident killed in that conflict.

Elder Robert Frost cited Price's life-long ambition to join his uncle, Gunnery Sergeant William F. Tinney, of Arlington, Va., in the service of his country with the Marine Corps. Tinney had made a career of the Marines and has been in the military for some 20 years. He had hoped to accompany the body of his nephew home, but arrangements to that effect could not be made.

Elder Frost also pointed out Price's willingness to serve in the military as being his own choice, and the outcome as something considered with his decision to serve. "Young Dwight went to Vietnam for one cause," said Frost, "and that was to fight for the freedom which is so dear to the minds and hearts of man."

. . . Traditional military burial services were

conducted at the Oak Grove Cemetery where Price's mother, Mrs. Maxine Price of 47 Edward Street, was presented with the flag which had draped the coffin of her son. . . .

TIMES RECORD [BRUNSWICK], 1 JULY 1968

COFFEE HOUSE JAMMED AT OPENING

BY ROBERT NISS

BATH—"It looks like Times Square," said one youth of downtown Bath on Friday night.

Indeed, Front and Center Streets were jammed with an unusual crowd, and the sound of guitars and singing was somewhat new to those who passed the concentration of the crowd at 9 Centre [sic] Street.

This was the opening night of The Bridge, Bath's new coffee house, and the turnout was beyond the expectations of coffee house officials. . . .

Barry Smith, the Bridge manager, stated that it was a "tremendously successful opening weekend, and we had more people than we could handle," referring to the extensive crowd which was unable to get into the coffeehouse [sic] and had to stand on the sidewalk outside the door.

. . . [Bill] Phinney attributed the initial success . . . to two simple factors: "People are pretty happy to have something free and the talent offered is good." Perhaps some people came to view Phinney's unusual painting which graces the wall of the coffeehouse [sic]. Done in "five shades of red," the painting "represents the whole group, the whole scheme of society enjoying a good sing." Such individual efforts as this are representative of the atmosphere generated by The Bridge. Any of the refurnishing which was not done by Smith was accomplished by local people showing a decided interest in the proceedings and hoping, in their own way, to speed the success of the venture.

The talent of which Phinney speaks is

arranged by Mrs. John Coombs of Bath. Friday night boasted the most extensive entertainment program of the weekend when six different people or groups showed up to participate. . . .

TIMES RECORD, 7 AUGUST 1967

'I AM CURIOUS' CANCELLED AT OPERA HOUSE

BATH—Area theatergoers curious about "I Am Curious (Yellow)" will remain so—at least for the time being.

The film, scheduled to open at the Opera House here tonight, has been cancelled and replaced with "Last Summer."

Opera House manager Robert Alexander said the head office of the chain which owns the theater called him yesterday and told him not to run the film. "They didn't tell me why," he said.

Alexander said he believed the replacement . . . was "preferable," even though it also is restricted to persons over 18.

"They will put anything in those damn Swedish films," he said. . . .

Alexander said the only thing he knows about "I Am Curious (Yellow)" is "what I read about it," and added, "That's bad enough."

He says the Swedes are working on one now that is "even worse," this one called, "I Am Curious (Blue)."

"It is supposed to be even worse," he said, but I can't see how it can be." . . .

TIMES RECORD, 19 NOVEMBER 1968

Back in February 1963, during one of those long and loud public debates in City Hall over the virtues of urban renewal, Charlie Burden had belittled the downtown's outmoded buildings. Then the lonely voice of Laura Sewall raised an interesting question. According to Burden, "It was in response to a remark that I had made. I said, 'There is one building downtown that has a piece of stone on it that's carved "1844." Well, that building is over a hundred years old!' " To Burden, such a structure had probably outlived its usefulness. Whereupon Mrs. Sewall spoke. "She stood up and said, 'Well, that's the most wonderful thing about it! It has wonderful character and it's old.' " Although it was lost in the snarl of subsequent arguments, Burden never forgot that remark.[15]

Neither did his opponent, Bud Shepard. At the time, Shepard's devotion to old buildings was strictly a matter of self-preservation: "I'm not a historian and I was young, you know. What the hell did I know about saving buildings? I was trying to save myself, I guess. . . . But the Sewall family is a very respected family in Bath." Mrs. Sewall, who apparently realized that she and Shepard had something in common, contacted him. "The first time I went up to talk to her—she invited me out to tea—it was a real joy. She was a lovely woman." Laura Sewall kindled in Shepard a sense that there was more at stake in urban renewal than he suspected: "She really won me over, because what she said was 100 percent right. And it didn't relate just to Bath. . . . She related it to the whole country."[16]

Why more of an issue wasn't made of historic preservation during the urban renewal controversy is a mystery. From the very start of their reports, Atwood, Blackwell and Young had stressed the distinction of Bath's historic architecture in and out of the downtown. That element, however, played almost no role in the arguments for or against downtown renewal. Bath's general disinterest in its architectural legacy is even harder to explain in view of the fact that, in response to mounting outcry about the destruction of historic buildings, the federal urban renewal program had made historic preservation a recognized part of its criteria. Elsewhere in New England, cities and towns were using such funds to save irreplaceable buildings.

Laura Sewall was in the vanguard of a nationwide preservationist mood that would snowball in the late sixties. It was largely propelled by revulsion at urban renewal's wholesale obliteration of historic buildings and neighborhood character across the country, and it was instrumental in putting the brakes on further destruction.[17] At the same time, the Johnson administration had become enamored of restoring the nation's beauty, which, since World War II, seemed to have taken a beating from highway projects, outdoor advertising, pollution, and indiscriminate development.[18] Accordingly, Washington now made available funds for the creation of public parks and recreation areas.

Another development was the National Historic Preservation Act of 1966, by which the federal Department of the Interior was empowered to maintain a National Register of Historic Places. The register's purpose was to protect buildings and districts deemed historically important by denying federal assistance to any project that would damage or alter their character after they were duly registered. It also made available, under certain circumstances, funds to help interested local agencies acquire important but threatened properties, and it offered tax benefits to owners of registered properties who would undertake their restoration. While hardly a federal giveaway program, the act legitimized a whole new set of options for American cities and towns whose identity had been threatened. Suddenly, preservationists, too often dismissed as idealistic aesthetes or reactionaries, were cast as realists.[19]

As Laura Sewall had tried to point out, Bath was a preservationist's dream, a potentially exciting case of what one historian called "negative preservation": hundreds of old and interesting buildings, some historic, that owed their survival to sluggish economics and benign neglect.[20] That was the picture that people like Bud Shepard tried to show Peter Cox when he came to the *Times* in 1965.

Cox's arrival was a most fortuitous coincidence for Bath preservationists, for he needed little prompting to see the beauty in the downtown's datestoned walls and antique storefronts: "I was as a child brought up in Washington. . . . We moved to Georgetown probably in 1945. It was gentrified in that period, from 1945 to 1950. . . . My father was from Portland, and I had always seen the waterfront there which was in terrible disuse in that period. I had been to Europe a couple of times and seen the stuff there. I was almost a history of art major, my brother is an architect, so I was very interested in that stuff." Cox was also bowled over by Bath's residential architecture: "I could see so many attractive things in Bath, coming in as an outsider. . . . I could see it as a beautiful town. I still see it as one of the most incredible residential areas in the world. Just one beautiful house after another. . . . And people thought it was a backwater!"[21]

At twenty-three, while editing the *Adirondack Daily Enterprise*, Cox had spearheaded a cleanup of Saranac Lake's waterfront by publishing comparative photographs of attractive waterfronts elsewhere. He tried a similar device in Bath. Shortly after his arrival, *Times* readers were treated to photographic spreads of such elegant, high-priced districts as Boston's Beacon Hill, whose quaint brick architecture, Cox's captions pointed out, bore a provocative resemblance to downtown Bath's. Only weeks after the defeat of urban renewal, having read the Blackwell Report, the new editor mounted a campaign for organized historic preservation as a way to revitalize Bath: "Most important . . . is the preservation of the best brick buildings on Front Street and the other good buildings about town. But first people have to be convinced that these buildings are really worth saving. As a newspaper, we intend to play an active role in the preservation of the best old buildings. . . . We also think Bath desperately needs a group interested in historic preservation.

"Such groups have been successful in Portsmouth, N.H. and Providence, R.I. Such a group could be successful in Bath.

" . . . Therefore, let this be an open letter to anyone interested in historic preservation in Bath. We hope you will give us a call or stop in to see us, and we will offer our full support.

"Along with city action, and private action by the merchants, an historic preservation group which can secure federal aid to preserve, not to tear down, will help in the rejuvenation of downtown Bath."[22]

Bath's awakening interest in historic preservation was certainly a psychological boost for sagging local morale, but it was nothing new to anyone who had read the Blackwell Report. That plan's emphasis on historic character had largely been contributed by consultant John Atwood, who, now that urban renewal was dead, was brought back to town by the Planning Board to revise the city plan in its new context. (Since the days of the Blackwell Report, Atwood and Blackwell had separated; the latter had developed Brunswick's master plan.) City fathers hoped that a new workable program might snag federal aid for such recreational improvements as a waterfront park.

Reporting to the Planning Board in late 1965 and early 1966, Atwood was most diplomatic, accentuating the positive. In view of how much time and how little action had transpired since the original plan had been adopted, he said, things could be much worse in the Shipbuilding City. Atwood put this nicely by praising the new public works department and other capital improvements and reaffirming the original plan's emphasis on Bath's residential and recreational attractions, which the city had now rediscovered. The death of urban renewal and the birth of Cooks Corner had at least weeded out the dreamy improbables, forcing planners and occupants alike to reduce their expectations for the downtown. Did Bath need to snag a major retailer for the downtown? Absolutely essential, said Atwood. Should the district be refurbished by "modern" facades on the old buildings? No; avoid the "cheap and shoddy." Instead, Bath should take advantage of its "historic past and its many unique older buildings to create a unified downtown with modern shops, but with an exterior reminiscent of the days when Bath was a major seaport."[23]

Given the go-ahead, Atwood assembled a plan that retained many of the old Blackwell Report's features. Presented in January 1967, it became Bath's comprehensive blueprint for the future. As before, the city's focal point was the unfulfilled downtown that could be rescued by a beautified, public-oriented waterfront, a one-way traffic loop (but no pedestrian malls), the presence of a magnet store such as the then-active co-op project, and the creation of a historic district to encompass the downtown and those nearby residential streets that constituted Bath's richest architectural trove. As before, the toughest of these to achieve would be the recreational waterfront. Despite improvements in the street itself and the erstwhile Parking District's acquisition of waterfront parcels, Commercial Street was a far cry from the complex of marinas, parks, and hotels the planner envisioned. To accomplish the plan, the city would need to purchase still more riverfront real estate. The other big municipal expense would be the cosmetic changes to downtown sidewalks, lampposts, power lines, and other components of the infrastructure to conform to the historical aesthetics of a nineteenth-century seaport. It should be added that Atwood was not an architectural purist bent on restoring Bath streets to historical accuracy. Instead, he told city fathers, Bath should strive for an atmosphere of antiquity.

Funding? Federal agencies did indeed offer money for specific recreational and historic projects; but, by and large, revitalizing the downtown would probably be a slow, bootstrap operation by City Hall, landlords, and merchants. Prerequisites for any outside assistance would be a rigid zoning code and relentless war against useless, dilapidated buildings. Although Council endorsed the plan, enough councillors found restrictive zoning and property condemnation so distasteful that little progress was made in those areas for years. But, all in all, the city had rebounded admirably from the urban renewal fiasco. Perhaps all the post-renewal adversity had sobered up its citizens about the need for prompt action. Perhaps the community had found a premise for its future that balanced the values of preservationists, developers, little guys, and bigshots—a plan everyone could live with. And maybe, by celebrating its distinctive legacy and surrendering the creation of a commercial Brave New World to such as Cooks Corner, Bath could recycle its lost pride, inherent civic strength, and battered individualism in a different direction.

After early 1967, Bath readers got their news from the Brunswick *Times Record*, wherein Peter Cox continued to wage his one-man war on municipal apathy. In August of that year, for example, Cox laid bare "Some Untruths about Bath": "Preconception number one is that the Bath Iron Works controls the city and no one can buck it. The fact is that the actual influence of BIW executives is less than it should be. At present, they go out of their way not to interfere and only come out when they consider a positive program has been initiated. . . .

"Preconception number two is that only a small group of people already in power can really exert influence. . . . I have spent two years looking for this establishment group, in the hope that I could get their support for projects, but I have not been able to find them, and I am convinced that no 'establishment' exists.

"Misconception number three is that people in Bath would violently oppose any change. On the contrary, I have found there is much real evidence they are desperate for new ideas and for some feasible program to get them out of the predicament of rising taxes without anything to show for them."[24]

Shortly after that editorial appeared, the city was abruptly confronted by a feasible program of stupendous proportions, one that would embrace the downtown plan, fix the tax problem, and bring the Bath Iron Works back into the community dialogue. The Navy was shopping for a shipyard to produce thirty highly sophisticated destroyers. The contract was worth well over $2 billion, and BIW had a fighting chance at winning it.

* * *

During the 1960s, Bath Iron Works underwent dramatic change. On the surface, BIW presented the image of a lean and competitive organization, but the company was actually less than robust.

During John Newell's presidency, which had commenced in 1950, BIW exploited the close personal contacts and influence that Newell, like his father, had cultivated at the Pentagon. For years, the Navy and the Iron Works had enjoyed mutual trust and close association. In the meantime, as the American merchant marine declined, commercial contracts were few and far between, and BIW management did not actively pursue that side of the shipbuilding business. The company had thus become ever more specialized in the art of building small, complex fighting ships.

By the sixties, however, defense contracting was changing. Under the administration of Robert McNamara and his vaunted "Whiz Kids," the Department of Defense abandoned the cozy relationships it had built up with contractors and moved to an almost-adversarial role in a relentless pursuit of lower defense costs. That, in turn, prompted suppliers to submit unrealistically low bids, even if doing so meant taking a loss, in order to eliminate long-range competitors and gain know-how with new weapons systems.

As the rules of the game changed, BIW found that its equity at the Pentagon was rapidly depreciating. Meanwhile, the company had paid its stockholders generous annual dividends and was debt-free, but it had not kept pace with technical changes in ship production, relying instead on its accumulated expertise and reputation for high quality. The obvious error of this strategy boded ill for the future. Profits at BIW, which had averaged 4.65 percent annually between 1956 and 1960, fell during the early sixties to below 3 percent of sales, and stock prices slid accordingly.[25] By 1963, underpriced BIW stock was a very good speculative investment.

In 1964, outsiders, notably William Kyle, president of a Milwaukee holding company, and John O'Boyle, a Texas investor, had purchased 20 percent of BIW's stock. In 1964, after the Iron Works had lost an important naval contract, Kyle demanded and won for himself and, later, O'Boyle, seats on the Iron Works board in the name of safeguarding their substantial investment. That ended BIW's days of direction by a board of insiders and congenial outsiders. Noting the chilly reception given him and O'Boyle when they assumed their board seats, Kyle was also incredulous at what he called the company's "roll-top desk management."[26] Big changes followed.

John Newell resigned from the Iron Works presidency in 1965 and was replaced by an outsider, James Goodrich, an executive from Todd Shipyards. Under Goodrich, the company diversified into commercial shipbuilding, undertaking construction of cargo vessels for the American Export Lines. That contract required some costly upgrading and expansion of facilities. The improvements were salutary and necessary, but the contracts lost money. In 1966, the Iron Works went $6.7 million into the red, posting its first loss since 1947.

Bath Iron Works was suddenly on lean times and without future prospects in Washington. McNamara's Whiz Kids had decided that efficient naval contracting required the Pentagon to contract with shipyards on a winner-take-all basis, awarding the whole pie to the lowest bidder instead of serving proportional slices to competitors. A single, massive award would presumably permit key shipyards to modernize adequately. The Pentagon had written off the rather old-fashioned shipyard on the Kennebec as too far from the sources of heavy capital and therefore unequal to the challenge of building tomorrow's high-tech naval vessels.

In March 1967, owing to turnover on the BIW board, and obviously hostile to the manner in which his company had so quickly become the instrument of high-rolling strangers, John Newell was forced to resign his director's seat, taking with him the magic of the Newell name that had given the Iron Works its distinctive local character. His departure must have been exceedingly painful, as, to a much lesser extent, was Bath's earlier repudiation of urban renewal, for which he had worked so hard. Newell sold his family home on Washington Street, retired to Florida, and played no further role in the affairs of the Shipbuilding City.

BATH-BUILT SHIP HIT OFF VIETNAM

BATH—The USS Ozbourn, a destroyer built at Bath Iron Works and commissioned 21 years ago this month, was hit by enemy shore-based artillery fire Saturday morning while she was patroling two miles off the coast of South Vietnam, just south of the demilitarized zone that separates the two Vietnams.

A spokeman said several shells were fired at the ship with two hits inflicting "minor damage" but no casualties. . . .

The enemy shellfire lasted about 10 minutes and was returned by the Ozbourn, but fog prevented an estimate of the amount of damage it inflicted on shore.

The 2,250-ton Ozbourn, 390 feet long, is the flagship of Destroyer Division 92 and had been assigned to support U. S. Marines fighting about 15 miles inland in "Operation Bunker Hill."

TIMES RECORD, 28 MARCH 1967

Following the board shake-up at Bath Iron Works, the company underwent radical restructuring. The Bath Iron Works, Hyde Windlass, and another BIW subsidiary, Pennsylvania Crusher (a maker of gravel and coal-crushing machinery), were each to be operated as subsidiaries of a new Delaware holding company, Bath Industries. Bath Industries simultaneously issued stock at a two-and-one-half-to-one ratio in lieu of BIW stock. The recently reorganized Iron Works board became the board of Bath Industries, with William Kyle as chairman. The new conglomerate immediately began to diversify, acquiring Kinder Manufacturing Company and Congoleum-Nairn. Within a few years, the shipyard on the Kennebec would be a subordinate part of a holding company involved mostly with the manufacture of home furnishings.

As it changed, Bath Industries liquidated Hyde Windlass as a separate entity, merging it into BIW, and, in 1975, divested itself of Pennsylvania Crusher.

The cumulative effect of this corporate mutation was massive in the city of Bath. From the departure of Newell to the erasure of Hyde, the changes were repeated and upsetting reminders that while Bath's economic eggs were in one basket, the basket itself now belonged to moneymen from away who had little interest in BIW's complex, intimate relationship with its host city. In addition, of the almost 4,000 people employed by the Iron Works in the late sixties, only a third lived in Bath. That meant that their paychecks and most of their business were enriching other communities.

The fact was, however, that the change and alienation at BIW looked worse than it was. For example, Goodrich appreciated the extent of community jitters and walked a tightrope, acting as a good citizen but assiduously avoiding the Big Brother image that had occasionally embattled the company. Remembering the Goodrich years, Pete Van Note recalled that "when I first came to town in chamber work, [Bill Haggett] was at the Iron Works in community relations. . . . Obviously, that put him and I in constant communication in terms of BIW and the community. I remember saying to him at one time . . . , 'What we really need is for BIW to . . . [give] brownie points . . . for middle management people being involved in community activities. It has to be a management thing that has to be passed down. We would like you to do this kind of work.' . . . He thought it made sense, being a native, and he and I went to see Jim Goodrich . . . and we made that pitch. Jim was positive. He agreed . . . , but he also pointed out that 'one of the things BIW is not, is about to make this a company town. It is a company town by virtue of this monster that is here but we're not about to run it, and we're not about to be accused of running it.' . . . I always thought that was an interesting, balanced view."[27]

Far more important than that was Goodrich's determination to see BIW through its modernization campaign, and to stay in the running for naval contracts. When the Navy announced that it would let a contract for a group of state-of-the-art gas turbine destroyers (DX), Iron Works brass were determined to bid. It was a long shot, but, on a winner-take-all basis, Bath might become the birthplace of literally dozens of future warships. Winning DX would more than double BIW's business and more than triple its work force.

The magnitude of the DX contract made it an issue of statewide, even regional importance, but its production demands were so great that whoever won it would need to invest enormous sums in prior expansion and modernization. On the Kennebec, such improvements would take at least $50 million, which made BIW the darkest horse among the six initial competitors. Many, like BIW, were subsidiaries of conglomerates, but they were reliably close to the sources of heavy capital the project required. For example, in Pascagoula, Mississippi, the Ingalls Shipyard, a Litton Industries subsidiary, received assistance to the tune of a whole new facility built by the state and leased to the yard. The Iron Works likewise appealed to the Maine Legislature for loan guarantees of $32 million, a sum so large as to require a constitutional amendment to raise the state's limit on such guarantees. Thanks to expeditious work by Governor Kenneth Curtis and Representative Rodney Ross, Jr., the necessary bills sailed through the Legislature and were passed in a statewide referendum in November 1968.

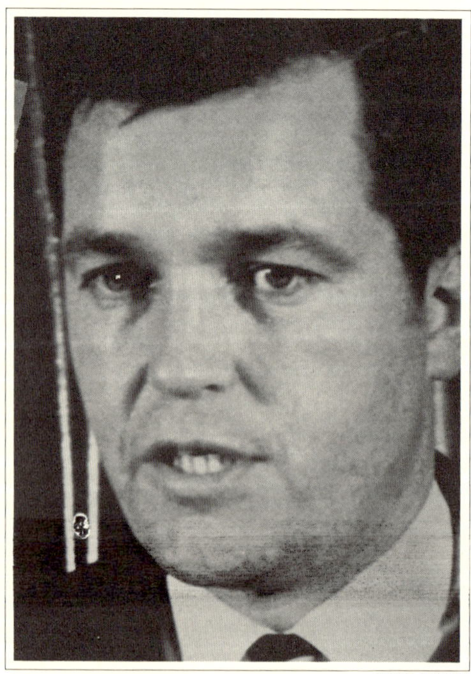

TIMES RECORD

Bill Haggett.

Mainers, too, saw the historical importance of the competition. "They gave us everything, in effect, that we asked for," recalled Bill Haggett. " . . . Good, solid support everywhere in Maine for that effort, a lot of concern about what would happen to the community."[28]

The possibility of an industrial bonanza won general support in Bath, where, urban renewal memories notwithstanding, BIW encountered almost no public sharpshooting. It was clear around the city that with the procurement changes in Washington, DX might be the company's last chance. As Van Note recalled, "It was that or nothing. Get into that game or there was no game. So it got into the game with everything it had, every resource it had."[29] In an amazing show of optimism, BIW waded into the competition, producing a 20,000-page proposal that survived the cut. Bath and Ingalls were finalists. "It was a David-and-Goliath-type competition all the way," recalled Haggett. "We were pleased the competition started with six companies. Four of them got knocked out before we did, and we were able to hang in there against Litton and compete all the way to the end. . . . It was a huge effort. We spent $10 million putting together plans and information. . . . Our price was right. . . . Furthermore, we just knew a lot more about building those ships than Litton did."[30] Bath expected to hear the Pentagon's decision by August of 1969.

The city government, meanwhile, had committed itself to providing BIW with the advance support it needed to win the contract. As with urban renewal, municipal expenses would be recouped in higher property taxes after expansion. Bath, in fact, would be showered with increased revenues once the contract was in hand. Furthermore, potential community growth virtually ensured future tax reductions. It is easy to see why the project looked so attractive to so many. Another of its selling points was that despite the massive physical changes it entailed, DX in no way conflicted with the plans to remodel the downtown.

As the DX countdown proceeded, the city expanded its own plan to accommodate the changes the new contract would require. They were colossal. In the official publication of the plan, which appeared in 1969, John Atwood stated that "DX will fundamentally effect [sic] the lives of all citizens of Bath and will have powerful economic and social effect throughout the region"—a neat case of understatement.[31] But the plan's enlarged frame of reference was historically significant. For the first time, Bath city fathers came to grips with the future of the entire region.

Winning DX would make Bath a very different place, far more changed than envisioned in the wildest dreams of the old Blackwell Report. For example, BIW would extend its riverbank facilities half a mile farther south along the Kennebec, filling in fifty acres of wetlands in the process. Such expansion would increase the payroll from 3,800 to 8,000 by 1975, which meant that 4,000 cars would arrive at the yard daily, mostly out-of-town vehicles traveling Route One. To handle such a crunch, Atwood planned a four-lane, limited-access boulevard, cutting through largely undeveloped land. It would whisk cars approaching from the west around the South End residential district to a BIW gate. "Such a new facility would easily provide for 2,000 to 2,400 vehicles per hour in each direction."[32] Cars approaching from the other side of the Kennebec, Atwood hoped, could be parked in Woolwich; workers would thereupon be shuttled by rail across the lower (Maine Central) span of the Carlton Bridge. Intown streets, including south Washington Street, which ran past BIW, would be widened, cut through, and put on a one-way traffic system.

The impact of DX upon Bath's critically short housing supply was expected to be similarly great. Growth would require 2,000 new dwellings, but, because of Bath's chronic shortage of space and sewerable land, most of these probably would be built in other nearby communities. In Bath, only about 450 acres, near Leeman Highway and adjacent to Lambert Park, looked suitable. Those sites might accommodate 500 modular homes.

The plan's coverage of service and cultural facilities was adroit. Atwood accepted the recent findings of the Maine Health Facilities Planning Council that hospitals in the Bath-Brunswick area should consolidate, eliminating duplication of effort, needless competition, and redundant service. With DX, the region should construct a single acute-care facility, relegating former hospital sites to outpatient and extended care, areas of health service that were gaining importance as the mean age of patients increased and Medicare entitlements challenged traditional hospital practices. The plan recommended another regional and possibly controversial step: creation of a two-year community college, the absence of which, wrote Atwood, was a "critically neglected area."[33]

Plans for the downtown mirrored the best of the Blackwell Report and the lessons learned thereafter about that district's options: "DX impact will mainly relate to improvements in the convenience shopping categories of retail trade and services. Bath downtown has been reduced in role by new regional retailing developments and even substantially enlarged employment at the Bath Iron Works and as many as 500 new facilities in Bath will not bring back the major chain stores which have migrated to suburban shopping centers. New roles must be found for downtown. . . . " Empty storefronts could be expeditiously converted into offices for DX personnel. The city should find funds to help the growing Bath Marine Museum relocate to the waterfront, preferably in the stately customs house, which the post office planned to vacate in favor of new quarters. Funding should also be provided for highrise housing for the elderly. Finally, city fathers must redouble their efforts to purchase and improve as much of the downtown waterfront—blocks' worth, if possible—for recreational use. Recreation would have a whole new meaning after DX. "To achieve the above goals will require that the city and its businessmen recognize two essential facts, 1) that Bath downtown will never play the central and even regional role it once played as a major shopper-goods center, and 2) that the waterfront and the old colonial [sic] brick buildings from the past are perhaps the major downtown asset. Needed is some outstanding design talent to enhance the colonial image (not planting a few trees and calling it beautification), and a willingness by private merchants to spend money in partnership with the city to create an image and intimate flavor of a 19th century seaport."[34]

Merchants would never be more willing to face facts and spend money than after the DX contract was in the bag, so Atwood's plan looked attainable at last. In addition, the aroma of imminent prosperity had attracted outside developers. By 1969, City Council was negotiating with firms competing for the privilege of building a large hotel on the waterfront, presumably to service the steady traffic of bigwigs from Washington and transients attached to the gigantic project.

In Washington, deliberations about the program lagged on. The Navy, dismayed at the high bids, held out for cuts. Maine and Mississippi politicians lobbied tirelessly for their constituencies, looking for some sign that the construction bonanza was going their way, for the award would be a telling indicator of their political prestige. Bath chewed its nails.

DX AND THE RUMORS

BY VERN WARREN

BATH—Despite nearness of the 30-ship DD963 (DX) contract award date and accompanying rumors, outcome of the $2.5 billion program still seems uncertain.

The only sure thing is that those who know aren't talking and those talking don't know.

Rumors are rampant. Many Bath Iron Works personnel maintain award of the contract is being held up for the outcome of union negotiations. They theorize the award is held up so the union can't use the huge contract—if it comes to BIW—as a lever to gain higher wages.

Other BIW personnel, and Bath residents as well, say a decision has already been made to award the contract to BIW and the Navy is simply holding up the announcement for some reason. That assumption is based on recent visits to BIW from high ranking military and civilian officials. "Why would they be here if the contract is not coming to Bath?" one office worker who refused to be identified asked.

One man stopped in at the Times Record

> office recently to say he heard "right from the top" that BIW is being bought by Hughes Aircraft. . . .
>
> Those and other stories are common. The truth is hard to find.
>
> The Navy Department and the Pentagon still refuse to pin down the award date. . . .
>
> William E. Haggett, assistant to the president at BIW also denied any tie between union negotiations and contract award. "It just isn't so," he said. . . .
>
> *TIMES RECORD*, 7 APRIL 1970

In June 1970, the Navy Department spoke at last. The entire DX award would go to Ingalls Shipyard. Why? It was a matter of price. According to Haggett, "Litton had taken a dive to stay in the bidding . . . [although] we couldn't prove that." In the final round of bidding, the Navy had inserted a provision that "allowed the winner to reprice the contract forty-two months after the ships were awarded. Litton took advantage of that and dropped their price about $10 million a ship. We dropped our price about $1 million a ship. And where the prices had been virtually the same, after the third round Litton ended up being $9 million per ship under Bath. Now, once that low bid was in there, it was duck soup for Senator Stennis and southern politicians to say, 'They've got the low bid and the contract.' "[35]

As chairman of the Senate Armed Services Committee, Mississippi Senator John Stennis certainly swung a great deal of weight. But in terms of the Defense Department's procurement procedures, a price differential of $270 million was hard to ignore, even if, as was hoped in Bath, BIW's superior track record in destroyer construction made its bid more credible. Efforts by Senators Margaret Chase Smith and Edmund Muskie to effect a division of the contract were to no avail. In Bath, DX had sunk, taking down highways, highrises, hotels, hospitals, houses, and tax relief with it.

Losing DX generated fears and rumors of BIW's demise, or possibly its sale by Bath Industries. "The day before that decision was announced," Haggett recalled, "we were planning on a very large investment, large facilities, rapid buildup in manning, lots of training programs, bringing a large cadre of engineers into the community, planning people, hiring a lot of production workers. And at day's end, we recognized that it was the only opportunity around. The day after we lost, we were back thinking in terms of alternative programs that could keep the shipyard alive. Employment dropped and we went through all of those problems that virtually every shipyard was experiencing in the early seventies (except those few that had one of these large programs). There was a lot of pessimism in the community, in the work force, and a lot of concern in the management of the company about how we were going to keep this place going."[36]

The DX flop did in fact unleash a movement on the Bath Industries board to unload the Iron Works, but William Kyle's control was just too tight. Kyle, regarded by many as a calculating moneyman, defied such characterization not only by fighting to keep the shipyard but also by strongly backing BIW President Goodrich's post-DX proposal for massive capital improvements. All this in the face of a flat statement from the Navy that BIW did not fit into its future contracting plans.[37]

So it was that, having hit bottom, the yard began to make itself competitive. Engineers sent to European and Asian shipyards returned with enough data on the latest construction techniques to design a new facility that promised enormous savings in production costs. The key to the new system was the ability to prefabricate and preoutfit massive ship sections under indoor, climate-controlled circumstances. The look of the Iron Works began to change. A new assembly building, aptly dubbed "The Green Monster" by outraged aesthetes, began to sprawl along south Washington Street. But the real symbol of change was a giant level-luffing crane—"the biggest in the Western Hemisphere"—which towered 400 feet over the riverfront when assembled in 1973. By 1975, BIW had invested $15 million in its new production system.

The yard kept busy with three more American Export freighters, a design study for a new type of naval escort vessel, five tankers for the Military Sealift Command, and four advanced roll-on-roll-off ("ro-ro") containerships for the States Lines. These commercial vessels were the guinea pigs for BIW's new production system, which proved to be full of bugs. Production schedules slipped badly and costs climbed as the yard struggled to make the system live up to expectations. By 1974, design errors, production tie-

TIMES RECORD

Boys play on Bath Street in the shadow of BIW's Green Monster. Somewhere beyond lies the Kennebec River.

ups, and rising costs of materials forced BIW to declare an $11 million loss, the second time in Goodrich's tenure that the yard had gone into the red.

This catastrophic loss, along with a bad year for Bath Industries generally, prompted still another administrative shake-up. Kyle brought in a pair of young turnaround specialists, Byron Radaker and Eddie Nicholson, to join his corporate team in Milwaukee and reverse Bath Industries' decline. The actions of Radaker and Nicholson rubbed a great many managers the wrong way, especially along the Kennebec. One of their first acts was to rename the corporation Congoleum in recognition of the relative importance of that side of the business. BIW, which had provided the financial leverage to organize Kyle's conglomerate in the first place, now took a back seat.

Radaker and Nicholson pursued the proverbial bottom line with a vengeance—selling, closing, or consolidating several subsidiaries and warning the rest to produce targeted profits or else. Nicholson told BIW brass that in view of its massive capital improvements, its performance was unacceptable; Congoleum, he said, could earn more by putting its capital in a savings account. Unless performance improved dramatically, Congoleum would divest itself of the shipyard.

Action followed words. Goodrich was made Chairman of the Board at BIW. He was replaced as president in July 1975 by a strong manager and manufacturing executive: John F. Sullivan. Sullivan's role was that of expediter and morale-builder; he had no shipbuilding experience. What he did have, he soon learned, was a modern and well-equipped shipyard with great potential, if it could iron out its new production system's problems and restore morale among disoriented managers and workers. Best of all, Sullivan found that BIW had its foot in the Navy's door once again.

In October 1973, BIW had received a contract to build the *Oliver Hazard Perry*, a prototype missile frigate whose design had been collaboratively developed by the Iron Works. By the time of Sullivan's arrival, the company was beginning outright construction of the *Perry*, the yard's first warship in ten years. Having at last mastered its sophisticated production system, BIW was able to demonstrate such productivity and cost saving that Congress authorized a fifty-ship program of *Perry* class (FFG) frigates. The Iron Works was again on the threshold of a long-term and lucrative relationship with the Navy.

THE DUKE STEALS THE SHOW AND THE CROWD LOVES IT

BY FAITH WOODMAN

BATH—Film star John Wayne was cast again in the role of "hero" Saturday as he "pushed" the 3,500 ton USS Oliver Hazard Perry down the ways and into the Kennebec River delighting thousands of spectators.

"The Duke," a guest of Bath Iron Works (BIW), and its parent company, Congoleum Corp., was a major attraction at the launching and stole the show by a perfect sense of timing.

After the champagne bottles were broken over the ship's bow at the end of the ceremonies, the Perry was scheduled to immediately slide down the ways and into the Kennebec River. But the frigate didn't budge.

And it wasn't until the attempts of 14 workers, using 50-ton air rams under the hull, and the tugboat Bath straining at the Perry's stern, did the ship finally move after a suspenseful two minute lapse. But all their efforts were out of the crowd's view. The crowd could only see Wayne and other dignitaries on the christening platform beneath the ship's bow.

Sen. Edmund S. Muskie and Rep. David Emery offered a little congressional muscle to the frigate's bow, but still it wouldn't move.

BATH IRON WORKS

> Wayne then casually strode across the platform and gave the Perry an effortless push. As he did the ship obediently slid down the ways. The crowd cheered and the horns from the nearby pleasure boat fleet tooted in salute. . . .
>
> *TIMES RECORD*, 27 SEPTEMBER 1976

The September 1976 launching of the *Perry* was a joyous one indeed for Bath. The company's profitability now showed the remarkable reversal demanded by the Milwaukee hotshots. Starting with a modest $1 million in 1975, the company's profit figures climbed rapidly, year after year, as additional naval and commercial contracts flowed in. Radaker and Nicholson dropped their talk of selling off the Cinderella of Congoleum, and BIW went on to capture the corporate title for return on investment. It was probably BIW's dazzling performance as a cash cow that motivated Congoleum's top management to enact a leveraged buyout of stock that took the conglomerate private by 1979.

BIW's long, agonizing haul from DX to FFG had taken the Shipbuilding City on a decade-long roller-coaster ride; but by the latter seventies, the company's future was secure for years to come. Much of the BIW story was played out in boardrooms and offices a long way from the Kennebec, a fact that escaped few Bath citizens in the seventies. In the meantime, the city, left high and dry when DX had vanished, was finding an independent identity.

Bath's road out of downtown shabbiness and public apathy was a long one. When DX had dashed hopes for the city's rescue, gloom once again set in. For a while, the most visible reminders of progress—although few called them that—were the frustrating, seemingly never-ending tie-ups caused by paving and sewer operations. Holes and detours on south Washington Street ("the Ho Chi Minh Trail") confounded traffic to and from BIW and kept Harry Ring and City Council under perpetual fire. So did the city's perennial battles over school budgets and municipal wages.

The post-DX letdown was not as bitter as the aftermath of urban renewal, but the similarities of the two fiascoes were unmistakable. In John Morse's view, the bottom might have fallen out had the Navy's repudiation of BIW been common knowledge: "After the DX was lost, the Navy told the Iron Works, 'Well, you'd better just go home and board up the doors, because we don't have any use for you anymore.' There was a period there that it probably wasn't splashed across the front page of the paper or anything like that, but the word was around town that unless Bath could come up with some new rabbit to pull out of the hat, that there wasn't that much future in shipbuilding. . . . Despite the fact that these things had been said and were being whispered about on the street, I don't think there was ever anything in the press announcing that. So . . . , perhaps not all the people knew how serious the situation was."[38]

But ten years of unproductive public debate had taken its toll. Citizens were just plain weary of Bath's chronic problems, especially when it came to the downtown. In addition, Bath people, like their counterparts across the nation, were pummeled by social pressures of the sixties and the prevalent sense that the nation's fabric had begun to unravel.

POLICE CHIEF SAYS DRUGS BECOMING INCREASING PROBLEM IN THE AREA

BATH—"We know that LSD, marijuana and other dangerous drugs are in the Bath-Brunswick area, and we're working on it," says Bath police Chief Robert E. Wagner, Jr. "This is a completely new area of investigation for this department, and for that matter for all police departments in this state." . . .

The police chief said that when he speaks of drugs being in the Bath-Brunswick area, he means specifically that they are within the city of Bath, and within the town of Brunswick, and in the other towns in this section. "We have the names of users in this area, including Bath," Wagner said.

. . . Wagner said he does not mean to alarm people, and that the extent of the use of drugs here, so far at least, seems to be more among youths slightly older than high school age, and that as far as he knows, use of drugs at Morse High School is minimal. . . .

TIMES RECORD, 24 OCTOBER 1968

WHO SHOULD RULE ON SHORT SKIRTS AND LONG HAIR?

"Forasmuch as the wearing of long haire after the manner of Russians and barbarous Indians has begun to invade New England contrary to the rule of God's word which

sayth it is a shame for a man to wear long haire . . . , wee the magistrates . . . doe declare and manifest our dislike and detestation against the wearing of such long haire, as against a thing uncivil and unmanly. . . . "
—Harvard College Book, 1649.

Three hundred years later and the cut of a youth's hair is still the concern of his well-clipped elder, although it is expressed in somewhat less shaggy language.

But there have been a few changes in the situation.

. . . the most significant change has been in attitude. A survey of the Bath-Brunswick area indicates that adults have given a little ground and are more tolerant of a boy's long hair and a girl's short skirt—but only to a point.

. . . Bath School Superintendent Clifford P. Tinkham explained that the school board's general guideline . . . is that personal appearance should not be such that it disrupts normal classroom activity.

. . . "We've tried to be reasonable," says Principal Moody Flint of Bath Junior high School. "Our only complaint is when a student's appearance distracts from normal classroom procedure."

. . . Flint said many parents are delighted that school officials take their sons in hand and convince them to get a haircut. This sentiment was backed up by a number of parents who were interviewed.

. . . Principal Raymond Farnham said Morse High School has nothing in writing regarding accepted personal appearance standards. Instead, he said, students are told at the start of the school year what is expected of them.

. . . "Fad clothing," Farnham said, is suitable for summertime and downtown wear, but not for school.

"If the girls want to wear miniskirts downtown, O.K., but they shouldn't wear them to school," he said.

"A quick word in the hall" is usually sufficient, said Farnham. . . .

TIMES RECORD, 18 APRIL 1967

LENGTH OF HAIR DISPUTE IN BATH LEADS TO A STUDENT'S SUSPENSION

BATH—James Hennessey, son of former State Legislator William Hennessey and Mrs. Hennessey of West Bath, was suspended from Morse High School yesterday for refusing to cut his hair which is longer than school board policy in Bath allows.

Hennessey, a senior at Morse, was given a chance to tell his side of the story yesterday in a meeting with the school board, school superintendent Clifford P. Tinkham, and Morse Principal Jascha French, as well as his own parents.

But, according to Tinkham this morning, the Hennessey boy refused to agree to have his hair cut. Therefore, Tinkham said, the board voted unanimously to suspend him from attending school until he does have it cut. . . .

Hennessey's brother Michael, a sophomore at Morse, also reportedly has hair too long for school policy. . . .

Michael told the Times Record he plans to follow his older brother's example and refuse to cut his hair even if he is suspended from classes because of his refusal to comply.

The Hennesseys' hair styles "created a disruptive influence in the school," Tinkham said today. "He (James) was challenging the right of the school board to have such a policy. . . . We hate to do things like this. . . .

"If you lose the fabric of control (of students), what is the future of education?" the school superintendent asked, emphasizing that the teachers and school administrators have authority and control over their students. Otherwise education would be chaotic, with no order at all, he said.

. . . James Hennessey was reached late this morning by telephone, and he said the school board's philosophy . . . "reflects the attitudes of society, generally speaking, in the United States. I don't believe anyone should lose his education just because of his appear-

> ance. To me, that's wrong. But apparently they figured my appearance was 'disrupting.' That's the word they used, 'disrupting.'"
>
> *TIMES RECORD*, 7 FEBRUARY 1969

Socially, politically, and economically speaking, the late sixties were a time of massive uncertainty in Bath, briefly reversed but finally made worse by the failure of the DX miracle cure. In the words of Ted Bradbury, a relative newcomer who defeated Red McMann for City Council in 1969, "I don't think in those days that this community had a very good sense of what it is to be a community. The people here for the most part didn't give a damn about each other. I can remember people saying to me, 'What do I care if downtown merchants make a living or not? What's that to do with me? If I don't have any kids in school, why should I have to pay a lot of taxes so that your kids can go to school? Why should I shop in downtown Bath if I feel like driving to Brunswick? I don't care if this community succeeds or it doesn't.' That was a very predominant, prevalent attitude."[39]

Yet the early seventies witnessed an extraordinary revival of public spirit, brought about by the joint efforts of merchants, city fathers, and historic preservationists, who at last perceived their common interests. Collectively, these groups transformed the city and restored its declining civic pride. Coincidence played a part in this revival; so did a few isolated incidents that for a while seemed unrelated.

When Colonel Henry Owen's history of Bath appeared in 1936, it contained an author's caveat: Owen had purposely avoided the maritime side of Bath's history because another book dealing with that topic would someday be written by Mark Hennessy. Hennessy, a local boy who had reported on Bath for the *Portland Press Herald* since 1925, had made it his life's ambition to write such a volume. In 1937, he completed *The Sewall Ships of Steel*, commemorating the twilight of Bath's Age of Sail, and over the years he assembled a bulging archive of research materials in the basement of his Center Street home. "I think Mark was one of the most popular men in the community," recalled Ray Small. " . . . He was good at his work. He had a cottage downriver right near me, so I used to see a lot of him. . . . Mark's place was up there in the woods a little. I could hear his typewriter going up there on the porch; he was working on that *Sewall Ships of Steel*. He'd go down there where it was quiet and work there during the summers."[40] Hennessy was also a fixture around downtown Bath. To young Dave Swearingen, who one day would edit the *Times Record*, he was both a good reporter and a picturesque character: "Mark often wore a trench coat similar to those depicted in cartoon works about newspaper reporters, but there was one sure way to tell the difference in a rainstorm. When it stormed,

MAINE MARITIME MUSEUM

Mark Hennessy.

he was the guy walking up Front Street smoking his pipe with the bowl upside down."[41]

Back in the thirties, Hennessy and such kindred spirits as Harry Webber (himself an expert on Bath's maritime affairs) began work on a maritime museum for the city. In view of Bath's rich and varied history, such an organization was long overdue and altogether necessary for civic pride. Another kindred spirit, Sumner Sewall, had taken a step of his own in that direction by displaying nautical memorabilia at the Sewall Company office for the pleasure of buffs and summer people, and he could testify to the popularity a museum might enjoy in the Shipbuilding City. In 1936, Hennessy, Webber, Sewall, and others established the Kennebec Marine Museum, Inc. The organization collected and exhibited noteworthy artifacts in City Hall. Whatever plans it might have had for further expansion were sidetracked by World War II and never subsequently resumed. The pictures and models adorning City Hall were gradually removed or left to fade into the institutional decor.

Bath's maritime history existed mostly in memory until 1962, when several interested parties established the Marine Research Society of Bath, dedicated to providing Hennessy with the necessary support to produce a regional maritime history. Enough money was raised to enable Hennessy, in the fall of 1964, to leave the *Press Herald* and begin writing. A few weeks after starting work, however, Hennessy learned he was terminally ill. He spent his last year of life cataloguing his files for some subsequent scholar's use. He died in September 1965. His project was given to William Avery Baker, a noted naval architect, scholar, and director of the Hart Nautical Museum at M.I.T. Baker's massive *Maritime History of Bath, Maine and the*

Kennebec River Region (1973) was a fitting, respectful tribute to Hennessy's forbearance.

Meanwhile, the Marine Research Society had involved itself in reviving the defunct local maritime museum, an idea the Blackwell Report had institutionalized as part of its erstwhile waterfront rehabilitation plan. In 1964, while the city was embroiled in the urban renewal flap, the Bath Marine Museum opened a storefront exhibit in the old Stetson's Furniture building at Center and Water streets. Its growth from that point on was truly remarkable.

The museum movement had three things going for it, not the least of which was the fact that everyone from Hennessy and Sewall on had been right: Bath's colorful past was important, interesting, and attractive to salts and landlubbers alike. In addition, the idea had appeal for well-heeled scions of Bath's old-money seafaring families, who could provide both the necessary artifacts and the funding to care for them. Finally, the society was overendowed with civic activists who provided the right spark. As Bill Mussenden put it: "Don Small was actually the first president of the Marine Research Society of Bath, and not much happened for the first year. Then Charlie Burden and myself were asked to join the Board of Trustees, which we did. I wound up succeeding Don Small, and the first thing I did was appoint Charlie as chairman of the museum committee, which was one of the brighter things I ever did in my life. He did a wonderful job, and we went on from there. . . . It was a success. As I recall it, we broke even the first year."[42]

The second year, thanks to the donation of a stately house on upper Washington Street by Camilla Sewall Edge, the museum moved into scenic and spacious quarters. Mussenden dropped out at that point, but Burden, who stumped for the museum with almost religious fervor, continued to be the sparkplug for growth and ambitious projects. By the late sixties, the institution had added an archive, filled "Sewall House" with artifacts, and was wrestling with the classic museum problem of how to manage growth and finances. To that end, it began to add professionally trained staff in 1972.

The museum board, a varied group of city leaders, civic activists, genteel retirees, and devotees of maritime history, was often perplexed by such a surfeit of opportunities that, at times, its reach exceeded its grasp. A city as historically rich as Bath, where the local heritage had for so long been dormant, offered limitless options for conservation of historic buildings, acquisition of old watercraft, accumulation of important artifacts, and publication of scholarly studies. The early tendency was to try everything. The trick, as trustees and staff members discovered to their distress, was identifying the options that were practical and, in the long run, affordable. By the mid-seventies, having acquired the dormant Percy & Small Shipyard in the South End (the last working yard from the old sailing days and

MAINE MARITIME MUSEUM

Sewall House, site of the Bath Marine Museum after 1965.

remarkably well preserved, thanks partly to its recent use as a Sears warehouse), the museum found itself land-poor: spread over several widely separated sites and in deep financial trouble. A massive fund drive and the retention of a permanent professional fund-raiser averted disaster, but it was henceforward clear that strict accounting had to replace the exciting, Quixotic ventures of earlier years.

The richness of its acquisitions gave the Bath Marine Museum national importance. Its value as a repository was doubled by the fact that it was, strangely, the only organization of a historical nature in the Shipbuilding City. And it served another important purpose by providing an inspirational rallying point for a wide variety of civic-minded individuals who shared an interest in Bath's historical identity.

Although there had been much talk about the historic significance of Bath's downtown architecture among the city's leadership, what focused the attention of the community at large upon preservation was a 1965 decision by two church congregations to reunite after more than a century and a half of separation.

Bath tradition has it that in 1801, members of the city's Congregational parish divided when they fell into disagreement about which way their proposed new church building should face.[43] There may have been other doctrinal differences among members, but in any case, by 1804, Bath had two Congregational churches. During the 1840s, both congregations moved to newer, larger buildings. One was the handsome, transitional Gothic Winter Street Church; the other, only two blocks south (and, incidentally,

MAINE MARITIME MUSEUM

Winter Street Church
as seen from the city park.

MAINE MARITIME MUSEUM

Central Church.

facing Washington Street in the same direction), was an English-style Carpenter Gothic masterpiece known as the Central Church.

Sally Haggett, a member of the Winter Street Church, reminisced later about the parallel development of the two congregations. "We were two blocks away from each other, and yet we carried on our religious activities completely independently. There were very few times when the two churches got together for anything. I knew people who attended the other church, I generally knew the other minister, but we didn't have joint fellowship days, swaps from the pulpit, that sort of thing. We operated completely independently two blocks away, and in a town of 10,000. We weren't mad at each other any more, although each obviously had pride in their own building and in their own minister, and in their own congregation. The architecture of the two buildings showed some of the division there, I think, in that we had one building that was . . . more of a traditional New England church. The other one . . . with the flying buttresses and the stained-glass windows, and the more English type of architecture. Those two kinds of architecture probably stood in our way a bit because you get very used to what you grow up with. We found this with our parishioners: they liked their own building."[44] By the 1950s, it had become evident to each congregation that it was in their best spiritual and financial interests to combine. It took years for that idea to win general acceptance, however. In July 1965, after lengthy and fastidiously diplomatic negotiations, both congregations approved a merger. One of the many sensitive issues to be resolved was that of a single site. In 1966, a joint building committee, no doubt attempting a Solomonic decision, recommended that both churches be superseded and that Winter Street's be razed so that a new church could go up at that site.[45] A published sketch of the proposed new building revealed a commodious structure whose cinderblock-and-steel construction would be veneered by clapboards and garnished with a perfunctorily "colonial" steeple.

Some Winter Street parishioners were of course aghast at the idea of tearing down a beautiful building that had been a local landmark for twelve decades. So was Peter Cox, who editorialized against its destruction. Acknowledging that economics and interparish diplomacy were important considerations in the decision to raze Winter Street Church, Cox added that "we simply want to introduce a third consideration: Aesthetics. We think the contribution the physical appearance of Winter Street Church makes to Bath should be considered. We think the members of the congregation who do consider this will be doing others in the city of Bath a great favor."[46] Other aesthetes joined the cry to save Winter Street Church, but not enough of them were parishioners. Late in May 1966, church members voted by secret ballot to replace the edifice. Responding to the mounting displeasure of preservationists, who knew little and cared less about internal stress on the merged congregations but who couldn't imagine the city skyline without Winter Street's lofty spire, John Morse, a member of the church's building committee, acknowledged the allure of the old church: "Morse confessed to 'having a love affair with the Winter Street Church steeple . . . ,' but declared, 'while it is a delight to the eye, it is a despair to the pocketbook.'

"He said the problem is that the steeple 'is so massive that it crushes itself.' Morse said it periodically develops leaks and the resulting water damages the interior of the church."[47] What Morse was speaking to, however, was an issue bigger than water damage and the desire of upper Washington Street's silk stocking set to keep the neighborhood looking nice. Winter Street was a historic fixture in Bath and integral to the city park's inviting ambience. If there was anything to the preservationist groundswell, or Atwood's plan, or the marine museum's dynamism, keeping that old building was a test case.

Preservationists had meanwhile contacted the National Trust for Historic Preservation and the Boston-based Society for the Preservation of New England Antiquities in an effort to establish the church's bona fides as an architectural monument. There was enough opposition to earn the building a stay of execution as other options were explored. But whose business was it, after all, to decide the fate of Winter Street Church? The issue so troubled parishioners that a movement arose to redivide the two congregations, although that option eventually was rejected. No further progress was made on the problem until the two co-pastors had resigned and a new pastor, the Reverend Ellis F. Eaton, was elected by the united congregation.

Eaton possessed the skills of a diplomat and no emotional commitment to either church building. He asked for and received a year to study the problem. In October 1969, Eaton recommended that the congregation dispose of both churches in a manner consistent with their architectural importance and build a new church on an entirely different site. These proposals were overwhelmingly accepted by the congregation.

At that point, the preservationist issue seemed to have gone elsewhere, because no concrete effort coalesced to save Winter Street. By 1971, the congregation had acquired land on Congress Avenue, approved plans for a new building of contemporary design, and started construction. But who would take Winter Street off its hands? Developers, it turned out, were interested in the choice location but not the white elephant standing on it. The most tempting offer, from the Bath Housing Authority, proposed the construction of a highrise apartment building for the elderly at the site. Pressed for money, the church's committee was sorely tempted by such propositions.

Just one week before the congregation was to vote on developers' offers, a small group of private citizens organized as Sagadahoc Preservation, Inc., with the initial objective of acquiring and preserving Winter Street Church. Sagadahoc Preservation, Inc. (SPI) was the brainchild of Dorothy Erickson of Bath, a member of the United Church who attended a meeting of the Maine League of Historical Societies in Bangor in May 1971. At the conference, she was encouraged by Earle Shettleworth, Jr., an architectural historian and preservationist (and future director of the Maine Historic Preservation Commission) to organize a community action group to rescue Winter Street Church.[48]

Returning to Bath, Erickson contacted kindred spirits, including Charlie Burden and Diane Francis, the latter a member of the United Church and a highly motivated civic activist, especially when it came to Bath's historic flavor. That was the nucleus for a hard-core group of awakened preservationists who formed SPI inside of two weeks, just before parishioners decided the fate of Winter Street Church, and in time to raise a small installment toward the purchase of that historic structure: about $5,000, a tenth of the rumored commercial value of the property.

On the Sunday before his congregation met to decide the fate of the old church, Reverend Eaton preached a sermon on "The Disposal of Church Properties." Three days later, assembled parishioners voted to accept SPI's meager $5,000 as payment for the church building.

The elated new owners, however, were now sitting atop a financial iceberg. Extensive fund-raising allowed them to make headway against the structure's deterioration. In 1973, the building was deeded to the expanding Bath Marine Museum, which exhibited and held symposia at the site. But Winter Street Church never outgrew its reputation as a money pit. The celebrated steeple, found to be almost two feet out of plumb at the top, was removed in 1981, and, for several years, Bath observers adjusted to the sight of the classic spire sitting incongruously in front of the truncated building

TIMES RECORD

Rebuilding Winter Street Church's truncated steeple in 1983.

while contractors, SPI activists, and museum brass hashed over the frightful expense of a proper recap. By the mid-eighties, the spire once again was in place, adding a priceless accent to the city skyline, but the church was in need of another new identity. The Maine Maritime Museum, as it was now called, was expanding dramatically at the South End, and had returned the church to SPI for readaptation. By then, Bath's Congregational churchgoers were peacefully established in their new quarters out on Congress Avenue.

Soon after saving Winter Street Church, SPI undertook the rescue of Central Church. In this effort the preservationists were aided by Jack Doepp,

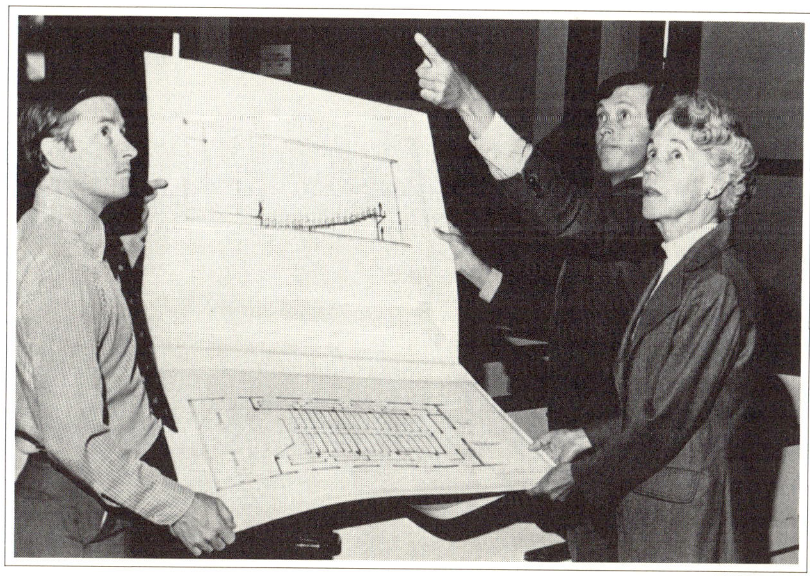

TIMES RECORD

Jack Doepp points the way to a performing arts center for supporters John Chapman and Jane Jermain in 1976.

a magnetic young New York designer of theater sets whose work with the Brunswick Summer Theater had encouraged him to establish a permanent performance center in the area. Doepp, who was willing to work gratis for two years toward accomplishing his goal, came to symbiotic terms with SPI in 1977. Central Church was recycled as a theater.

The new performing arts center came to be known as the Chocolate Church because it had been puristically repainted in its original—and to some, hideous—brown color. ("That's taking historic preservation too far," remarked one observer in disbelief at the paint job.) Doepp, meanwhile, had ambitious plans to modify the interior for better audience comfort and performance standards, despite inevitable financial risks. Local citizens once again rose to the occasion and organized as the nonprofit Performing Arts Center at Bath (PACB), to qualify the venture for state and federal assistance.

It proved to be a major struggle. Gate receipts at the Chocolate Church covered performers' fees but made almost no headway against the $50,000 annual expenses of maintaining the structure. The bedazzled PACB board soon realized it needed a business-oriented manager and a theater specialist, but could not afford both. The dilemma induced a great deal of acrimony on the board. In 1980, Doepp, whose dynamic presence had become synonymous with PACB, returned to New York. Thereafter, the center eked out a dogged but difficult existence under a succession of directors, living on grant monies and the proverbial generosity of Bath's deep-pocketed citizens.

By the 1980s, the Center for the Arts at the Chocolate Church (CACC), as it was now called, offered a wide variety of programs: local dramatic and musical productions; concerts by visiting classical, jazz, and folk musicians; comedy presentations; and art exhibits. Besides providing a spot in which local people could enjoy live performances by out-of-town artists, the center provided a showcase for the region's creative artists and performers, who were migrating to Maine in ever-increasing numbers. But the building showed serious structural deterioration, necessitating exhaustive fund-raising by its tireless supporters to maintain the historic structure and, eventually, to upgrade the interior to professional acceptability. Meanwhile, CACC events took place in satellite locations such as Winter Street Church or Morse High's auditorium.

The indefatigable determination of the supporters of the museum, SPI, and the Chocolate Church—in many cases the same individuals—was partly a throwback to Bath's philanthropic traditions; but in another sense, it constituted an interesting new phenomenon, for it aroused the interest of able individuals previously uninvolved in civic affairs. Such activities had special appeal for retired executives with time on their hands; eager young professionals seeking a nonpolitical route to community leadership; elitist members of the teacup set who saw a chance to give Bath a little polish;

and people of all backgrounds with a professional or amateur devotion to art, history, and the material culture with which Bath was so lavishly endowed. As one insider commented, "All those people who don't show up at Morse High basketball games now have something to do with their leisure time." All those people also constituted a prodigious new source of talent and civic determination that, during the seventies, brought its weight to bear on the malingering issue of Bath's downtown.

Herbert (Bud) Caverly, elected to City Council in 1968, was a dentist by profession and a man with deep roots in Bath. An informed, outspoken, maverick conservative, Caverly seemed to thrive on the national confusion of the sixties and its local repercussions, and he had an unusual zest for press and radio coverage, which he cultivated to shake up right- and left-wingers alike. Over the next fifteen years, Caverly remained a self-conscious gadfly, although his positions sometimes riled opponents and, as in 1970, lost him voter support. Describing his first days as a councillor, Caverly recalled a confrontation with the venerable Charlie MacDonald: "We'd get together [over dinner] and talk about who was going to be chairman and who was going to do what and everything. I remember old Charlie MacDonald saying, 'Who the hell are you? You don't represent anybody. You're a doctor.' I said, 'You old bastard, I get one vote the same as you do, and you're going to find out who I am!' And, you know, Charlie and I became the closest friends you would ever see, personally, politically, and everything. But we started off like that. . . . Charlie respected someone that did his job, did his homework. You didn't have to agree with him all the time if you did your job."[49]

Like MacDonald, Caverly spent a great deal of time on homework, but the style of the latter was substantially more strident. Caverly had a way of making even motherhood issues sound controversial. For example, during the period of the DX expectation, he went on record that "It's about time the City of Bath, instead of saying we're going to live or die because of DX," pursue other options, and that "Bath, Maine, should get off its rear end" and entice other industries to locate in town, as though that had somehow escaped previous notice.[50] After DX went south, Caverly and his Council friend Ted Bradbury tried to drum up a City Council commitment to support the historic seaport ideas of John Atwood. The historic district idea was hardly new, but, after DX, it too was in jeopardy. Caverly went to the Planning Board. "At that Planning Board meeting, I made a statement. I said, 'Look, we voted down urban renewal, we've lost the DX program. Bath can . . . do one of two things. It can either do something or it can die.' That's the way things were. I said, 'Why not take our heritage and what we have down here for buildings and go backward? . . . Let's go backward . . . and restore downtown as nineteenth century.' [The response was] 'Dumb!' 'Stupid!' 'Who wants that?' " One of Caverly's pet projects for the imagined downtown seaport was a motorized trolley car to circle the business district and provide a note of nostalgic atmosphere. "Stupidest goddamn thing they ever heard."[51]

One reason, certainly, for City Hall's reticence about downtown restoration was that its advocates collectively presented a surrealistic view of the past. Before DX, Atwood had advised city fathers to try for a general impression, not a painstaking restoration; good advice, in view of tight money and the recent demolition of many of the downtown's earliest structures. When Atwood had called for a "colonial" seaport, he apparently meant one that reflected Bath's nineteenth-century heyday, inasmuch as there were no colonial buildings in the district. To Caverly, looking backward meant reviving the downtown's turn-of-the-century ambience, complete with streetcars. Another "historical" touch discussed at the time was the possibility of a "pirate ship" that would cruise the Kennebec for the amusement of visitors, an idea that was enough to send preservationists heading for the hills. Another motif was to adorn all of Front Street's stores with a copper awning that would pull the group together architecturally while suggesting something vaguely quaint about old-time Bath. If nothing else, these fanciful invocations of bygone days showed that there were many ways to reinvent the wheel.

The other stumbling block to going backward was, as always, financial. Caverly, Bradbury, and another forceful advocate, Bud Shepard, insisted that the project should be accomplished with local funding in the event that HUD or other governmental agencies declined to help. That was enough to send such councillors as Charlie ("Where is this money coming from?") MacDonald heading for the hills.[52]

But, at the risk of a pun, history was on the side of the advocates. Bath really looked as though it would die after DX. There was another difference between this push and previous renovation schemes: The city now was home to an emerging cadre of preservationist go-getters who did not flinch at big projects. Robert Chadwick, the new, dynamic director of the Chamber of Commerce, prodded Council into creating the Ad Hoc Committee on Downtown Restoration to study the situation and make recommendations for municipal action. Bath Iron Works donated $5,000 to get the committee started and urged that it choose John Morse, popularly labeled as the man "who owns half of downtown Bath," as chairman. Having the downtown's shrewdest, biggest, and quietest landlord on board was an auspicious demonstration of commitment.[53]

The committee included Morse, Atwood, Caverly, Shepard, Chadwick, Charlie Burden, Harry Ring, City Solicitor Carl (Skip) Stinson, City Codes Officer Alden Grant, and six other citizens. According to Morse, "The plan was to get the city to do their part first, up front. This would then cause the property owners to fall into line and redo their stores."[54] As a beginning, Atwood obligingly reduced the melange of restoration ideas to a basic, "twelve-feet-up-and-twelve-feet-out" cosmetic facelift of Front Street: widened, brick sidewalks, pocket parks, benches, shrubs, replacement of existing signs with simple wooden signboards, and installation of a single, awninglike canopy extending along all storefronts.[55] The plan was expandable according to how much money became available. Atwood had raised hopes that half of the public expense would be covered by HUD. In September 1971, there was a heated public hearing on spending city monies for such a project, a replay of all the old arguments for and against urban renewal. The proposal was indeed controversial, but it was officially approved as a working concept by city fathers.

City Council's acceptance of the necessity of sprucing up the downtown was an important milestone, because activists could at last stop debating the principle of the idea and turn their energies to the task at hand. But moving from that generality to the gritty specifics of even a modest facelift was going to be difficult. As it stood, the project fell between two stools: The proposed quick fix was too piddling and historically slapdash to please diehard preservationists; yet it looked too costly to hidebound conservatives, who were bound to resist expenses that appeared frivolous or even harebrained. Nor did federal funds materialize to defuse that problem. A month after its acceptance, Morse sadly reported that "the program doesn't fit for beans with anything the federal government has to offer."[56] Persistent and argumentative approaches to HUD failed to change Uncle Sam's mind. Without such help, the city's cost was estimated at $365,000, and that meant a larger tax burden—if the conservative Council would accede to the Ad Hoc Committee's recommendations. Council's cooperation was by no means certain. In May 1973, a local radio station editorialized that "despite the enthusiasm of the Ad Hoc Committee . . . the whole concept of Bath restoration has never really caught on. . . . With all that has to be done in Bath . . . , no councilman in his right mind could authorize $350,000 to be spent on restoration ahead of such things as sewers, schools, streets, or trying to lower the tax rate rather than raise it!!! . . . "[57]

BATH'S NEW PALACE THEATER IS NO MORE

BY MARILYN BENNETT

BATH—"Well, I guess that's the end of the Grand Olde Opry," an interested on-looker said as the last section of the Bath Opera House on Center Street came crashing to the ground. Workmen and heavy equipment completed the tedious job of demolishing Bath's last theater and all that remains is a tidy smooth-surfaced lot.

. . . "It was a damned hard job," foreman Jack Shaw commented on razing the theater, when the last of the debris was hauled away. "It took longer than we thought—mostly because we salvaged anything we could as we went along."

Bricks, stained [glass] windows, the marquee and other materials were sold to individuals or kept by the owner Nicholas Kakos or went to the demolition contractor—whatever the agreement happened to be.

"It's too bad," some said, as the work progressed. Small groups of people gathered daily to watch the proceedings. "She really doesn't want to come down, does she," one retired man said as the clamshell hammered away at the well-constructed building which resisted the battle. . . .

TIMES RECORD, 16 NOVEMBER 1971

DENTAL CLINIC HAS A HOME

BY ROBERT FORKEY

BATH—Bath Iron Works Corporation deeded some land and the former Bath Railroad Station building to the city last night. BIW stipulated the building be made available to the Jess[i]e Albert Memorial Clinic.

The clinic, organizing since February, will provide dental care for children of the poor in Lincoln and Sagadahoc counties. William E. Haggett, BIW's vice president for marketing, presented the city council with a warranty deed for the property. A one-dollar fee was charged the city to make the transaction legal.

. . . The federal government funded the project with $37,000 as of July 1. To get that, workers for the clinic, including Mrs. Hattie Webber of Merrymeeting Community Action Inc. and Mrs. Pat Christopher of Wiscasset, had to raise a local share of $12,500. Some of that money is still in pledges. . . .

TIMES RECORD, 22 JULY 1971

'EVERYTHING WILL BE VERY MOD'

The 'Grok Shop' All Set to Open

BATH—The Grok Shop, a combination boutique and head shop, is opening Monday on Front Street in the former Maine Coastal Electronics Building. Owners and operators are Skip and Jeanette Greenleaf and Dusty and Kay Lambert, two young area couples.

Geared to attract young and old alike, the shop will carry clothes designed by Wayne Harris, unusual games and puzzles, records, tapes, scented and sand candles, jewelry, belts, hats and other accessories. In fact, it will carry everything that can be found in most other head shops and more.

Among the Grok Shop's more unusual characteristics is a beautiful hand painted design on the window, a huge zodiac sign which forms the focal point of one wall, a b[l]ack light room with b[l]acklight posters, a free visual effects display and a game corner.

. . . Speaking about the store, Dusty said, "everything will be very mod" and clothes will be "one of a kind originals."

According to Dusty, the two couples chose to locate in Bath because "the need is great" and because the location "offers all kinds of opportunities." . . .

TIMES RECORD, 21 MAY 1971

By 1971, the creaky issue of downtown renewal and its handmaiden, higher taxes, were again losing momentum. But late that year, flushed with its Winter Street victory, the newly formed SPI turned its attention to the downtown. Things began to happen. Taking its own approach to restoration, the fledgling group hired architectural consultant James Ballou of Salem, Massachusetts, to tour the area with members and thereby generate ideas on how individual structures could be treated to improve the basic theme. That marked the beginning of a unique, three-way partnership among the Ad Hoc Committee, the Chamber of Commerce, and SPI, a union designed to formulate a long-range program and win its acceptance by the Planning Board, City Council, property owners, and downtown merchants—groups never known for their ability to work together in the past, or for any devotion to historic preservation. The difference this time, however, was the determination of several diverse organizations in the city to mobilize cooperatively to achieve an agreed-upon goal. The convergence of energy that resulted infused new vitality into Bath's civic and political affairs.

To establish a visible presence, SPI, the Ad Hoc Committee, and the Chamber of Commerce printed up "Downtown Restoration" stationery bearing all three organizational letterheads and began to gather information to fortify and expand the restoration concept.[58] Pulling together, the groups practiced a symbiotic division of labor. While the Ad Hoc Committee worked on improvements that could be made at public expense, SPI investigated steps that were affordable and possibly beneficial to property owners and shopkeepers, always pushing for more substantial and authentic restoration. To that end, volunteer artists Judy Barrington and Jim Stilphen, assisted by dogged researchers who combed Bath for antique photographs of Front Street and studied traditional paint schemes, prepared an enormous rendition of what Front Street would look like when properly restored.

Assuming that seeing would be believing, the joint organizations held a public meeting at Winter Street Church to unveil the SPI panorama. Only seven businessmen attended. Undeterred, SPI developed a new approach, tackling downtown merchants one at a time. At every meeting with a prospect, the Downtown Restoration people came well prepared, complete with an artist's rendition of how the building in question would look after salutary changes, and a data sheet suggesting color schemes, window and door treatment, and special structural considerations. By late 1973, twenty-six presentations had been made by SPI volunteers, representing many thousands of dollars of contributed time and effort.

Ray Clemons, owner of Wilson's Drugstore, took the first step, renovating his storefront in 1973. In October of that year, a heartened City Council accepted the Ad Hoc Committee's Atwood-based agenda of brick sidewalks, landscaping, pocket parks, benches, and modified streetlights. (Because it would be expensive to build and difficult to mount, the proposed block-long canopy had been discarded—much to the relief, no doubt, of preservationists.) City Council thus moved from agreement in principle to a promise to participate. As preparations for the municipal improvements were made over the next two years, more storefronts were restored privately. By 1976, more than a dozen had undergone restoration. The long-debated transformation of downtown Bath was a reality.

The comeback of downtown Bath is a classic example of how, in civic affairs, motivated volunteers can outperform official public servants. The critical edge in this case was the unflagging work of Sagadahoc Preservation volunteers, who continually and successfully pushed for higher standards of restoration. Within SPI, the most vital element was probably Margaret (Peggy) Chapman. Chapman and her husband, John, had arrived in the area in 1962 and were restoring their 1779 home in Days Ferry, across the Kennebec from Bath, when they became involved in the Bath Marine

TIMES RECORD

Peggy Chapman, sparkplug
of Bath's downtown restoration.

Museum and Sagadahoc Preservation. John was SPI's first president, but Peggy, who chaired the Downtown Restoration consortium, proved to be the sparkplug for upgrading the district.

Peggy Chapman was possessed of a warm but gently forceful manner. Engaging and well informed, she knew what she liked when it came to authentic restoration, and she was not intimidated by opposition, no matter how formidable. Like many in SPI, she faced the fact that Front Street was an admixture of buildings—Federal, Victorian, fake Georgian, and straightforwardly twentieth century—that somehow blended well together into a "historic" atmosphere redolent of the late nineteenth century. "We urge you to remember," she admonished downtown merchants, "the goal is to restore Bath to a flavor of the middle to late 1800's when it was the wooden shipbuilding capitol [sic] of the nation. This does not mean Colonial Williamsburg or even colonial Boston. It is not Deerfield, Sturbridge Village or Strawbery Banke in Portsmouth. We should not have Georgian entrance ways, or tiny paned windows. Our signs should not be rustic wood, nor should they use 'Olde English' Script. We should avoid plastics and the use of garish colors. Our restoration would give Bath a rare flavor which will be good for Bath and you. . . . "[59]

Chapman would probably be most remembered around Bath for her crusade for appropriate street lighting. The city's engineering plans called for existing streetlight poles to be shortened and, in deference to restoration, fitted with "colonial" brackets holding high-intensity mercury vapor lamps. Such lights were, of course, an attempt at economy, and planners had assumed they had taken the cheapest route. But besides being historically incongruous, such fixtures would bathe the downtown with garish light. Chapman would have no part of such a compromise, and she made that position clear to the president of Central Maine Power.[60]

Determined SPI activists searched for an alternative to the proposed "colonial" lighting. Two members journeyed to Newburyport, Massachusetts, whose once-shabby but historic downtown had undergone a comprehensive restoration of great charm and character that was nurturing new, life-giving business. Architecturally speaking, downtown Newburyport could serve as a model for Bath. A key part of its historic atmosphere was its use of imitation nineteenth-century gas lantern fixtures, invisibly powered by buried electrical cables instead of unsightly overhead wires. When asked, Central Maine Power affirmed that Bath could easily install such fixtures on Front Street. Furthermore, such a change was well within the city's budget for downtown renovation.[61]

But such a change was not accomplished without more selling. By July 1975, it was time for city fathers to stop planning and commence work. To demonstrate once and for all the irresistible benefits of restoration and thus win the hearts and minds of business and Council holdouts, the downtown consortium organized two bus trips to Newburyport. According to John Morse, "We . . . took all the Council who would go, and all the shopkeepers who were willing to go and so forth. . . . What we wanted them to see was the brick sidewalks and particularly the streetlights. [We] had a nice afternoon and evening; had dinner down there and so forth. Everybody seemed to have a good time." On the trip home, SPI volunteers intensely proselytized among the heathen, taking advantage of the good impression made in Newburyport. "We got back and the reports and responses were all favorable with one exception who shall remain nameless. He had somehow hunted around the back streets of Newburyport until he found somebody that said that what they had done down there had been a disaster, and he came back and reported on that."[62] But the expedition had been an overwhelming success. Two days after the trip, City Council gave final approval to the downtown project: $422,000 worth, including imitation nineteenth-century gas lantern streetlights. The tripartite Downtown Restoration group thus acquired a fourth willing partner: the Bath City Council. The way was now clear.

The long road to City Council's acceptance of downtown restoration had been lengthened by more obstacles than pinchpenny tradition. Bath, in fact, was encumbered with other massive concerns in the early seventies, including construction of a sewage treatment plant, difficult wage negotiations with unionized city employees, conflict with the Water District, and turnover in the city manager's office after Harry Ring's retirement in 1972. Ring's immediate successor, Jerry Maxwell, proved so controversial that his support of the program probably alienated councillor support. All of these issues may explain why the movement for a waterfront park, like the matter of historic preservation, was spearheaded by private individuals more than by city fathers.

Creative readaptation of the Kennebec riverfront had been an important element of all of Bath's various self-improvement plans. During the DX period, when the city anticipated a bonanza of tax revenue and developers painted rosy pictures of waterfront hotels, the recreational attractions of the waterfront had gotten a new lease on life, but they faded quickly in the aftermath of BIW's 1970 tailspin.

It could not be said that the waterfront had escaped its perennial unsightly aspect. The city's share of the landscape amounted only to two lots on Commercial Street, where a variety of old wooden structures had lived and died. After acquisition by the Parking District, the parcels had been cleared. By the seventies, one was a parking lot; the other, just to the north, was a kind of desert and occasional storage depot. In between was a plot owned by John Chapman. Farther to the north, at the Coal Pocket, a scrap business was shredding junk cars for shipment to Newfoundland. While committees were discussing how to restore Front Street, the waterfront one block east was a wasteland.

Surveying the situation late in 1971, Linwood Temple remembered how, as a boy, he had enjoyed the river's recreational attractions. Over the years, he had watched the waterfront go downhill or succumb to various commercial uses. He felt strongly that people should have easy access to the Kennebec, even if it meant no more than a place to sit and enjoy the movement of the water. Noting the city's small share of the riverfront, he decided to act before it was too late: "In the seventies, the city fathers, being what they are (they're always looking for a larger tax base), were talking about selling the property. . . . A few of us got our heads together, primarily myself to start with, and said, 'Really, that's the only city land where people can get to the waterfront, and it should be saved for the people. We ought to have a park there.' "[63]

Temple and his friends contacted the Planning Board, which was sympathetic. The board, in fact, recommended to Council that the Chapman lot be optioned for purchase, thus consolidating the city's waterfront holdings, and that the whole parcel be officially dedicated as a park. Once so designated, the park's status could not legally be revoked by future members of Council.[64] But time was of the essence if City Council was thinking of selling the land.

Temple's grassroots movement to set aside a park drew favorable coverage in the *Times Record*. It also won the support of the increasingly influential *Maine Times*, a brainchild of Peter Cox and John Cole, who had left the *Times Record* in 1968 to start a statewide environmentalist paper. (Cox's grubstake, incidentally, came from an interesting source: "When I went to

Bath, my father bought me some stock in the Bath Iron Works. . . . In those days, it split and doubled and tripled, and that was my starting money for *Maine Times*.")[65] By 1972, John Cole's classy brand of environmentalism had made him almost a guru to opponents of big business, clumsy government, and agencies that posed a possible threat to Maine's "quality of life." It was therefore significant when Cole took up Temple's cause.

In January 1972, Cole used his *Maine Times* editorial column to publish an open letter to Temple, extolling the virtues of a waterfront park and using precise imagery to express the need for all Mainers to conserve what was left of their disappearing heritage: "When I worked for the *Times Record* in Bath five years ago, my office was just a few yards from the center of the city property. . . . At that time, the city was using the area for outdoor storage of construction materials for the new sewage treatment plant. On warm days I would sit there among the sand piles and stacked pipes, watching the Kennebec move by, making mental plans for the property, thinking even as I did that the city fathers would almost surely sell the place to a motel builder, or some other sort of commercial hustler. But, quite wonderfully, the land hasn't been sold; and now it looks as if you can save it."[66]

Temple's and Cole's fears came true in the spring of 1972, however. Pinched, as always, between tax revenues and needed expenditures, city fathers ignored Temple's lobbying and the Planning Board's recommendation, opting instead to sell off one parcel of waterfront land. Cole told Temple he would raise the $50,000 necessary to purchase the city's lot and Chapman's property for a park, but matters moved too quickly.[67] To the outrage of citizen activists and the Planning Board, City Council sold its marketable parcel to a Brunswick development firm, BathPort Limited. BathPort had bought the Chapman land, which gave the developers critical leverage in negotiating with the city government. The company proposed to build an expansive complex of offices, stores, and a restaurant described as "a very high-class affair"—provided it could snag the city's lot.[68]

The proposal was ambitious and attractive to conservative, sharp-penciled councillors. (And, inasmuch as the Shipbuilding City was decidedly light on restaurants of any description, the promise to provide a good one must have sounded particularly attractive.) Although its $4,000 offer was far below competing bids, City Council sold to BathPort.

From a municipal perspective, the transaction was a mistake. BathPort completed only part of the proposed complex, so the high hopes of city fathers for new businesses and a higher tax base were crushed. Furthermore, in a period of growing local interest in historic architecture, the completed BathPort structure looked stridently discordant: a series of sharp-angled, barnboarded modules whose aggressive modernity seemed at war with the rest of the downtown. (For several years, however, BathPort was home to an ambitious nouvelle cuisine restaurant; but that establishment eventually succumbed to rising rents, and its space was taken by BIW for offices.)

After one waterfront lot was sold off, the public's toehold on the downtown waterfront amounted only to about sixty feet of frontage, not much for future planning or expanded recreational use. And even that was in jeopardy. According to Temple, "We tried to persuade the city to set it aside as a waterfront park. They still wanted to sell it. So we got a petition together, went to the City Hall, and said, 'Look; if you don't do it, we'll have a referendum.' They said, 'Okay, let's have a referendum and see what the people want.' They did, and . . . 75 percent of the vote went for a city waterfront park."[69]

The referendum took place in June 1972, but little progress was made until May 1974 when, impatient with the delay, Temple mobilized Bath's Rotary and Garden clubs and called for other support. One Saturday, a crowd of volunteers of all ages descended on the lot to spread loam and plant grass, collectively nudging the spot from a lot to a minipark of sorts. The finishing touches, aided by a state grant, were in place by October 1976.

Although measured against the erstwhile visions of such men as Blackwell, Atwood, Temple, and Cole, the park was undeniably small, Bath now had a restful waterfront enclave featuring walkways, trees, grassy knolls, and an unobstructed view of the river. Furthermore, in the parlance of the day, it could truly be called a people's park.

TIMES RECORD

A 1977 aerial view of the downtown waterfront shows the new waterfront park in the left foreground. On the right is the controversial BathPort complex. Farther upriver, a bulk hauler idles at the Coal Pocket.

But it was not called a people's park. In 1985, City Council unanimously designated the area the Linwood E. Temple Waterfront Park. The new name was embedded in a decorative boulder in one corner of the minipark in 1986. It commemorated another example of decisive action by private citizens willing, if necessary, to take matters in hand to achieve long-standing but unattained goals.

* * *

While the waterfront park was taking shape, preservationists scored another architectural coup just three blocks away. With the completion of a new post office at Washington and Vine streets, the General Services Administration needed to dispose of its former post office, the old customs house. The city got it for $62,500, planning to use it as a magnet for further

TIMES RECORD

Bath's handsome customs house, acquired and rehabilitated by the city.

revitalization. Although many in Bath had considered the elegant structure a perfect permanent site for the expanding Maine Maritime Museum, the building, elaborately rehabilitated with a whopping $450,000 HUD grant, became home for the District Court and a variety of private businesses.

By 1977, when the Ad Hoc Committee disbanded, the old-time aspect of Front Street was in place and inviting to passersby and new businesses alike. Front Street was by no means a replica of Bath in its nineteenth-century heyday, but it had undeniable character and a look of antiquity. And by avoiding slapdash cosmetics and half measures, the downtown had, like Newburyport, escaped the fey, come-hither cuteness and gimmickry that characterized many New England tourist traps.

No newcomer could possibly appreciate the enormous difference brick

TIMES RECORD

Restored Front Street, complete with brick sidewalks, plantings, and old-style lampposts.

sidewalks, appropriate street lighting, selective planting, underground electrical cables, and the continuing restoration of storefronts had wrought in the once-bedraggled district. That such a turnaround had occurred in the exact area the Bath Urban Renewal Authority had once targeted for wholesale demolition made it all the more dramatic to natives.

Economic and aesthetic rationales aside, downtown restoration was of major importance to the city of Bath because, for the first time in memory, city fathers, the Chamber of Commerce, property owners, merchants, and interested volunteers—the entire social, business, and political infrastructure—had pulled together. In the process, the city had perhaps found an identity that would harmonize its past glories with its future expectations. Evidence of that was the growing number of historic houses undergoing restoration in every section of town, and the new businesses that capitalized on Bath's air of salty antiquity.

Bath's rediscovery of its historic character—a movement that germinated with the Marine Research Society, grew during the crusades to save the Winter Street and Central churches, and bloomed with the downtown's tortuous renaissance—was of national importance as an example of what local effort could accomplish largely on its own steam. It did not go unnoticed. The turnaround received substantial coverage in regional and national broadcast and press media and, in May 1977, the National Trust for Historic Preservation presented its President's Award to the Maine Maritime Museum, Sagadahoc Preservation, the Bath Area Chamber of Commerce, and the Bath City Government for their exemplary, cooperative, preservationist achievement.

Whether or not the movement could produce the economic miracle Bath

TIMES RECORD

Representatives of Bath's cooperating organizations pose before Winter Street Church after receiving the National Trust's President's Award in 1977. Left to right: Mary Donnell (Mel) Rogers (Sagadahoc Preservation, Inc.), Herbert (Bud) Caverly (Bath City Council), Diane (Di) Francis (Maine Maritime Museum), and John Morse, Jr. (Ad Hoc Committee on Downtown Restoration).

TIMES RECORD

Restoration continues on Front Street, 1981.

sought remained to be seen. The struggle, however, had been worthwhile, in more ways than one. Reviewing his committee leadership, John Morse recalled that "Charlie [MacDonald], early on almost to the end, fought tooth and nail against the city doing the things that we did: the brick side-walks, the lamp poles, and all that sort of thing. . . . When it was over and the job was done and the results began to come in, I was absolutely delighted that Charlie came to me and said, 'Well, you know, you were right and I was wrong. This is a great thing. I'm glad it happened, and I want to congratulate you for carrying the ball for so long.' I think that probably that was the most touching thing that ever happened to me."[70]

Notes

1. Bartlett M. Van Note, Interview, Bath, July 1987.
2. Ibid.
3. Alan Robert Miller, *The History of Current Maine Newspapers* (Lisbon Falls, ME: Eastland Press, 1978), p. 130.
4. Peter W. Cox, Interview, Georgetown, ME, July 1987.

5. Ibid.
6. Ibid.
7. BDT, 26 July 1966.
8. *City of Bath Annual Report*, 1962–1963.
9. Editorial, TR, 28 September 1967.
10. *City of Bath Annual Report*, 1968–1969.
11. Stephen Hopkins, quoted in BDT, 27 April 1966.
12. Van Note interview.
13. Ibid.
14. Morse interview.
15. Burden interview; see also BDT, 17 February 1963.
16. Shepard interview.
17. Arthur P. Ziegler, Jr., and Walter C. Kidrey. *Historic Preservation in Small Towns: A Manual of Practice* (Nashville: American Association for State and Local History, 1980), p. x.
18. John Robinson, *Highways and Our Environment* (New York: McGraw-Hill, 1971), p. 272.
19. Ada Louise Huxtable, *Will They Ever Finish Bruckner Boulevard?* (New York: Macmillan, and London: Collier-Macmillan, 1971), p. 4.
20. Marius Peladeau, quoted in Neil R. Peirce, *The New England States: People, Politics, and Power in the Six New England States* (New York: W. W. Norton, 1976), pp. 418–19.
21. Cox interview.
22. Editorial, BDT, 2 August 1965.
23. Ibid., 19 January 1966.
24. "Maine Times," TR, 17 August 1967.
25. Snow, pp, 465–66.
26. William Kyle, quoted in "An Old Shipyard Moves In New Ways," *Business Week*, 14 March 1970, pp. 148–50.
27. Van Note interview.
28. W. Haggett interview.
29. Van Note interview.
30. W. Haggett interview.
31. Community Planning Services, *DX (DD 963): Municipal Program, City of Bath, Maine* (Bath: Community Planning Services, n. d. [1969], p. 1.
32. Ibid., p. 20.
33. Ibid., p. 58.
34. Ibid., pp. 68–69.
35. W. Haggett interview.
36. Ibid.
37. Snow, p. 485.
38. Morse interview.
39. Theodore E. Bradbury, Interview, Bath, August 1987.
40. R. Small interview.
41. David L. Swearingen, "Compassionate Man," TR, 17 September 1985.
42. Mussenden interview.
43. Rev. Franklin H. Blackmer, *Notes about Churches in the Lower Kennebec*

Valley, 1607–1976 (Bath: Greater Bath Council of Churches, 1976), p. 15.

44. S. Haggett interview.
45. Ibid.; Bowker interview.
46. Editorial, BDT, 17 May 1966.
47. Morse, quoted in BDT, 20 May 1966.
48. Dorothy Erickson to Earle Shettleworth, Jr., Bath, 27 May 1971 (Margaret E. Chapman, comp., Personal File on Sagadahoc Preservation, Inc.).
49. Herbert T. Caverly II, Interview, Bath, 29 July 1987.
50. Caverly, quoted in TR, 5 February 1970.
51. Caverly interview.
52. TR, 16 June 1970.
53. Gloria Hutchinson, "New Dawn for Bath," *Down East*, February 1980, p. 89.
54. Morse interview.
55. TR, 2 December 1970; 6 January 1971.
56. Morse, quoted in ibid., 6 October 1971.
57. Radio editorial, quoted in Margaret E. Chapman, "How to Organize a Main Street Revitalization Project: A Case Study—Bath, Maine" (typescript of a speech presented at the Conference on Main Street Revitalization, Boston, December 1977), p. 6 (Margaret E. Chapman, comp., Personal File on Bath Downtown Restoration).
58. Margaret E. Chapman to Ralph L. Snow, Woolwich, ME, 21 October 1987.
59. Chapman to Bath Merchants, Bath, n. d., quoted in Chapman, "How to Organize a Main Street Revitalization Project," p. 8.
60. Chapman interview.
61. Ibid.
62. Morse interview.
63. L. Temple interview.
64. John Carey to Linwood Temple, Bath, 14 January 1972 (L. Temple, comp., Personal File on Bath Waterfront Park).
65. Cox interview.
66. John N. Cole to L. Temple (editorial), *Maine Times*, 28 January 1972.
67. Cole to L. Temple, Topsham, ME, 22 February 1972 (Temple file).
68. TR, 6 March 1972.
69. L. Temple interview.
70. Morse interview.

6

"A Lot Going for Us"

One of the last holdouts against downtown renovation in Bath was Norm's Pantry, a hole-in-the-wall luncheonette whose decor consisted mainly of manifestos deploring municipal policies and signs proclaiming the virtues of its unique bill of fare ("The Watergate Sandwich [It Won't 'Bug' You]").

On a chilly morning in 1980, while awaiting an order of Norm's flapjacks, one of the authors overheard an exchange typical of the eatery's regular clientele. Over in a corner, nursing a cup of coffee, sat a weathered veteran of the Iron Works wearing a blue BIW jacket. In walked an acquaintance of similar description. "Why, Bill," said the latter in the ironic, flat accent of the true downeast humorist, "What are you doin' here? I thought you was in Florida!" Without looking up or missing a stir, Bill muttered, "I ain't got my grant yet. When I get my grant, *then* I'm goin' to Florida."

Bill's retort was a salty summation of two local trends: the increasing immigration to Bath of educated, even academic professionals from away, many of whose career agendas were fueled by grantsmanship; and the growing involvement of the city in programs dependent on state or federal funding. Both trends were substantially changing Bath's character, completing a fifty-year process by which the community had debated, then sampled, then exploited, and finally expected as a matter of course to get governmental assistance to achieve its objectives.

Perhaps the most important example of Bath's creative use of state and federal monies was in the field of housing, an area that had been crying out for action since before World War II. Given its limited space and conservative attitudes, Bath had never been overendowed with acceptable housing, but by the 1970s the need was especially severe for several reasons. For one, life expectancy was increasing. For another, the structure of the family was changing: fewer parents lived with their children after their working years were over. But meanwhile, the cost of living was climbing faster than retirees' Social Security and other benefits.

In Bath, rising living costs for the elderly was one of the biggest reasons why tax increases were a volatile issue. As always, the city's chief funding source was the property tax, and, as taxes rose relentlessly, elderly householders on fixed incomes were in a bind because the city offered no low-rent public housing. Hence, such councillors as Charlie MacDonald, mindful of the tax trap for the elderly, battled relentlessly to keep costs down and new projects under control.

By 1967, Bath taxpayers had sustained a tax increase of 70 percent in constant dollars since World War II. BIW's 1969 phaseout of Hyde Windlass reduced the tax base by $1.5 million, a step that took on major importance after BIW lost the DX contract. Obviously, tax relief was nowhere in sight for private householders. Would people on fixed incomes have to sell out to escape the bite? Where would they go?

City fathers perceived that a possible solution lay in the construction of comfortable, attractive, low-rent housing for retired persons of limited means. A new Bath Housing Authority (a semiprivate municipal corporation like the Bath Water District) was created specifically for that purpose, and its board began seeking federal construction grants. The federal Department of Housing and Urban Development offered a variety of such programs, including those that paid construction costs, guaranteed construction loans, or paid various rent subsidies. The Bath Housing Authority sought a "turnkey" program in which a developer would design and build a project, turn it over to the city when completed, and be paid an agreed-upon price by HUD. But there was a quid pro quo: HUD stipulated that such grants would only be made upon evidence that the community was meeting the housing needs of low-income groups. In the late sixties, the BHA had no desire to involve itself in that kind of program.

In 1970, BHA member Bud Caverly went to Washington to see what the BHA could do about housing for the elderly. He got some good news from HUD: "[Charles] Pace, a Nixon appointee . . . , called me into his office. . . . He said, 'Do you need something in Bath? . . . I need a place to build middle-income housing.' I said, 'We can certainly use middle-income housing.' Nixon had put together this Operation Breakthrough. [Pace] said, 'Find me some land and I'll give you something.' I came back and found him some land, and I put together the package with the Housing Authority and with the Council very quietly. It sounded good. It was a very bad thing."[1]

Operation Breakthrough was a Nixon administration program designed to encourage private investment in public housing. As Caverly and the Bath

Housing Authority learned, it had strings attached. For example, 10 percent of the units built under the program had to be rented to persons who fell into the low-income category. Although the BHA wanted to stay out of low-income housing, a figure of only 10 percent was attractive. In further negotiations, the BHA struck a deal with HUD whereby 20 percent of the proposed Operation Breakthrough units would be rented to low-income families, thereby absolving Bath of any further responsibility for low-income housing. In Bath, entrepreneurs Sherwood Francis and Red Mulligan came forward, and, by 1972, the 200-unit "Sherred Village" was underway in a wooded site on Oak Grove Avenue, near Lambert Park.

One of Operation Breakthrough's priorities was to keep down construction costs by resorting to premanufactured housing modules trucked to the site. In Bath, the concept proved to be a disaster. After the city had built the requisite roads and installed water and sewerage lines, the wood-frame modules arrived stacked on flatbed trailers like so many children's building blocks. They had been designed—shades of Hyde Park—for a wholly different environment than Bath's. Set on crawl-space foundations with insulation more suitable for the Sunbelt, the units were plagued with freezing pipes and related problems that took several years and many thousands of dollars to correct. Because of those circumstances, the developers had to rent the first 20 percent of the completed units to low-income families to create cash flow. Once that was done, "Shredded Village" became stereotyped as a low-income housing project—which discouraged an elderly clientele.

Likening the Sherred Village episode to the disappointment of BathPort, which likewise delivered far less than was expected, Caverly, its instigator, regretfully admitted that "you have to be very careful if the city is going to be involved in something that sounds great. You've got to cross every 't' and dot every 'i' rather than take someone's word for what it is going to be, because BathPort is not what we were promised and, again, Sherred Village is not what we were promised either."[2] The Bath Housing Authority had much to learn about getting something for nothing from Uncle Sam.

The saga of "Shredded Village" was as nothing compared to the concurrent embarrassment over another BHA-HUD project, Washington House. A monolithic, fifty-four-unit highrise apartment building, Washington House was to be exclusively for the elderly. The Bath Housing Authority worked out the details of design, cost, and specifications with a Massachusetts developer. Upon its completion, the BHA was to purchase Washington House from the developer with a grant provided by HUD. The building was to be operated thereafter by the BHA.

The site chosen for Washington House was the northwest corner of Washington and Center streets, opposite the Chocolate Church. The spot was convenient and, it was hoped, would provide an economic cornerstone for the downtown. The site selection was part of HUD's strategy to locate housing near downtown business sections so that occupants could get about without public transportation. But, as Raymond Gaul, BHA director during the project, put it, "It should have been obvious (and I'm sure it was to them, although they ignored it): You paid a high price for downtown real estate. In this case, there was a perfectly good building which had housed the old Sears store and a chain of grocers . . . , a perfectly good building which they tore down in order to do this building. Now that doesn't come cheap."[3] Building on expensive real estate drove up the project's cost, which displeased HUD, despite the fact that the costly locale conformed to the agency's guidelines. Concern about overall costs forced some compromises in the building's design.

Besides its great expense, Washington and Center was a chancy place to put up a large building. Part of the structure would stand on ledge, the rest venturing out on a no-man's-land of clay and mud that had once been a tidal creek. All this caused some very costly construction problems. Pete Van Note, who became the BHA's director in 1977, later recalled that the builder drove a seemingly endless number of pilings "sometimes sixty feet into the ground . . . , trying to find rock. They couldn't believe what was happening. . . . But by the time they got the base under it, there obviously wasn't money enough to finish it. . . . Then, in the course of putting the shell up, [they] were constantly asking for more money." In over their heads with a second mortgage by 1973, the developers were unable to persuade HUD to authorize more expenditure. To economize, the builder substituted components that did not conform to specifications. Then came accusations of skimpy construction. "HUD said, 'There will be no more money,' " Van Note explained. "In the final analysis, the contractor said, 'That's all. Without any more money, I quit,' and he just simply walked."[4]

The project went nowhere for more than a year, as the various parties argued over a solution. Canal Bank, holder of the first mortgage, foreclosed on Washington House and sold the empty shell to a private Maine housing firm, Shelter Group, which at last completed the long-awaited building, reportedly at twice the original cost estimate. Shelter Group retained control over the structure after its completion. Despite its painful history, Washington House filled quickly.

After Canal Bank took over Washington House, the BHA undertook some much-needed restrategizing and decided to pursue more conventional funding routes. With the assistance of HUD construction grants, it completed two attractive and successful housing projects for the elderly off Congress Avenue: The Anchorage (1977), a group of semidetached, wood-frame, one- and two-story dwellings; and The Moorings (1979), a three-story wood apartment building. SeaCliff (1982), another three-story building, was completed with the assistance of a bond issue floated by the Maine State Housing Authority. The projects were convenient to a new suburban-style complex, the Bath Shopping Center, which went up in 1977. In 1984, the

TIMES RECORD

SeaCliff gets its finishing touches, 1982.

BHA also rehabilitated the old Dike School as housing for the elderly, renaming the structure Dike Landing and bringing the total available housing units to 138.

These projects more than achieved their purpose. Rents were based upon the ability of tenants to pay, which in 1987 averaged about $140 per month including utilities—about $300 below the going market price. As director of the BHA, Van Note had no trouble filling the complexes. Furthermore, he could boast that Bath's was the only housing authority in the Northeast that did not rely upon a rent-subsidy program.

A private housing development noteworthy for its innovativeness was Aegis Apartments, undertaken by John Morse in the mid- and late 1980s. As BIW expanded west of Washington Street, the company offered to give the existing houses on its acquired land to anyone who would move them. Morse took several large old homes, relocating them on land just off Congress Avenue near the BHA developments, where they were refurbished, divided into apartments, and finished in exteriors appropriate to their period, creating an instant neighborhood whose character was reminiscent of the rest of Bath.

The development of public housing in Bath was important for several reasons. Although it proved a painful training ground on which city fathers learned the ropes of federal and private financing, it provided an acceptable living alternative for residents whose incomes could not keep pace with the city's rising tax rates. And by doing so, it defused much of the tax controversy, liberating city fathers to undertake programs deemed essential without undermining the well-being of elderly citizens.

The creation of public housing for the elderly was also significant in another way. As property owners sold out to take advantage of the newly available housing, their homes were often purchased by a conspicuous group of outsiders for whom Bath was an irresistible spot for settlement: professionals seeking to escape the rat race of city life, well-fixed retirees for whom Bath's attractions far outweighed its drawbacks, and wealthy searchers after "The Good Life in Maine," for whom Bath was an economic bargain, taxes and all. At long last, Bath's scenery, historic character, and cultural offerings were exerting a pull on outsiders, making the Shipbuilding City a fashionable address.

Another program, albeit a temporary one, helped rescue Bath from its financial paralysis: federal revenue-sharing, which went into place in 1972,

TIMES RECORD

Just off Congress Avenue and Leeman Highway, 1976.

contributing almost $277,000 to the city's budget in that year alone.[5] The infusion of federal monies for several years thereafter makes a consistent analysis of the city government difficult, but it is apparent that spending continued to spiral, the tug-of-war between spenders and savers was alive and well in City Council, and the position of city manager continued to be controversial indeed.

Harry Ring, who had taken over the city manager's seat in 1961, retired in 1972. His longevity as city manager was indeed remarkable. Ring had a tremendous capacity to absorb the criticisms and impositions of the changing roster of councillors, meanwhile plugging away for the programs he wanted. Bud Caverly, a hard man to please, conceded that Ring had been "an old-time manager who had moved up from clerk and kept things under control." Ted Bradbury, equally finicky, deemed him "an excellent administrator. He got a lot done with very little." All of this despite a relationship to successive City Councils whose members were inclined, "more often than not, to find fault with him, even to the point of holding him up to [public] ridicule."[6] Ring's fifteen years as city clerk had equipped him admirably for the manager's job, for in the ordinary course of business, he was in a position to meet virtually every citizen of Bath. Furthermore, it was the clerk's responsibility to take the minutes of each Council meeting, which afforded Ring a firsthand opportunity to watch and learn. Councillors might come and go; Ring was the permanent fixture in City Hall. Probably no one in the city knew more about the real workings of the government or had more access to the public.

As manager, Ring accomplished a great deal. He streamlined city operations by consolidating various departments. He launched a program to upgrade and equip the public works department and retained a city engineer (a position that, though it proved salutary, was later abolished by referendum). That was the basis for the city's long-deferred program of street and sidewalk repair, and for the construction of Congress Avenue, which redirected and accelerated development in Bath, as the later BHA housing and the Bath Shopping Center would prove. Ring was also instrumental in Bath's adoption of the state retirement plan for city employees.

The manager played a central role in the city's water-pollution control program, one of the first in Maine. Upon his retirement, he told City Council that his most gratifying achievement in eleven years as manager was persuading the federal government to increase its contribution to Bath's water treatment system from 30 to 55 percent, a change that saved the city $1 million.[7]

During the sixties, with federal and state assistance, Bath had undertaken a massive project to provide a drainage system for storm and waste water that would be routed by pumping stations to a riverside treatment plant in the North End near the sardine cannery. Uncle Sam and the state of Maine picked up most of the tab for the work. As Ring put it, the project "covered almost the entire period that I was in there as manager from the planning to its completion. The original system had eleven pump stations and the main treatment plant, covered about two and a half to three miles . . . , and took a lot of planning. Of course, you had to go right up through the main streets of Bath, and the BIW was mad at us for several years because that covered [the area] right in front of the plant for about . . . a year [the notorious "Ho Chi Minh Trail"]. . . . But it was a necessity, and we got in on the plan early to try to get the funds. We were very fortunate, and we got 55 percent federal [aid], I think, 25 percent state, and the rest from Bath."[8]

Although moving quickly secured mammoth outside assistance, such haste carried a heavy price tag for future years. When at last the city's plant was fully operational in the early seventies, it proved unequal to its task because, for reasons of economy, it had been built without the capacity to separate storm water from waste before treatment. As a result, the treatment plant often literally overflowed with excess effluent, a problem that would take decades and millions to upgrade to acceptability.

While the city's sewage treatment system plant was abuilding, a water crisis developed that precipitated a showdown between City Council and the Bath Water District. In June 1970, the pipeline under the Kennebec broke and Bath found itself without water. Bath citizens learned to their surprise that the Water District had long ago abandoned its original underwater pipeline, apparently relying upon the single line laid in the thirties to last forever. There was, in other words, no backup from Nequasset Lake to Bath. Antique pumps were activated at Thompson Pond in West Bath, but they soon sucked that supply dry. Standpipe water, retained in Bath for fire emergencies, was liberated for public use as the District rushed to repair the ruptured line and install a long-overdue new one.

Inasmuch as the water crisis occurred just as the bad news about DX arrived, it may have seemed worse than it was. In any case, riding a wave of public outrage over the shortage and demanding not one but two lines, councillors accused the Water District's three trustees of violating public trust and called for their replacement. The Water District, however, was immune to such demands, just as it was not legally liable for the inconvenience of the pipeline breakdown.

The old line was repaired and work commenced on a single new one. Then, incredibly, the pipe ruptured again. Though it was quickly restored to operation, that second failure seemed to justify Council action against the District's management. In November 1970, when his term was up for renewal, Water District Commissioner Baer Connard (who had replaced Pete Newell on the District board in 1940) was not reappointed. Who should replace him? According to Pete Van Note, "The night that the meeting came up, I happened to be sitting in the hall. I don't think there were more than four people in the room as viewers, and they really didn't have a name. One of the councillors, I remember, turned around and looked at me in the room and pointed at me. And I got chilled and I thought, 'Oops! I know what *he's* thinking about!' " Van Note took the job. "I was young and brash and I figured there wasn't anything I couldn't handle."[9]

Van Note's appointment was at first little more than symbolic, inasmuch as he was but one of three trustees. He introduced a bill in Augusta to increase the number of Water District board seats from three to five. Before that bill took effect, the two other incumbents died, "so that one year after I had become a member of the board . . . , we were sitting there with five [new] trustees, and I got elected president of the board. . . . I was the senior member!"[10]

Needless to say, the new District was more reflective of changed times and responsive to public opinion. It spent more than $3.5 million on new underwater pipe, pumping stations, and underground street pipelines. (The work was coordinated with the city's sewerage construction to minimize disruption of traffic.) It managed to accomplish the program without drastically raising rates. To preclude another crisis like the one in 1970, the

District phased out Thompson Pond as a backup facility and worked toward a long-range solution that took years to accomplish: the linkage of Bath's and Brunswick's water systems so that one could supply the other in an emergency.

The Water District received a pleasant surprise during its upgrading process because new meters revealed exactly where pumped water was going. For years, vast amounts had been flowing to the Iron Works, about twelve times more than the company had been paying for. The discrepancy was due to the company's spurts of expansion that had overrun former streets, houses, and businesses. As Van Note later explained, "When they were public streets . . . , there were water mains all through those streets and there were hydrants down in there. As the yard expanded and surrounded them, those water mains were still there and those hydrants were still there, and water was available through the water mains and through the hydrants. I don't think necessarily it was anything that anybody had thought about, but when the shipyard or the ships needed major water to fill tanks or whatever, they used water [from the district]. Today they use over 50 percent of the water that the Water District pumps."

A new master meter for BIW permitted a precise accounting. The District revised its bills upward and waited for an explosion on south Washington Street. It never came. "Finally," recalled Van Note, "there was a day with a social situation, I believe, with Bill Haggett. He knew where I stood with the water company, and there was small talk about how things were going down there. He said, 'Well how are things going at the water company?' And then he kind of looked at me and said, 'You ought to be in pretty good shape considering the bills we've been paying lately!' "[11]

NEWELL FUND TOTALS $4,532

BATH—Today is the final day of the Edward F. Newell Fund which was launched in December to assist the Chief Deputy of the Sagadahoc Sheriff's Department. The fund, which this morning totaled $4,532.07, was started to help defray medical expenses for Newell.

Wounded in a shooting incident while on a routine call in Phippsburg in late November, Newell has been hospitalized since for amputation of his lower leg. He is presently undergoing therapy treatment at Bodwell House, Brunswick, and visits his home here occasionally.

TIMES RECORD, 29 JANUARY 1971

EDWARD NEWELL RECEIVES BANK BOOK

BATH—Sagadahoc County's Chief Deputy Sheriff Edward Newell received a bank book for a total of $5,420.07 Thursday, to conclude the fund which was started for him earlier in the Winter.

Fund treasurer, Warren Higgins made the presentation to Newell at his home, 20 Newton Rd., where the deputy is recovering from a leg wound he received in November. . . .

TIMES RECORD, 26 FEBRUARY 1971

One of Harry Ring's sources of popularity was his reputation for economy; but, as has been seen, he was anything but a pinchpenny. In fact, during his years as manager, city expenses increased 80 percent in constant dollars. Schools naturally accounted for the largest share of the increase, with expenditures for education rising 77 percent. Public works outlays went up by 64 percent. The city's bonded debt also increased, of course, but the debt as a percentage of valuation declined from 8.2 to 5.8 percent in the Ring years, reflecting more realistic valuation methods and Bath's improved capacity to meet that debt.

Ring's administration, in summary, brought about a low-key but steady increase in spending for city services, raising city outlay to a level that was, in constant dollars, seldom exceeded by his successors in the seventies and eighties. Ring was thus to a large part responsible for shifting Bath's priorities from obsessive concern with the tax rate to concern for the quality and quantity of municipal services.

Among Ring's most useful traits were his patience with city fathers who disliked or misunderstood the managerial system, and his consequent avoidance of destructive standoffs with Council. The price he paid for that accord was acceptance of Council's unofficial kibitzing in departmental affairs and minimal prestige for the manager's office.

There is a school of thought that insists it is the function of a city manager to bring professional leadership, permanence, and long-range thinking to a government whose elected legislators and policymakers are amateurs serving very short terms. Inevitably, such councils as Bath's focus on the immediate concerns of the electorate; that, after all, is democracy. But councils that operate by consensus, as Bath's usually did, seldom act decisively before an issue has attracted public attention. Managers, who implement policy over the long haul, must sometimes take responsibility for the long haul and guide—perhaps lead—councils toward confronting strategic issues. At that point, the line between legislators and executive necessarily blurs and friction occurs. Thus, friction, not accord, is a sign that a manager is doing his strategic job.

Because of the urban renewal issue, it is impossible to characterize the Bath City Council of the mid-sixties as consensus-oriented. But as far as council-manager relations went, the Ring years were not confrontational; Ring even kept his distance from the urban renewal battles. Beneath the workaday surface, however, hostility to the managerial system was still present, as Ring's successors found out.

Jerry Maxwell came to Bath from Carbondale, Illinois, where he had served as assistant city manager. In late 1972, he had beaten out a roster of forty-five applicants for the job of Bath city manager. He brought to his new job youthful self-confidence, enormous drive, and the ambition to make a name for himself. These attributes, coupled with an undiplomatic candor and the inability to suffer fools gladly, led to some exciting times at City Hall.

It is significant that city fathers chose a man so unlike the bland, homegrown Ring. But times were changing. Inflation was growing alarmingly. Federal revenue-sharing and other programs of assistance posed a managerial challenge. Maxwell, obviously, had been hired because he possessed the professional training and experience Bath would need to keep pace with its rising municipal expectations. His arrival was thus seen as another step toward professionalism in city government. But city fathers soon learned that, professionally speaking, they had a tiger by the tail. As Councillor Hayward Newcomb admitted after Maxwell was making changes, "He's definitely the type of guy we had in mind when we hired him, but whether he is more than we wanted remains to be seen."[12] Or, as Robert Forkey, the *Times Record*'s observer, put it, "It was as if the city had been a car long idling at the curb and Jerry L. Maxwell came by, jumped behind the wheel, slammed it into gear and floored it."[13]

Jerry L. Maxwell was very touchy about the demarcation between manager and City Council, particularly where the latter's responsibilities were concerned. He pushed through a charter revision that redefined the relationship between the city manager and Council, and he guarded the prerogatives of his office tenaciously.

Maxwell often confronted Council with issues it was inclined conveniently to overlook. A good example, which occurred shortly after his arrival, was his handling of problems at the ailing sewage treatment plant. Maxwell pulled on a pair of rubber boots and went to see for himself what was wrong. He soon was embroiled with the plant's very reputable Boston designers, forcing them to admit a number of design faults and help pay for corrections. He then developed a long-range plan for improving the sewerage system's overall efficiency.

It was Maxwell who embraced the downtown renovation concept and brought the city fathers around to participating. He was also instrumental in launching the project to acquire and adapt the customs house for commercial use. He followed through on established programs such as a playing field complex on Congress Avenue and the ongoing improvement of Bath streets and sidewalks. He was protective of municipal employees, militating on their behalf for higher salaries and shielding them from the criticisms of an increasingly restive Council. Issues such as the appointment of department heads and the workings of municipal departments were out of bounds for Council, regardless of how much that offended city fathers.

It offended city fathers a great deal. The comfortable old-boy network that Ring had accepted suddenly short-circuited. The matter of administrative autonomy was hardly new, but Maxwell interpreted it liberally. The manager was not loath to pursue important objectives on his own initiative in the name of expeditiousness. When a controversial decision had to be made, he preferred to apologize to Council after the fact than to ask permission beforehand. His revised budgetary procedures increased his independence. "We went from a modified accrued budget under him to a cash flow situation," explained Caverly, who was reelected to Council in 1975 as an outspoken opponent of Maxwell's management. "Departments and their budgets meant nothing. You took from this one to fund that one. At the end of the year you ended up alright. Fine; but you couldn't read a budget under Jerry Maxwell on a bet. . . . "[14]

Maxwell's irksome brand of independence and competence had soon divided the city's legislative and executive elements into hostile camps. But he had his own power base. He retained the city clerk's position for himself, as had Ring. He appointed a full-time city planner, Paul Bracciotti. His handpicked police chief, Robert Picucci, was the very model of a newfangled law-enforcement official, not a hometown policeman. At one point, Maxwell instituted the practice of taking regular City Council meetings to the community by holding sessions in various neighborhoods. He thus garnered enormous popular support from professionals and younger residents, people who felt no reverence for the Establishment and were fed up with Council's characteristic dithering. He enjoyed a favorable press for the same reason. (He also benefited from the *Times Record*'s increasingly explicit, crisis-oriented coverage of city affairs.) But, ironically, his style had exacerbated the problem of council-manager relations, because city fathers were kept in the dark about important issues too often and too long. The arcane system's success relied entirely upon the manager. In 1976, late in Maxwell's tenure, Caverly summed up the situation: "I think Jerry's built a system here that works for Jerry and I'm not sure if it works for anyone else."[15]

Maxwell rode out some serious attacks. In March 1974, Charlie MacDonald inquired of the city solicitor what legal means there were to dismiss Maxwell. There followed a closed-door meeting that, as Bob Forkey avidly reported, was "punctuated by raised voices and table pounding that could be heard outside the closed conference room at city hall. The executive session lasted more than two hours and capped days of rumors of a move afoot to oust Maxwell."[16] When the voices calmed and the table-pounding stopped, the emerging councillors were noncommittal about the topic of conversation and about their obviously smoldering displeasure with the manager: precisely the sort of thing Maxwell's defenders would call dithering. But Maxwell's management required a public perception of City Council as essentially reactionary, incompetent, and bent on obstructing progress. It was bound to wear thin after a while.

One of the most contentious Maxwell administration issues was the conduct of the police department. Unconcerned about the reaction of City Council, which characteristically took great interest in such matters, Maxwell had struck another blow for professionalism and autonomy by appointing Robert Picucci as police chief. A highly trained professional, Picucci regarded his job as one of executive management. Accordingly, he distanced himself from the workaday street routines of police work, to the consternation of city fathers, who had had enough of that sort of thing in Maxwell.

Meanwhile, the national trend of societal alienation had reached Bath, and the problem of aimless, obstreperous groups of young people disturbing the peace had assumed serious proportions. Picucci's solution was to enroll youngsters in a police-sponsored program of community service—a tactic, critics said, that coddled offenders. When Bath police cracked down on such offenders, critics objected to the stern measures. Sniping at the police department was a way of getting at Maxwell.

BATH'S 'GREASER'S GRAVEYARD': THERE'S NO PLACE TO GO

BATH—To the regulars, it's called "greaser's graveyard." To police and city officials, it's simply the Water Street parking lot, one of the so-called trouble spots in the city where young persons congregate late at night.

. . . The city council recently passed ordinances prohibiting drinking in the lot, establishing an 11 p.m. curfew and governing disorderly conduct.

The action has resulted in frequent arrests there for disorderly conduct, drinking and a variety of violations. Public attention has been focused on the "Water Street problem" in light of recent public statements by District Court Judge Paul A. MacDonald who frequently dismisses some of the cases brought by Bath police.

MacDonald's statements, in turn, have angered some city officials who say the ordinances must be enforced to control problems in the lot.

. . . "We seem to be in an age where disrespect for the law in general, specifically to the police officers, is more predominant than it was four or five years ago," [Police Officer Orinton] Haines said. . . .

Councilor Herbert T. Caverly offered a similar view. He said the city should provide recreational activities, but is not required to establish a place for people to gather and break the law.

"That is against the law and they're infringing on the rights of others. I will not give them a place to go do that. Their thing is illegal and it's not going to be tolerated."

TIMES RECORD, 28 JULY 1976

YOUTH MAKING ELDERS UPTIGHT

The Crowd and the Library's Image

BY FAITH WOODMAN

An elderly woman said she was disgusted. Another said it was embarrassing and degrading. Still another said people were afraid and kept away.

These women, one a patron and the other two librarians of Patten Free Library, were referring to the behavior of some youths who gather in the parking lot and sit on the library steps. . . .

"We're not objecting to all the young people out here per se," said librarian Ruth Graffam. "What we are objecting to is the drinking and the language, and because it is so crowded. People get a bad picture of the library."

. . . The young men complained of being bored. They said they wished the city had year round recreational facilities which were free or inexpensive to use. They said they gathered at the parking lots to drink because

> they couldn't afford to go to bars. "The only difference between the older folks and us," one man said, "is we sit here and drink and they sit home and drink." . . .
>
> *TIMES RECORD*, 30 JULY 1976

As anyone who remembered Ralph Mittendorf, Nathan White, and Stanley Judkins could predict, it was simply a matter of time before accumulated frustrations would precipitate Jerry Maxwell's departure. In 1976, Council held a unique "judicial trial" on a variety of charges that had been leveled at the manager by councillors, city employees, and others. Caverly, who as Council chairman presided over the hearings, found little substance to the complaints. But in August of that year, Maxwell handed in his resignation, having taken a manager's position in Claremont, New Hampshire. Picucci left soon afterward.

The Maxwell administration's financial impact upon Bath cannot be assessed precisely because accounting procedures were changed during the period. The high inflation rate of the seventies must also be borne in mind. While overall expenditures climbed nearly 24 percent, expenditures in constant dollars peaked with Maxwell's first budget, then slowly declined. Debt as a percentage of valuation remained constant. As for priorities, expenditures for education climbed 1 percent in constant dollars; police and fire department outlays increased by fully 34 percent. By contrast, expenditures for public works declined by 38.6 percent by the end of Maxwell's term. Throughout the period, Bath's tax rate declined 6 percent in constant dollars, without an equivalent increase in valuation, largely because of increased federal revenue-sharing. Debt in actual dollars increased slightly but in constant dollars declined by 18 percent, again reflecting the inflationary impact.

Opinions about Maxwell's contribution to Bath, sharply divided in 1976, would soften over time. Maxwell had left his mark, having at least eked out a foothold for executive professionalism and a constituency to support it. A decade after his departure, his adversary Caverly believed Maxwell had accomplished his mission, which was "to bring the City of Bath out of the nineteenth century kicking and screaming. . . . He was an antagonist to the council, defied the council, did things his way. They got done. . . . If it were not for Jerry Maxwell, we would not have the community that we have today."[17] Ted Bradbury deemed him "an able administrator. He needed a council around him that would rein him back because he was a very gung-ho type guy. But I think that's easier to deal with than the other way."[18]

Bill Kay, who directed the Chamber of Commerce in that period, believed that "Jerry was outstanding in his leadership to this community, and he was probably a little bit ahead of his time. . . . I think had we not had a strong city manager at this time that possibly the restoration program wouldn't have moved ahead as well. He seemed to work well with the people that wanted this restoration program. . . . I don't think he did anything in Bath that wasn't fully to the long-range benefit."[19] Larry Cilley, Maxwell's successor, believed Maxwell had accomplished his mission as manager, knowing he would move on to bigger things: "He, in fact, did do what he said he wanted to do: to bring Bath kicking and screaming by the legs to the twentieth century whether they wanted to come or not. He certainly had no interest in tenure; it was more a case of creating footstones."[20]

Larry Cilley's term as Bath city manager was also a case of creating footstones. Cilley was a Maine native but didn't look it. A seasoned California county administrator, he was urbane in appearance, reflective of mind, and had a sophisticated knack for understanding local issues in a larger context. In 1976, Cilley was planning to develop a private real estate business in Maine but heard that "Bath was looking for a city manager here. We had some conversations, and they wanted me to do it. It looked like my experience might be good for them, and it was a good opportunity to transition back from California, to come home, so we did that. I signed a three-year contract to do the city manager thing." Cilley, who was selected from a field of 150 applicants, saw an opportunity to complete the refinement of the managerial system. What faced him immediately, however, was the fallout from previous years: "Books in bad shape, people burnout, false promises, irate taxpayers, a debt that was going to affect tax rates for the next few years, no monies left in the reserves, an angry council that wanted to keep the momentum going and didn't have the money in their pockets to do it. And . . . I was going to work these miracles with my California experience."[21]

Cilley worked no miracles over his three-year term, but his years in office did provide a breather in which City Council and the manager could sort out problems and clear the air somewhat. Cilley's relaxed, philosophical demeanor also helped soothe frazzled nerves at City Hall. The new manager separated his position from that of the city clerk, with the latter position going to longtime assistant clerk Beverly Henrikson. As Caverly put it, "We had a manager who was looking to go into business . . . and wasn't going to rock the boat."[22]

Much of Cilley's time was spent revamping the accounting system. He put the city on a program budget so that Council could see exactly where expenditures were going. (The format did not outlast his administration, however.) He brought Bath's business year into alignment with the state's. Cilley's other financial concern was the damaging effect of national inflation on Bath's expectations. What emerged was a move for retrenchment, a withdrawal from high expenditures for revitalization. Accordingly, although actual dollar amounts increased during Cilley's administration, expendi-

TIMES RECORD

VIPs look over bath's award-winning downtown. Left to right: Senator Edmund Muskie, Councillor Andrew Hart, City Manager Larry Cilley, and Councillor Charlie MacDonald.

tures for city services declined in constant dollars. The debt, in constant dollars, remained fairly stable, varying between 2.4 and 2.9 percent of the city's valuation. There was a noticeable decline in funding of the once-favored public works department, whose budget dropped below public safety, where it remained thereafter.

Strategically speaking, renewed emphasis was placed upon stimulating private enterprise, a tactic that was paying off in the downtown. Cilley actively promoted business development in Bath, although private projects pursued for the downtown did not materialize. One such was a multilevel parking garage and office tower proposed for the rather seedy area of Water Street between Elm and Center, formerly home to the American House and, later, the erstwhile "Greaser's Graveyard" hangout for Bath youth. The project would have been a decisive step toward reducing Bath's perennial parking problems—problems that were worsening as expanding BIW recruited more out-of-town workers—but it never received enough support to go beyond the basic concept.

Another opportunity, which popped up suddenly in 1979, involved the city with a Cleveland developer who proposed a spectacular project for the waterfront, still the area of least creative use and most potential. The planned development was to be called Captains' Walk, Cilley recalled, "and it was going to be fifty shops and specialty shops. K mart was going to come in, but they weren't going to do their usual K mart theme. They were going to dress it up with a brick building and have a large parking lot in back. We had federal financing to do it."[23] The federal government would have provided an Urban Development Action Grant (UDAG) to cover costs of street, water, and sewer work. Here, possibly, was a last chance for low-risk urban renewal.

At Cilley's behest, three councillors quietly flew to Cleveland to discuss the matter before rumor took control in the downtown. Caverly, one of the three, returned elated by the prospect: "There would have been a motel, there would have been . . . a lot of other stores, restaurants, etcetera. At that time the estimated taxable value to the city would have been $50 million."[24] The project, it was thought, would combine with Washington House and the readapted customs house to anchor the now-attractive but still-fragile downtown economy. Might the city achieve, at last, the long-sought escape from overdependence on the Iron Works?

No sooner had the delegation returned to Bath, however, than word about Captains' Walk rippled through the downtown. It touched off a blitz of opposition. Once the matter was out in the open, it didn't have a chance against public opinion. As Caverly recalled, "The downtown merchants at that time took the position, 'This [district] was given to us. It's ours. You can't change it or add anything to it.' That was not the philosophy under which downtown was redone. . . . "[25] How times had changed in downtown Bath. For better or worse, the new shopping center off Congress Avenue, anchored by a Shaw's supermarket but no large department or discount store, had ended some of the uncertainties about the downtown's commercial future. And, at a public hearing on the issue, fears were expressed that Captains' Walk would draw "the wrong kind of people" to the city. Furthermore, as Cilley put it, "A lot of the Bath bluebloods and the carriage trade on Washington Street . . . liked Bath the way it was. . . . "[26] To the consternation of Cilley, Caverly, and the Cleveland developers, who thought the plan would be a shoo-in, the City Council voted against the requisite UDAG grant and the matter died. Thus ended the last attempt to put a big retail store in the downtown. Meanwhile, Commercial Street continued to be a Cinderella as the downtown continued its conversion into a district of specialty shops.

TIMES RECORD

Bud Caverly.

Just a few years earlier, Bath citizens might have been dazzled by such a plan as Captains' Walk; but, in defense of merchants, bluebloods, and carriage traders, it could be argued that an Early Americanized K mart on the banks of the Kennebec was not the most sensitive use of Bath's waterfront, especially in light of all the effort to maintain the integrity of the district's historic character and the controversy surrounding BathPort. (Peggy Chapman described the architectural cosmetics proposed for Captains' Walk as " 'colonial' in the A&P sense of the word," and Bud Shepard, who considered the project a gauche monstrosity, would ever after refer to it as "Caverly's Folly.")[27] City Planner Paul Bracciotti's obvious displeasure with the concept also helped discredit it. Another symptom of the changed times was Cilley's disinclination to push the matter the way his predecessor might have done: "I was trying to promote a diversification of interest. . . . But it didn't happen and I was not a Maxwell complex. I simply suggested ideas and told them how to do it and how it could be accomplished. I figured you're smart enough to reach out and approve of things that were good for you. If you weren't, that's okay. I'm not so sure that philosophy is a good one. . . . I was getting tired. I didn't have much time or patience with the pettiness that was entrenched, and so I turned my attention to cleaning up City Hall, getting good people who would do good jobs, and cleaning up the messes in the books and the finances."[28]

Ray Gaul, a retired naval officer and former director of the Bath Housing Authority, replaced Cilley in October 1979, when the latter went into private business. A native of Reading, Pennsylvania, Gaul had seen enough of Maine during his Navy years to prompt him and his family to settle in the Bath area. Gaul was a known quantity. His military career had equipped him with formidable management and engineering credentials and the confidence that came from command: "When I took the [city manager's] job, it didn't matter to me whether I had a contract or not, because I wasn't in this for a career. I had already had two careers; I didn't need a third one. And we really didn't need a contract; but if they felt better about having a written contract, fine, that was okay with me. I told them, 'If it ever gets to the point where I feel I'm no longer contributing something that is worthwhile, you won't have to fire me, I'll quit.' "[29] Gaul was dedicated, scrupulously honest, painfully blunt, fiscally conservative, and a hard-liner when it came to waste in government.

He intended to run a tight ship. A hundred days into his administration, in a *Times Record* interview, Gaul stressed that waste was rife in City Hall. Most of the problem, he said, was poor personnel management: "The only way you can cut waste is by working closely with department heads and pointing out to them that their deficiency results in inefficiency."[30] Gaul's Navy-style, head-on approach soon put him into conflict with many of the city's employees and councillors.

By his own admission, Gaul knew little and cared less about the tendrils of Bath's grapevine and the bureaucratic informalities that, to him, spelled mismanagement. In short order he had run afoul of both. By early 1980, he found himself in conflict with the public works department when he forbade employees to use city equipment to snowplow their own driveways after logging hours clearing city streets.[31] A few weeks later, he faced a grievance from the police union when an officer was denied use of a police vehicle to go home for lunch.[32] These matters commenced a pattern of adversarial relations that dogged Gaul for two years of his term.

In a concurrent, well-publicized incident, Gaul threatened to dismiss Paul Bracciotti unless he submitted paperwork detailing planning expenditures by a specified date, an exchange that took place not in the sanctity of executive session but in a public meeting of City Council. Bracciotti, who as city planner had prepared grant applications worth millions to Bath, was incensed, and the following day asked Gaul for an apology. Gaul refused and Bracciotti resigned on the spot.[33] Then, in an apparently unrelated matter, popular City Clerk Beverly Henrikson proffered her resignation. According to the city charter, the clerk was responsible to the manager but answerable to Council for the conduct of her office, which may explain why, when faced with Henrikson's possible departure, Council convened a closed-door meeting with Gaul to review the latter's personnel problems to date, after which Henrikson withdrew her resignation and received a salary increase from Council.[34]

Gaul ran into other problems with councillors. When, for example, he tried to respond to a complaint about hazardous pollution seeping from a private dump used by BIW, the matter was dismissed as a neighborhood feud. The fact that Gaul's son Allen was a member of City Council during his father's administration led to rumblings about conflict of interest.

Gaul, meanwhile, had presented himself as dedicated to keeping city government within its means. Accordingly, his first budget, for fiscal year 1980–81, saw the inflation-driven process hit bottom at the lowest level of spending—in constant dollars—since the 1969 fiscal year. The next year, however, spending rose dramatically: 26 percent in constant dollars. The city debt also increased in both constant and absolute dollars as Bath bonded the first phase of its sewage-treatment improvement program.

During Gaul's tenure, several key city employees left. Complaints against the manager mounted, running the gamut from allegations that morale was tumbling among city employees to accusations that, in preparing his budget, he had underestimated federal revenue-sharing figures. Of course, Gaul was by no means solely to blame for the deteriorating situation. Council had not given up the old habit of interfering with the manager and the conduct of his duties. The source of many complaints was the propensity of unhappy city employees to go around Gaul and complain to city fathers, undermining both the chain of command and the statutory division of powers. Bath's council-manager system, it seemed, still operated at the convenience of City Council.

What followed could have been the plot for a two-act comic opera except for the damage it did to the city's reputation. City Council fired Gaul. Gaul took the city to court, where it was found that Council had had insufficient grounds for his dismissal, and won reinstatement and three months' worth of back pay. A year later, Council and Gaul finally came to terms, for by late 1981, Gaul had decided that "even if I had the wisdom of Solomon and had all the skills anybody could ask for, anything that I proposed at that point in time would have been turned around. In effect, I was hurting the city more than I was helping it because of this thing that had grown up between the Council and myself. As a result, I said, 'Hey! Here I am getting to a point where I don't even want to get out of bed in the morning and face that office down there. What am I doing this for?' So I finally resigned."[35]

By late 1981, Bath had regained the notoriety she had earned twenty years earlier with municipal professionals as a place where a manager was a short-timer.

Like his two predecessors, Peter Garland was a man who did not really need the job of Bath city manager. Garland had spent forty of his fifty-eight years in Saco, where he had served five terms as mayor in the fifties. In 1960, in an unusually harsh, mudslinging campaign, Garland, an archconservative Republican, won a seat in the U.S. House of Representatives, where he served until 1963. Since then, his employment had included stints in Maine as manager of Gorham and, from 1974 to 1981, Searsport.

Garland and his wife, a Bath native, came to the Shipbuilding City to

TIMES RECORD

Peter Garland.

retire. When he assumed the vacant manager's position in October 1981, he received the inevitable warnings from professional colleagues: " 'Oh my God! Don't go there,' they all warned me. 'They will eat you alive,' which indeed they were doing." But Garland had a great deal more rough-and-tumble political experience than his predecessors; so, looking on the bright side, he could see the job's inherent challenge: "Any half-decent person couldn't possibly fail, because the only way you could go is up. You couldn't go any lower."[36] To protect himself, Garland signed a three-year contract.

In 1982, as an additional precaution and, it was hoped, a cure for the confusion over division of powers, a review committee rewrote the city charter to delineate more clearly the roles of both Council and manager. But, of course, the old ways went on. By 1982, some councillors persisted in giving orders to department heads and staff. Others retained their suspicion of professionals from away, sometimes to the point of outright, pointed snubbing of city employees.[37]

The prestige of the manager's office reached an all-time low. In the spring of 1983, during a Council meeting on the forthcoming annual budget, Charlie MacDonald carelessly characterized Garland and his department heads as dishonest, cheating misappropriators. Although those remarks were clearly not intended as a showdown for the system, Garland took them as such: "This situation . . . [involved] a few individual councillors, but the rest were condoning what was going on, and so they were equally as guilty, virtually, by the fact that they said nothing. So I submitted my resignation in July of 1983 to the Council sixteen months in advance. . . . I didn't really want to resign, but I felt it was important that I bring it to a head, and I wanted to make an issue in that fall's municipal election here, and make my position clear, because I felt that I had a good feeling for the general public in Bath."[38]

That fall, support of the council-manager system was the key issue in the election. MacDonald did not seek reelection, which relieved Garland, "because I didn't want to do battle with him, being a personal friend. . . . "

TIMES RECORD

Charlie MacDonald at the time of the 1983 council-manager showdown.

In December 1983, "The newly elected Council, as they took their seats . . . , all pledged their support to the council-manager concept and to the manner in which it should be administered and in support of myself and the policies that I was trying to carry out. And from that point forward, it has just been an ideal situation."[39]

Financially speaking, the situation was characterized by an increase in total city expenditures in both absolute and constant dollars. For 1984–85, the city spent $10,506,106, ending the period with a bonded debt of $5,219,000. In constant dollars, however, Bath's total outlays were only marginally higher than a decade earlier. More significant was the steady decline in constant dollars of the city debt: By the end of 1985, it constituted but 2.3 percent of Bath's total valuation. Needless to say, Garland remained at City Hall beyond his contractual three years.

Contributing to the city's healthy financial condition was the slackening of national inflation; another factor was an enormous surge of outside interest in the region as a desirable place to visit or reside. Maine was enjoying a tourist boom, which of course was good for the economy. More important, by the mid-eighties, Bath was undergoing a wave of "gentrification": immigration of working and retired professionals, whose arrival drove up property values and, accordingly, the tax base.

The reason for the migration of upscale families and individuals to the area was an effect of changing values wherein "quality of life" superseded the traditional "standard of living." More and more Americans were without geographical roots, pursuing professional, creative, or service careers that permitted them to live where they wanted. Others took advantage of rapid transportation or electronic communications to move their work stations where they pleased. When looking for greener pastures, such people characteristically placed great importance upon affordable property, a leisurely pace, convenient recreational activities, an unpolluted environment, and regional character.[40]

Long a refuge for artistic individuals seeking a quiet life and/or inspirational surroundings, Maine had been a target for countercultural, back-to-nature migrants and farsighted professionals since the sixties. The movement snowballed after the easing of the energy crunch of the mid-seventies. By the eighties, Bath, heretofore overlooked in favor of other coastal communities, had become a magnet for professionals and white-collar retirees, thanks to its recent beautification, cultivation of cultural facilities and organizations, and affordable housing. (It was, of course, Bath's own champions of a higher "quality of life" who had lately magnetized the city for such outsiders.)

The influx of outsiders created a spectacular rise in real estate values, housing starts, and development schemes. Bath city fathers, who once wrung their hands at local stagnation, now burned the midnight oil trying

TIMES RECORD

Gentrification in Bath: before . . .

R.L. SNOW

. . . and after

to cope with growth pressures and the inadequacy of the city's 1983 comprehensive plan and land use code. "The Bath area is going through a metamorphosis which is a little scary and threatening to our value structure," wrote realtor Larry Cilley in the *Times Record* early in 1987. "Nevertheless, the change is being controlled by vigilant government officials who have given considerable forethought to exactly how to grow so that we don't become victims of uncontrolled growth."[41]

Brave words. Because growth pressures in Bath seemed to have come out of nowhere, forethought about exactly how to grow was inevitably limited—a safeguard but no guarantee of a smooth process. For example, Bath's forethought included possible ways to improve snarled traffic flow, including a second bridge across the Kennebec and a bypass from Congress Avenue to the South End—which, if implemented, were likely to exacerbate growth pressures. Garland was a little less sanguine about the future: "If there's a postage stamp in this community that's for sale, someone will come along and buy it and try to develop it. . . . We were late because the developers went to all the easily accessible, available spots first, but now they're finding Bath and they are just pouring in on us. . . . It's been creeping up the coast, and we're going to be as bad in this area in the not-too-distant future as they are in southern York County now. People don't realize it, but it's

TIMES RECORD

Gentrification in Bath: before . . .

R.L. SNOW

. . . and after.

R.L. SNOW

Upper Washington Street in 1988.

coming, it's inevitable, and there's nothing we can do to stop it. All we can do is make the best of it. I hope in another year we'll be able to get a full-time city planner back on board because we need . . . to plan at least to absorb this development which is taking place."[42]

Besides its pressure on available space, the influx of newcomers would have a profound demographic impact on Maine in general and Bath in particular. For one thing, it pumped new money and ideas into communities like Bath that just a few years earlier were singing the blues about the future.[43] For another, most of the arrivals were of childbearing age, which would have an exponential effect on static areas.[44] Propelled by enthusiasm for their adopted home, such people were apt to be active, and probably political, in the community. And they brought with them high expectations. It was thus just a matter of time before "carpetbaggers" were a force to be reckoned with.

Immigration to Bath made a neat fit with the restored downtown. By the time the last sidewalk brick was in place on Front Street, merchants and owners had accepted the fact that the district would never again become a solid shopping area now that shopping centers were stealing the retail thunder. But the period architecture and inviting storefronts of Front Street did attract specialty shops willing to cater to tourists' and new residents' upscale taste for wine and cheese, art supplies, local crafts and gifts, gourmet kitchenware, cocktails, and nouvelle cuisine. Some of these emporiums were playthings of proprietors who did not need to turn a profit. Others, miscalculating the market for luxury goods, folded and were replaced by new hopefuls.

Observing the turnover, Ted Bradbury wondered if the district shouldn't be earmarked for offices or even housing: "We keep trying to have a downtown where people are going to shop, and our store owners keep changing. . . . This year it is a place selling pine boards, and then next year it's

TIMES RECORD

Brie and Chablis: gentrification in Bath.

a bread place, and after that they're selling doilies. All these specialty shops, and they don't seem to be able to stay throughout the winter."[45] Longing for the days of now-vanished fish and meat markets, Laura Ridgewell likened the new downtown stores to the scented potpourri some of them sold: fragrant but insubstantial.[46]

WEAVER OPENS SHOP IN DOWNTOWN BATH

BATH—It took a move from New York City suburbs to a small city in Maine to put weaver Susan M. Kenlan in contact with people.

In Montclair, N.J., Kenlan wove custom fabrics for wholesale orders. She rarely saw the people who wore her elegant silk shawls or scarves, carried her clutchbags or reclined on her upholstery fabrics.

But Loom-in-Essence, the combined workshop and display space she opened this month at 23 Center St. in Bath, changed all that.

. . . Kenlan began weaving nine years ago. "I went to school to be a lawyer," she recalls. "In college I took a weaving class and just really gravitated toward the textiles."

. . . A summer vacation brought her to Midcoast Maine at a time when she was ready for a change. Kenlan and her assistant . . . packed up the business and moved to Bath. Two looms are set up in the 23 Center Street space where the weavers work above Ernie Back's newsstand. . . .

TIMES RECORD, 29 JULY 1983

PENELOPE'S WEB HAS NEW OWNERS

BATH—A familiar shop on Front Street has had new owners since last summer. Sisters Diane Wilhelm and Susan Bilodeau bought Penelope's Web and have increased its inventory.

Bilodeau has been running the store this fall, as her sister lives in Ohio.

. . . Owning a business is something Wilhelm and Bilodeau have wanted to do for about six years. Bilodeau just recently started knitting sweaters but Wilhelm and their mother have been knitting for a long time. They are originally from Bath.

They eventually plan to offer knitting and macrame classes. . . .

TIMES RECORD, 31 OCTOBER 1984

CRUISE SHIP SURPRISES TOWN WITH STOP HERE

BATH—American Cruise Lines caught the city by surprise this week when it called Monday to say the 210-foot motor vessel Savannah planned to tie-up at the public dock today at 1:30 p.m. for an overnight stay.

In May, the Connecticut firm notified the city that it had canceled its plans for its ships to stop in Bath this year.

"We had a wild few days," Mary Ella

Rogers, president of Sagadahoc Preservation Inc., said today. SPI was asked Monday to arrange a bus tour, as it had in the past, for the ship's passengers.

Rogers said SPI lined up two buses and two guides. . . . The cruise line indicated it planned to stop four more times this summer in the City of Ships.

. . . Since 1982, the ships have stopped in Bath for one night, and last summer's visits stretched to two nights. ACL contracted with the city . . . to ask that it provide tie-up space for the vessels.

That request led to the setting of two dolphin moorings off the Waterfront Park, part of a two-year $122,000 improvement project. . . .

TIMES RECORD, 18 JULY 1985

CHEVY DEALER TO CLOSE, SHIPYARD LEASES LOTS

BY SUSAN LAMB

BATH—Dodge Chevrolet plans to close by the end of this month and consolidate with Bill Dodge Oldsmobile, Inc. of Brunswick, Rupert Hurd, owner of the 108 Center St. business, said today.

Hurd has signed a three-year lease with Bath Iron Works, which plans to use three Dodge Chevrolet lots for employee parking. . . .

The three lots . . . are located between Leeman Highway and School Street. . . .

TIMES RECORD, 19 OCTOBER 1982

BIW DROPS PLEA TO HALVE ITS CITY TAXES

BY CHRISTINE KUKKA

BATH—Bath Iron Works announced today it was withdrawing its request that the City of Bath reduce by nearly one-half BIW's current property tax assessment.

After a series of meetings between BIW

officials and Bath Assessor Michael Austin, the two parties have agreed to an in-depth reappraisal of shipyard properties for the tax year 1984–1985.

. . . "This is a compromise that is the best for both worlds," Austin said. "I told them that I have always felt confident in my appraisal and if there was any error at all it would never be of the magnitude that they were discussing."

Earlier this year, BIW, which pays 36 percent of the city's property taxes, hired a firm to perform an appraisal of BIW property in Bath.

In a draft report to Austin, International Appraisal Co. of New Jersey asked for a tax abatement that would have halved the property taxes BIW pays to the City of Ships.

Apparently the appraisal company is going to take a back seat while Austin performs an in-depth, building-by-building reappraisal of the shipyard.

. . . The last time the city performed a building-by-building reappraisal of the shipyard was in 1977 when the Cole-Layer-Trumble Co. did a citywide revaluation.

. . . If BIW were able to halve its valuation, Bath homeowners could pay an additional $260 a year on an average home. . . .

TIMES RECORD, 1 JULY 1983

The most substantial factor in Bath's economic health was the growth of BIW, which in the 1980s paid 35 percent of Bath's property taxes.

TIMES RECORD

The Bath Iron Works was in a highly competitive position by the end of the 1970s. It had completed a long and agonizing modernization process under Jim Goodrich, then ironed out its sagging morale under John Sullivan. Because Congoleum had become a closely held private company, BIW no longer published the details of its business, but there is no doubt that business was extraordinarily good: an estimated annual pretax profit of 15 percent between 1979 and 1985.[47] BIW's stock-in-trade was still the ongoing FFG program, wherein the shipyard on the Kennebec vastly outperformed its competition. Between 1977 and 1987, BIW turned out twenty-four FFGs.

The very nature of FFG contracts also contributed substantially to BIW's profits. For one thing, the company did not have to lowball to beat out competitors' bids. For another, the contracts' inflation clauses provided that any cost savings would be shared between the Navy and the shipyard on a sixty-forty basis. As BIW's production system reached full swing, it realized large savings on each successive ship, which the company duly split with Uncle Sam. All twenty-four FFGs, including the last, which was held up by a four-month strike, were delivered ahead of schedule, some by as much as six months.

Sullivan, continuing Goodrich's policy, mixed civil with naval construction, all of it reportedly profitable. But the days of commercial deepwater shipbuilding were numbered. Federal subsidies for such work were almost gone, and foreign yards were drastically underpricing commercial work. For the Iron Works and its competitors, naval construction was about the only long-range hope. Pressed for space as always, BIW flirted with a proposal to move its lucrative ship repair operation to Boston, but opted instead for

TIMES RECORD

Portland after a controversial statewide referendum approved a Maine bond issue to finance the facility in 1981.

The Iron Works won contracts in two important naval programs, thanks in part to the Navy's abandonment of winner-take-all awards. In 1983, after the lead contract went to Litton, BIW became a second supplier for the Aegis cruiser, a vessel equipped with elaborate electronic fire-control systems designed to handle multiple threats simultaneously. The Aegis program was to extend through the 1980s. In 1985, after several hectic years of design and development competition ("the Destroyer Wars"), BIW won the lead ship contract for DDG-51, another high-tech vessel believed to be the Navy's last major surface-ship program of the century.

BIW had had its share of management problems since the John Newell days. In the eighties, as it grew and evolved in corporate structure, it had to face problems with the labor force as well. Employment had increased dramatically. In the 1981–83 period, it reached the highest peacetime level in BIW's history, 8,500 workers, then it declined as commercial work wound up and the FFG program moved toward completion. Most of the rank-and-file hailed from out of town. Hundreds of workers commuted daily to Bath, some from as far away as a hundred miles, lured by a wage scale that was almost the highest in the state. Around BIW's fifty-four-acre Bath site, houses and stores were razed to provide parking lots for vehicles, and pity the poor motorist who found himself in the area when the afternoon whistle blew, unleashing a horde of cars, buses, vans, and motorcycles that scat-

DON HINCKLEY, *TIMES RECORD*

The wrong place at the wrong time: Washington and Center streets during a BIW shift change, 1979.

tered frantically in all directions. The days of a local work force that management knew by first names were long gone.

Labor relations at BIW, which had worsened as the company went through its metamorphosis, improved again by the late seventies. Flush with success, and basking in the glow of media attention, the company scrupulously praised its work-force productivity. At launchings, union officials were included as VIPs, and speeches invariably noted the contribution of BIW labor. But the company had, in the main, purchased good labor relations via generous wage and benefit settlements with the unions. As BIW grew and its productivity became legendary, labor's expectations rose.

In 1983, having signed a labor contract, BIW management had to formulate its strategy to win the all-important DDG. Litton, BIW's principal competitor, had lately negotiated concessions from its work force. In Bath,

TIMES RECORD

where wage scales were higher than Pascagoula's, management approached the shipbuilders' AFL-CIO local for concessions in return for profit sharing. The rationale was to keep BIW in the running for DDG by paring down costs in advance. Negotiations proceeded. In 1984, after the union apparently had offered a wage freeze, management proposed a contract calling instead for lower starting wage scales, more cross-trading of skills between workers, and an end to seniority rules. On the advice of union leadership, the work force rejected the proposal.

Contributing to the breakdown was the suspicion among the rank-and-file that the moneymen in distant Congoleum, whose leveraged buyout had taken the company's financial details behind closed doors, were preparing to sell BIW and needed a sweet labor contract to do so. Assurances by Bill Haggett, the company's new president, that Congoleum did not call the shots were apparently unconvincing.[48] Despite demands by the union that

BIW document its expressed need for concessions, management persistently declined to reveal its financial picture.

The union resolved to strike when its contract expired, and did so in July 1985. BIW, meanwhile, had snagged its DDG award. The strike, which lasted ninety-nine days, came at a slack time, so its impact was blunted. In September, the work force caved in and bitterly accepted a new contract with more concessions than it had rejected the year before.

With a concessionary labor contract and the lead contract for DDG, Bath Iron Works was a hot property. In August 1986, Congoleum's owners broke up their conglomerate, selling BIW to Prudential Insurance Company and a Wall Street firm, Gibbons, Green and VanAmerongen, for an estimated $400 to $500 million.

The new owners were reportedly prepared to recognize the autonomy of the shipyard management. For their part, Haggett and his team faced several long-range challenges. Would the company's labor strife erode its fabled productivity? Did BIW have the technical know-how to complete the incredibly complex ships it had contracted to build for the rest of the century? Was the Kennebec riverbank a viable spot for future shipbuilding? Were there alternatives? These were questions of regional, possibly national, importance.

BIW's last FFG, the frigate *Kauffman*, went down the ways to the traditional accompaniment of whistles, horns, cheers, and snapping pennants, on 29 March 1986, after which attending dignitaries were treated to an elaborate buffet reception at the Brunswick Naval Air Station.

If a visiting *Kauffman* VIP had had time to explore Bath, he or she probably would have been surprised by the contrast between first impressions and familiarity.

Most visitors to Bath approached by car from points west along Route One's scenic divided highway. Reaching the top of Witch Spring Hill, our VIP would first have glimpsed the distant towering BIW crane, then noted that the attractive countryside had given way to Leeman Highway's short but sign-encrusted strip development: a stretch of new and old service stations and assorted pocket-size establishments designed to make life convenient if not pleasant for motorists. Facing Leeman Highway was the Holiday Inn, Bath's only motel. The old Sedgwick, where VIPs used to stay, had burned down more than a decade earlier. Across the highway from the Holiday Inn was the small but crowded Bath Shopping Center, complete with a McDonald's drive-through restaurant. How many travelers, beholding all this, had decided to keep moving?

Easier said than done, perhaps. If our visitor were unlucky enough to be on Leeman Highway when the afternoon shift change occurred at BIW, he would have had plenty of time amid the gridlock to take stock of the view below the Carlton Bridge's viaduct. The prospect was interesting, even

R.L. SNOW

Looking north on Long Reach in 1988. Contrast this view with its counterpart in Chapter One.

pleasant. To the north was a panorama of steeples, cupolas, and a couple of blocks' worth of inviting, antiquated commercial section. There were holes in its skyline where old buildings had been cleared away so that hundreds of cars could park on the empty spaces.

To the south stretched the intriguing complex of the shipyard, with several naval vessels on the ways or alongside in the ice-strewn Kennebec. It was an impressive sight. Aside from an idle bulk hauler rusting at the Coal Pocket a few blocks north, the warships and their attending tugs were the only large vessels in a river that once had teemed with ships of all descriptions. Traffic on the Kennebec was seasonal, and for fun. If it had been summer, our visitor would have noted dozens of small pleasure craft buzzing upriver and down or neatly clustered near the city's tiny waterfront park.

A look around town would make any VIP forget the gasoline-alley look

R.L. SNOW

Commercial Street and the Carlton Bridge in 1988. Contrast this view with its counterpart in Chapter One.

of Leeman Highway. Front Street featured congenial spots for a lunch or dinner break (one restaurant was rumored to have been named for an erst-while city manager) a few doors down from Bud Shepard's clothing store. Even in late winter, there were several shops where a visitor could buy souvenirs of the Shipbuilding City and its products, and, perhaps, wonder who at home might enjoy a T-shirt emblazoned, "FRIGATE IS NOT A DIRTY WORD IN BATH, MAINE." The obligatory ride up north Washington Street revealed swank, old-money homes restored to their one-time splendor. Every neighborhood, in fact, had its share of big and small houses of historic character undergoing repair and restoration.

Watching the *Kauffman* go down the ways at BIW, a visitor would have noted the nearby Carlton Bridge, which in recent years was often jammed with cars regardless of season. The talk around town was about traffic, tourism, carpetbaggers from away, and, of course, how long the boom would last.

Bath's struggle to make headway in a changing world had been constrained by its peculiar geography, its history, and economic forces beyond its control. In many ways, the long haul since the Depression had been a case of muddling through, wherein the city reacted to big and small emergencies, then rested on its oars until the next crisis arrived. Its preoccupation with a low tax rate afforded a handy excuse to avoid expensive

TIMES RECORD

Old and new at a Morse High School reunion, 1983: Sillie Niles, Class of '08, and Scott Harrison, Class of '83.

municipal programs. For years, its treasured self-image of sturdy individualism offered a philosophical rationale for avoiding community action and made citizens wary of governmental aid, despite the fact that the city had been directly aided by Uncle Sam since the thirties. Also complicating Bath's progress was the fact—although few would admit it—that there was a wide gap between the values of its blue-collar and its white-collar citizens.

By the eighties, the city at last had gotten its political house in order. It had come to terms with financial reality and mastered the art of tapping outside funding sources for its vital needs, as the accomplishments of the Bath Housing Authority demonstrated. It had also learned the art of community action, as the exemplary downtown renovation proved.

Bath's desire to reduce its overdependence on one industry had been a recurrent, frustrating theme for decades. In the eighties, changing national attitudes and tastes offered the Shipbuilding City the opportunity to exploit further the potent resources of natural beauty and historic character that were proving so appealing to tourists and newcomers.

Creative management of its scenic and historical assets would require several massive efforts. The city would have to continue its circumspect planning and vigilant zoning so that the development crunch and traffic control did not eat Bath alive, as had happened elsewhere in Maine.

Simultaneously, city fathers would have to assume more of the burden of providing recreational and cultural facilities. Because of the assiduous plugging by Red McMann, Bath had been well equipped with outdoor athletic fields, and city fathers had lately taken an interest in promoting boating facilities, but Bath had little else to offer. (Somewhere in City Hall accounts lurked a swimming pool fund, decades old, that might be dusted off for recreational purposes.)

Bath taxpayers enjoyed an excellent library, marine museum, arts center, and educational opportunities (at the YMCA) at almost no municipal cost, thanks to the legendary generosity of local citizens living and dead. In 1986, for example, the Chocolate Church's supporters completed a major fund-raising drive that covered the building's renovation and conversion, and the Maine Maritime Museum raised $7 million for a massive new building to be built in the South End next to the Percy & Small Shipyard that was likely to become a major regional attraction. Times were changing, however. The resources of private individuals, however generous, were finite, and there were signs in 1986 that major local benefactors were approaching burnout. If the high and rising demands of future tourists and upscale newcomers were to be met, city support of Bath's cultural and recreational service organizations was a must.

Any successful strategy for exploiting the city's physical assets had to include creative use of the still-neglected, still-bedraggled waterfront. Because Bath remained seriously short of lodging for tourists and business visitors, there were repeated rumors and murmurs of a major hotel/restaurant/

recreational complex that would go up at or near the Coal Pocket, or behind the old customs house near the Bath side of the bridge. Presumably, by the late eighties, Bath citizens would be receptive to such a project and savvy enough about zoning, architectural integrity, and economic reality to give the nod. Meanwhile, integration of Commercial Street and the Kennebec riverbank with the historic downtown remained the biggest missing piece in Bath's revitalization.

To make the most of available state and federal aid and avoid duplication of effort, Bath would have to adopt a more regional attitude and plan accordingly. The parochialism of past years, however satisfying psychologically, was a self-indulgence that citizens could no longer afford. It still flourished in Bath, however. For example, when the Bath Marine Museum, taking a larger view of its mission, rechristened itself the Maine Maritime Museum, some charter supporters were outraged by the sellout, and the new name was still a small source of disapproval in the late eighties. Nonetheless, recommendations for the pooling of some services by Bath and Brunswick were at least a generation old, and had been specified further in the city's 1969 DX plan. If state and federal funding agencies saw fit to include Bath, Brunswick, Topsham, and nearby communities as a single entity, perhaps the Shipbuilding City should do the same. Yet several attempts at establishing a regional approach to planning in the greater Bath-Brunswick area had come to nothing.

There were signs that regionalism was coming by stages. Brunswick developers were making large investments in Bath and vice versa. And, after long negotiations, the boards of Bath Memorial and Brunswick's two hospitals resolved to consolidate in 1987. Connecting the Bath and Brunswick water districts for mutual emergency assistance was another positive step toward a larger view of asset management.

Despite recent successes, there was still hard work and much risk to be undertaken if the community was to improve its quality of life, diversify its economy, and achieve a measure of long-range security. It was worth the effort, of course. In any case, did Bath have a choice?

Old-timers in the Shipbuilding City prided themselves on their traditional conservatism despite the younger generations' litany that the city was behind the times. But lately, an old phrase about the state of Maine seemed applicable to Bath: The city was behind the times in the right direction.[49] To be sure, much from the old times was still visible in Bath. Even the decidedly unantiquated Iron Works continued the city's unique tradition. Everywhere there were reminders of past glory.

Occasionally there were reminders of past disasters. Take the Great Flood of '87, when March rain and melting snow swelled the Androscoggin and Kennebec, inundating low ground and threatening bridges. In Bath, spectators lined the riverbank to watch the cresting water take its captive houses

TIMES RECORD

and assorted debris on a ride to the sea, and, perhaps, to salvage something of value. Looking at the high water, old-timers said it was nothing compared to 1936. *That* was a disaster. Perhaps. But youngsters knew they would remember '87 for fifty years or more.

NOTES

1. Caverly interview.
2. Ibid.
3. Raymond A. Gaul, Interview, Bath, August 1987.
4. Van Note interview.
5. *City of Bath Annual Report*, 1972–1973.
6. Caverly and Bradbury interviews.
7. Harry E. Ring to the Bath City Council, Bath, 1 November 1972 (PFL).
8. Ring interview.
9. Van Note interview.
10. Ibid.
11. Ibid.

12. Hayward Newcomb, quoted in Bob Forkey, "Move Afoot . . . to Remove the City Manager," TR, 28 February 1974.
13. Robert Forkey, "Collision for Hard Driving Manager?," ibid.
14. Caverly interview.
15. Caverly, quoted in TR, 26 July 1976.
16. Forkey, "Move Afoot. . . . "
17. Caverly interview.
18. Bradbury interview.
19. William Kay, Interview, Bath, August 1987.
20. Larry Cilley, Interview, Bath, September 1987.
21. Ibid.
22. Caverly interview.
23. Cilley interview.
24. Caverly interview.
25. Ibid.
26. Cilley interview.
27. Chapman and Shepard interviews.
28. Cilley interview.
29. Gaul interview.
30. Gaul, quoted in TR, 22 January 1980.
31. TR, 1 February 1980.
32. Ibid., 6 March 1980.
33. Ibid., 7 and 8 February 1980.
34. Ibid., 7 February 1980; Gaul interview; Beverly Henrikson, Interview, Bath, October 1987. Henrikson declined to discuss the matter during her interview.
35. Gaul interview.
36. Peter A. Garland, Interview, Bath, October 1987.
37. Ibid. Calculated, even cruel snubs went back at least as far as the Maxwell years (Caverly interview).
38. Garland interview.
39. Ibid.
40. This rationale is discussed and defended at length on Maine terms in Richard Salstonstall, Jr., *Maine Pilgrimage: The Search for an American Way of Life* (Boston: Little, Brown, 1974).
41. Larry Cilley, "Revitalization in Bath," TR, 6 February 1987.
42. Garland interview.
43. See, for example, Peirce, p. 48.
44. Gregory Jackson, George Masnick, et al., *Regional Diversity: Growth in the United States, 1960–1990* (Boston: Auburn House Publishing Co., 1981), p. 37.
45. Bradbury interview.
46. Ridgewell interview.
47. Allan Dodds Frank, "Bath Money Works," *Forbes*, 10 September 1984, p. 58.
48. Ibid., p. 62.
49. Cilley, "Revitalization in Bath"; Cilley interview.

APPENDIX A

CITY OFFICIALS 1936–1986

MAYOR: 1936–1948

1936–38: Arthur Sewall
1938–39: Donald N. Small
1939–40: Arthur Sewall
1940–41: Robert H. Haskell
1941–46: Walter C. Rogers
1946–47: Dominique J. Tardif
1947–48: Donald N. Small

CHAIRMAN, CITY COUNCIL: 1948–1986

1948–49: Merritt A. Mitchell
1949–52: Rodney E. Ross, Jr.
1952–53: Stanley R. Hunter
1953–55: Merritt A. Mitchell
1955–56: Ronald C. Oulton
1956–59: Merritt A. Mitchell
1959–61: John F. Leonard
1961–62: Arthur E. Hutchins
1962–63: Frank E. Harvie, Jr.
1963–64: Merritt A. Mitchell
1964–65: William E. Haggett
1965–66: Elford A. Stover, Jr.
1966–67: C. Lloyd Hooker
1967–68: Edward J. Cummings
1968–69: Abraham E. Greenblatt
1969–71: Henry A. LeClair
1971–72: Alex Wasilewski, Jr.
1972–73: Charles F. MacDonald, Jr.
1973–74: Scotchy Doyle
1974–75: Andrew J. Hart
1975–76: David M. McKellar
1976–77: Herbert T. Caverly II
1977–78: John M. Lydon
1978–79: Herbert T. Caverly II
1979–80: Thomas E. Perry
1980–81: Herbert T. Caverly II
1981–84: David A. King
1984–87: John M. Lydon

BOARD OF ALDERMEN: 1936–1948

Anderson, Alden H.: 1944–46
Bowie, John F.: 1942–44
Bragg, Ralph W.: 1936–39
Burgess, Alexander, Jr.: 1938–41
Butler, Joseph A.: 1946–47
Carter, Harold J.: 1941–42
Cook, Randall F.: 1945–46
Cooke, John F.: 1945–46
Cooper, Lancelot H.: 1946–47
Drake, Frederick E.: 1937–39
Duley, William H.: 1940–41
Eaton, Philip A.: 1943–47
Emery, George W.: 1936–38
Footer, Edward A.: 1940–42, 46–47
Fortier, Frank T.: 1937–38

Gediman, Arthur W.: 1936–37, 41–43
Gillies, James A., Jr.: 1945–46, 47–48
Grant, James R.: 1947–48
Haskell, Robert H.: 1936–38
Hunt, J. Frank: 1940–42
Hunter, Stanley R.: 1946–48
Kingsbury, Ernest G.: 1941–44
Larrabee, Howard C.: 1946–47
Legard, Forrest C.: 1939–41
Luke, Roger M.: 1943–45
McInnes, Duncan: 1941–42
Mitchell, Merritt A.: 1938–40, 47–48
Newell, John R.: 1942–45
Oliver, Philip H.: 1942–44
Parks, Charles E., Jr.: 1940–41
Pinkham, Thatcher B.: 1937–38
Plummer, Charles W.: 1946–47
Powers, Henry M.: 1938–40
Reeks, Alfred G.: 1944–46, 47–48
Robbins, Edward M.: 1936–37
Robinson, Joseph A.: 1947–48
Robson, William O.: 1937–39
Rogers, Walter C.: 1940–41
Rothwell, Edmund A.: 1944–45
Sheldon, Leburton D., Jr.: 1947–48
Shepard, Charles A.: 1942–43
Small, Donald N.: 1939–40
Temple, James W.: 1939–40
Thayer, Charles A.: 1941–46
Turner, Frank H.: 1936–37, 39–40
Whittemore, Ellery E.: 1938–39
Woodman, Horace B.: 1936–37

BOARD OF COMMON COUNCIL: 1936–1948

Allenwood, Guy: 1946–47
Anderson, Alden H.: 1942–44
Anderson, Herbert L., Jr.: 1941–42, 47–48
Annis, Louis D.: 1946–48
Avery, Harold S.: 1938–39
Bailey, Woodbury: 1936–38
Benson, Donald H.: 1941–43, 47–48
Blair, William S.: 1938–39
Blake, Howard E.: 1944–45
Bowie, John F.: 1941–42
Brooks, Harry H.: 1945–46
Burden, Alexander P.: 1938–40
Butcher, Kerwin B.: 1941–42
Cahoon, Earl P.: 1936–37
Carter, Harold J.: 1938–41, 43–45
Chaney, John A.: 1947–48
Child, Harold W.: 1939–40, 46–47
Clement, Chester W.: 1941–43, 45–47
Comeau, James A.: 1943–45
Cooke, John F.: 1944–45
Coombs, Charles A., Jr.: 1940–44
Coombs, Isaac C.: 1945–46
Crooker, Wilbur H.: 1939–40
Cummings, Thomas J.: 1946–48
Day, Walter F.: 1938–41
Donnell, William T.: 1936–38
Dunton, Frank O.: 1939–41
Eames, Linwood: 1944–45
Eaton, Philip L.: 1942–43
Emery, George M.: 1943–44, 47–48
Eseley, Louis P.: 1936–38
Fenn, Converse F.: 1943–45, 47–48
Footer, Edward A.: 1938–40
French, Carl G.: 1944–45
Gaudet, John D.: 1945–46
Gay, Ralph: 1936–38
Gediman, Arthur W.: 1937–38, 46–48
Grant, James Russell: 1946–47
Green, Langdon E.: 1942–44
Green, Robert D.: 1944–45
Greene, William L.: 1939–40
Haggett, Charles L.: 1939–40
Harrington, Harold H.: 1939–40
Hart, Eugene G.: 1940–41
Hart, John E.: 1936–37, 38–39, 40–42
Haynes, W. Linwood: 1945–46

Henderson, David S.: 1936–37
Hunt, J. Frank: 1939–40
Hunter, Stanley R.: 1941–46
Jackson, Mark A.: 1938–39
Jean, Clarence L.: 1940–41
Jewett, Donald M.: 1942–43
Jones, James A.: 1943–45
Kennerson, Walter I.: 1945–46
Kidder, Charles H.: 1943–44
Kingsbury, Ernest G.: 1940–41, 44–45
Knight, Harry L.: 1942–43, 44–45
Lake, Vernon B.: 1936–37, 47–48
Larrabee, Howard C.: 1945–46
Leavitt, Edgar D.: 1938–39, 41–42
Legard, Forrest C.: 1936–38
Leonard, John M.: 1940–41
Lermond, Earle B.: 1942–45
Longley, Cyrus W.: 1941–43
Lovett, Jasper H.: 1946–48
Luke, Roger M.: 1941–42
Lyden, Walter G.: 1947–48
MacElman, Donald E.: 1946–47
MacKinnon, Clyde L.: 1945–48
McCabe, Alfred P.: 1942–43
McCausland, Edgar B.: 1938–39
McFadden, Roscoe C.: 1936–37, 45–46, 47–48
McLaughlin, Joseph A.: 1938–40
Marchetti, Joseph: 1940–41
Marks, William P.: 1938–39, 40–42
Marsh, Oscar R.: 1947–48
Martin, Cedric A.: 1945–46
Mitchell, Merritt A.: 1937–38, 46–47
Morse, Earl P.: 1937–39
Morse, Franklyn W.: 1946–47
Morse, Herbert R.: 1937–38
Mullaney, John E.: 1940–41, 46–47
Mullin, David P.: 1940–41
Murray, Kenneth M.: 1945–48
Mussenden, William F.: 1947–48
Newell, John R.: 1940–42
Oliver, Philip H.: 1940–42, 46–48
Oliver, Roger A.: 1943–44, 45–46
Oliver, William W.: 1940–41
Osborne, John F.: 1941–43
Parks, Alfred A., Jr.: 1939–41, 46–47
Parks, Charles E., Jr.: 1939–40
Perry, Carleton W.: 1945–46
Pierce, Roger W.: 1936–38
Pinkham, Thatcher B.: 1936–37
Pletts, Robert C., Jr.: 1942–43
Plummer, Charles W.: 1944–45
Plummer, William F.: 1942–44
Plummer, William F., Jr.: 1944–45
Povich, Morris S.: 1942–43
Pratt, E. Melvin: 1945–48
Pratt, Foster M.: 1940–42
Prentiss, Lewis E.: 1943–46
Reeks, Alfred G.: 1943–44
Robbins, Edward M.: 1938–40
Robinson, Roland B.: 1943–45
Robson, William O.: 1936–37
Rodick, Harris T.: 1936–38
Rogers, Elmer W.: 1938–39, 42–43
Rogers, Gardiner D.: 1938–40
Rogers, Walter C.: 1936–40
Ross, Rodney E., Jr.: 1947–48
Rothwell, Edmund A.: 1941–44
Savage, Melvin H.: 1936–38
Sheldon, Leburton D., Jr.: 1946–47
Shepard, Charles A.: 1939–42
Small, Charles T., Jr.: 1937–39
Small, Donald N.: 1936–37
Small, Harold P.: 1936–39, 41–43, 44–45
Small, Ralph F.: 1937–38
Smith, Bartlett O.: 1936–38
Snowdon, Rupert A.: 1940–41
Sterling, Frederick A.: 1945–47
Stinson, Carl E.: 1939–40
Stover, Elford A.: 1942–44
Tabor, David D.: 1939–42
Tardif, Dominique J.: 1936–38
Thomas, Edward P., Jr.: 1942–46
Troop, Harold L.: 1944–46
Turner, Frank H.: 1937–38
Turpie, William: 1945–46
Wallace, Stanley E.: 1936–37, 39–40, 41–42

Watson, Theodore F.: 1943–44
Webber, Elbridge E.: 1938–39
Weston, Waldo R.: 1938–39
Wilson, Paul B.: 1946–48
Witham, John O.: 1943–47
Woodman, Horace B.: 1937–38

CITY COUNCIL: 1948–1986

Adams, Oscar S.: 1950–52
Allen, Jesse W.: 1949–55
Atkinson, Edward G.: 1955–64
Bailey, Boyd L.: 1956–59
Bates, Delmar E.: 1949–51
Berkery, Edward G.: 1963–65
Berry, Paul A.: 1967–69
Billings, Leon J.: 1965–67
Blair, Grace: 1956–58
Bradbury, Theodore E.: 1969–71
Brewer, Robert E.: 1954–56
Burden, Ralph, Jr.: 1972–74
Burgess, Richard: 1978–80
Butterfield, Andrew M.: 1948–50
Carter, Harold J.: 1969–70
Caverly, Herbert T., II: 1968–70, 75–79, 80–81
Chadwick, Laura Lee: 1980–83
Clark, Byron: 1952–54
Comeau, David J.: 1983–
Comeau, Melvin: 1952–54
Cooke, Harry E.: 1952–55
Cooper, Lancelot H.: 1948–50
Couture, Louis O.: 1951–55
Cummings, Edward J.: 1964–69
Cummings, Thomas J.: 1948–50
Dickson, David C.: 1948–50
Doyle, Scotchy: 1970–74
Dutton, Charles W.: 1975–77
Fenn, Converse G. : 1948–49
Filler, Stephen A.: 1982–
Finn, Charles J.: 1977–80, 82–83, 86–
Gaul, R. Allen, III: 1977–82
Gediman, Arthur W.: 1948–67
Grayson, Arthur: 1979–80
Greenblatt, Abraham E.: 1967–69
Grill, John A.: 1971–73
Guild, Eastham, Jr.: 1951–55
Haggett, William E.: 1964–68
Hart, Andrew: 1972–77, 78–
Harvie, Frank E.: 1958–63
Hecht, Joseph: 1952–54
Hill, James W.: 1969–71
Hinds, John J.: 1973–76, 83–87
Hooker, C. Lloyd: 1963–66, 68–70
Hunter, Stanley R.: 1948–57
Hutchins, Arthur E.: 1950–52, 59–62
Jaeger, Hector: 1982–
Jordan, Edward A.: 1975–76
Kelley, Dorothy E.: 1974–77
King, David A.: 1980–86
King, Marc N.: 1961–64
Kingsbury, Ernest G.: 1967–69
Kuzmickas, Dennis: 1985–86
Lawson-Stopps, Ruth: 1986–
LeClair, Henry A.: 1967–73
Lee, Edward J.: 1957–61
Leonard, John F.: 1954–56, 59–61
Libby, Hilton F.: 1965–67
Lydon, John M.: 1975–78, 80–82, 83–
MacDonald, Charles, Jr.: 1955–56, 61–62, 63–79, 80–83
MacElman, Harold W.: 1948–52
McGuiggan, James: 1954–56
McKellar, David: 1973–80, 82–85
McMann, Edward J.: 1963–65
McPhee, Wesley: 1955–56
Madden, Joseph H.: 1948–50
Main, Archibald M., Jr.: 1950–54
Marchant, Paul: 1957–59
Marco, Wesley: 1952–54
Marsh, Oscar: 1961–64
Meyer, Donald J.: 1973–75
Mitchell, Merritt A.: 1948–49, 51–52, 54–61, 62–64
Murphy, G. Thomas: 1955–56
Murray, Martha: 1971–73

Nadeau, Richard: 1979–82, 86–
Newcomb, Hayward A.: 1971–75
Oliver, Philip H.: 1952–55
Oulton, Ronald C.: 1952–56
Owen, William W.: 1949–50
Pecci, Clarence T.: 1970–72
Perry, Donald F.: 1952–64
Perry, Thomas E.: 1977–80
Quimby, Everett M., Jr.: 1970–72
Quimby, Richard A., II: 1974–78
Redlon, Richard O.: 1968–70
Rioux, Timothy: 1978–80
Rogers, Walter C.: 1948–49
Rogers, William R.: 1961–62
Ross, Rodney E., Jr.: 1948–52
Rowe, Harvey V.: 1954–56
Sarkis, George A.: 1962–68
Savage, Milton H.: 1969–71
Sheldon, Leburton D., Jr.: 1948–49
Sides, Andrew B., Jr.: 1961–62
Skillings, Warren P.: 1966–68
Small, Gerald T.: 1976–83
Small, Harold P.: 1949
Sonia, Harold J.: 1949–52
Stinson, Lucy E.: 1972–74
Stover, Elford A., Jr.: 1964–66
Sturtevant, Arthur E.: 1950–52
Tanguay, Oscar J.: 1957–58
Temple, James W.: 1956–61
Thurlow, Etta M.: 1948–52
Tibbetts, Charles H.: 1981–
Trafton, John F.: 1962–64
Wagner, William O.: 1955–57
Wasilewski, Alex, Jr.: 1970–72, 74–75

City Manager: 1948–1986

1948–52: Ralph F. Mittendorf
1952–55: Nathan C. White
1955–61: Stanley W. Judkins
1961–72: Harry E. Ring, Jr.
1972–76: Jerry L. Maxwell
1976–79: Larry D. Cilley
1979–81: Raymond A. Gaul, Jr.
1981– : Peter A. Garland

City Clerk: 1936–1986

1936–42: John W. Gilmore
1942–44: Chesley L. Hutchins
1944–46: John W. Gilmore
1946–72: Harry E. Ring, Jr.
1972–76: Jerry L. Maxwell
1976– : Beverly Henrikson

Fire Chief: 1936–1986

1936–37: Charles E. Parks
1937–40: Scott Morse
1940–64: Richard J. Frates
1964–72: Charles W. Swearingen
1972 : Willard McCabe
1972–81: Norman C. Kenney
1981– : Ronald Clark

Chief of Police: 1936–1986

1936–38: Walter L. Whitney*
1938–42: Joseph A. Butler*
1942–47: Percy W. Kingsbury*
1947–48: Langdon E. Green*
1948–53: Frank L. Moriarty
1953–58: Edward L. Gaudreau
1958–73: Robert E. Wagner, Jr.
1973–77: Robert P. Picucci
1977–83: Charles R. Bruton
1983 : Lawrence Dawson (Acting Chief)
1983–87: Thomas Landers

(*City Marshal)

CHAIRMAN, BOARD OF EDUCATION/SCHOOL COMMITTEE: 1936-1986

1936–40: William L. Skelton
1940–41: Allan Spear
1941–51: Edwin A. Andrews
1951–54: Henry A. Powers
1954–56: John M. Conley, Jr.
1956–59: Robert Perry
1959–60: Linwood Temple
1961–62: C. Lloyd Hooker
1962–63: Linwood Temple
1963–64: Abbott Fletcher
1964–65: Donald Small
1965–66: Edward Butterfield
1966–67: Linwood Temple
1967–68: Abbott Fletcher
1968–69: Donald Small
1969–70: Edward Butterfield
1970–71: Lawrence Boardman
1971–72: Abbott Fletcher
1972–73: Warren Skillings
1973–74: Edward Butterfield
1974–75: Lawrence Boardman
1975–76: Abbott Fletcher
1976–77: Elford A. Stover, Jr.
1977–79: Sally Haggett
1979–80: Diane Moyer
1980–84: Sally Haggett
1984–86: Arthur Grayson

BOARD OF EDUCATION/SCHOOL COMMITTEE: 1936-1986

Andrews, Edwin R.: 1940–52
Bell, Oliver W.: 1959–61
Boardman, Lawrence: 1967–75
Brewer, Ralph W.: 1954–59
Burden, Alexander A.: 1946–49
Butterfield, Edward: 1962–74
Conley, John M., Jr.: 1952–56
Dearborn, Carl R., Jr.: 1959–62
Dunton, Arthur J.: 1936–43
Dutton, Charles W.: 1977–81
Fitzgerald, Duane D.: 1975–76
Fletcher, Abbott: 1961–76
Grayson, Arthur: 1980–86
Haggett, Sally: 1976–86
Hooker, C. Lloyd: 1949–52, 54–62
Hunt, J. Frank: 1943–47
McCurdy, Dana: 1977–83
McKellar, William: 1983–86
Marchetti, Joseph, Jr.: 1981–85
Mayo, Arthur, III: 1974–76
Miller, Justus H.: 1942–46
Mitchell, Merritt A.: 1963
Moyer, Diane: 1976–80
Mulligan, Brian: 1985–
Noyes, Albert S.: 1941–46
Perry, Robert: 1952–59
Powers, Henry A.: 1946–54
Skelton, William L.: 1936–40
Skillings, Warren: 1969–73
Small, Donald: 1962–69
Smith, Alden G.: 1936–40
Smith, Marion L.: 1947–54
Spear, Allan: 1936–41
Stover, Elford A., Jr.: 1973–77
Temple, Linwood: 1956–67
Towne, Selwyn H., Jr.: 1940–42
Wade, Earl: 1959

SUPERINTENDENT OF SCHOOLS: 1936-1986

1936–38: Clinton D. Wilson
1938–42: John Parker
1942–45: Harland A. Ladd
1945–64: Loring R. Additon
1964–78: Clifford P. Tinkham
1978–86: Patrick Donahue

APPENDIX B

Library Trustees 1936 & 1986

1936

Trustees

Walter S. Glidden
President

Arthur K. Purington
Secretary

Omar W. Folsom

William S. Newell

Harry B. Sawyer

William S. Shorey

Langdon T. Snipe

Ex Officio

Arthur Sewall
Mayor, City of Bath

Donald N. Small
President, Bath Common Council

Nonvoting

Charles C. Low
Treasurer

Allan Spear
Curator

Daniel Williams
Auditor

Librarian

Margaret R. Foote

1986

Trustees

Susan Hummer
President

J. William Lister
Vice President

Joseph Allen

Margaret Bertocci

Jane Chapin

William F. Haney

J. Franklin Howe

Nancy St. John

Stephen Singer

Raymond Small

Donald A. Spear

Jane Stevens

Ex Officio

David King
Councillor, City of Bath

Peter A. Garland
Bath City Manager

Nonvoting

John C. Marsh
Treasurer

Loraine P. Crosby
Secretary

Librarian

Gary Berger

APPENDIX C

Publication Sponsors

Publication of this book
was made possible through the
generosity of the persons
listed on the following pages.

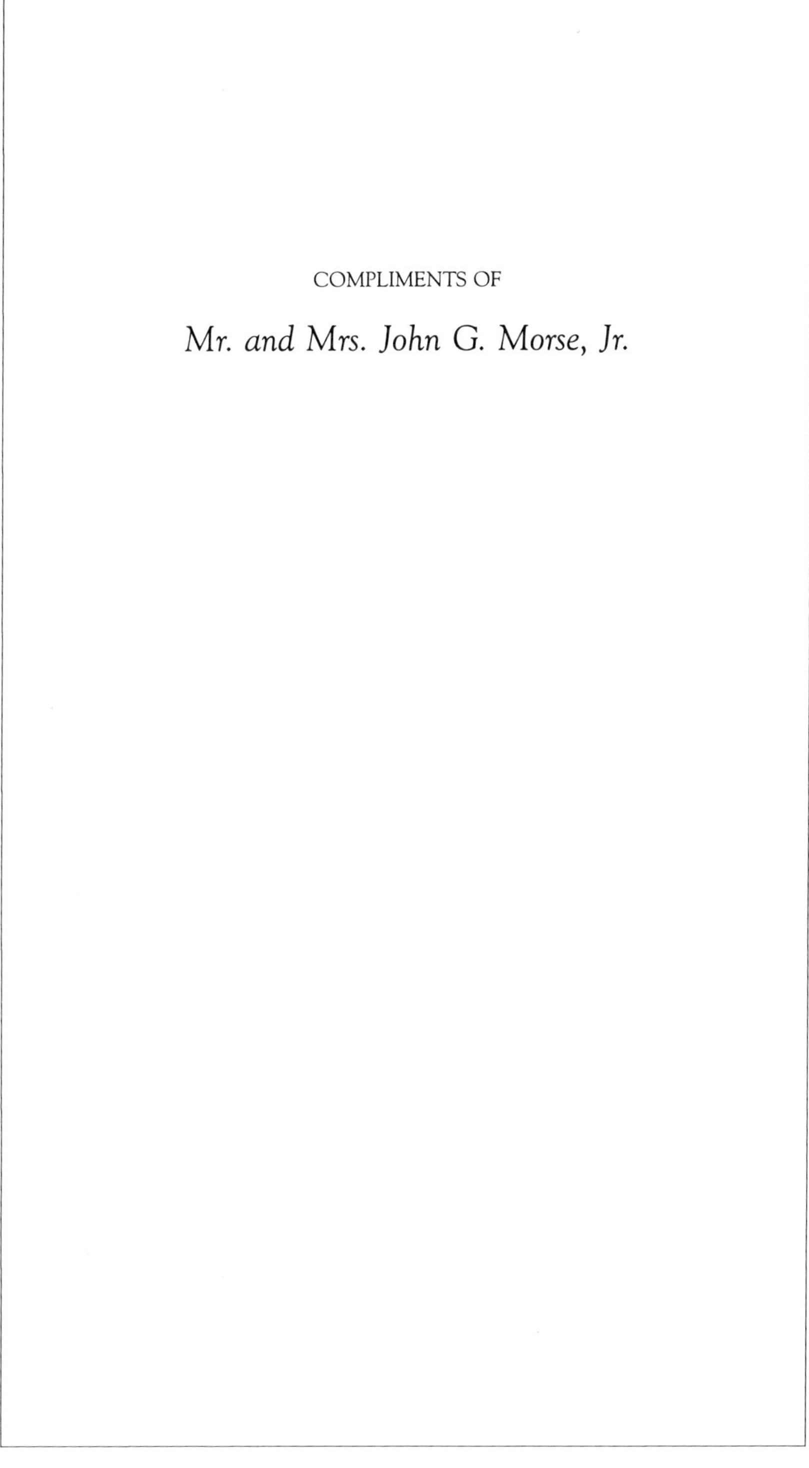
COMPLIMENTS OF
Mr. and Mrs. John G. Morse, Jr.

Dedicated in memory of all of
those citizens of Bath who have served
the City in an elective capacity
since its original incorporation
as a Town in 1781 through 1987.

BATH CITY COUNCIL

1988

Charles H. Tibbetts CHAIRMAN	Ward 6
Andrew J. Hart	At Large
Stephen A. Filler	At Large
Charles J. Turcotte	Ward 1
Maurice Cunningham III	Ward 2
H. Hector Jaeger	Ward 3
Richard D. Nadeau	Ward 4
David J. Comeau	Ward 5
Ruth Lawson-Stopps	Ward 7

A grant

toward the funding

of this publication

was made by

THE DAVENPORT TRUST FUND—

a trust created

under the will of

the late George P. Davenport

which continues to serve

as a legacy to

the City of Bath.

This history is dedicated
to the people of Bath
from your friends at
BATH SAVINGS INSTITUTION.

In memory of

Jacob Smith, M.D.

Bath's "Dr. Jake"
1909–1978

To all who have lived and worked on the sea;
to all who have built Bath ships;
and to all who would preserve that heritage.

MAINE MARITIME MUSEUM

BENEFACTORS

Mr. and Mrs. E. Barton Chapin, Jr.
Capt. and Mrs. Charles F. Richelieu
J. Franklin and Beverly P. Howe
Sandra W. and David R. Weiss
Mary Newell Guild
Bath Iron Works
The Times Record
Sumner A. Hawley
Mr. and Mrs. J.W. Lister
John William Voorhees
Friends of Patten Free Library
Thompson, Desmond and Payne
Mr. and Mrs. William E. Haggett
John and Karin Carter
First Federal Savings and Loan Association
In memory of Wilmer I. and Eleanor T. Voorhees

PATRONS

Gary Berger
Carl and Lucy Stinson
Frederick H. and Judith P. Clarke
Diane C. Francis
John F. Cooke
Marion Dean Shaw and Robert P. Shaw, Jr.
David A. King
Mixon Family of Meadowbrook Camping Area
Mr. and Mrs. Raymond C. Small
In memory of Harry L. Day, Trustee 1945–1953
In memory of Carol E. White
Charles E. Burden, M.D.
David R. Flaherty
Mr. and Mrs. R. Allen Gaul

SPONSORS

George and Nancy St. John
Robert E. and Marcia E. Foulger
Allan G. and Shirley B. Anderson
John D. and Margaret M. Chapman
Mr. and Mrs. J. Michael Conley
Steven and Kathleen L. Buttner
Mr. and Mrs. William F. Haney
Michael and Ann Badham
Carol and Red Mulligan
Ruth F. Attaya
Mr. and Mrs. Foster M. Pratt
Harry B. and Beatrice T. Shepherd
Mrs. John F. Dougherty
Clare K. and Velma D. Fulton
Edward M. and Margaret K. Butterfield
Oscar R. Marsh
Willard H. McCabe
Fred H. Summerton
John J. McMullen Associates
Mr. and Mrs. Daniel L. Lord, Jr.
Mr. and Mrs. William F. King, Jr.
Bert's Oil Service
T & R Associates
Leonard and Alma Litchfield
Guy and Ruth Allenwood
Patricia B. Raven
William D. Sewall
William and Marilyn Rogers
In memory of Bart O'Donnell
The Cabin
Louis F. Ricciardone, O.D.
Bruce A. Verrill, D.M.D.
Mr. and Mrs. Ira E. Parry
WJTO AM730/WIGY FM106
Richard J. Largay, D.D.S.
Warren A. Higgins
Mr. and Mrs. Frank A. Donnell
Ronald C. Oulton
Mr. and Mrs. Frank A. Givin
Samuel A. Johnson
Dana L. McCurdy, O.D.
Reinhold and Maud Steussy
Carolyn M. MacElman
Mr. and Mrs. Joseph Henry Davis
Day and Hoch, Attorneys at Law
Fitzgerald, Conley, Haley and O'Neil
Vance L. Horne, D.M.D.
The Rev. and Mrs. L.E. Hodgkins
Alison and Tyler Kuzmickas
CHR Realty
Elizabeth Houghton Trott
Mr. and Mrs. Francis Bertrand
John A. Ross
Shelley B. Holland, D.C.
I. Benjamin Young, D.D.S.
In memory of Henry M. Baribeau, Sr.
Roebuck Real Estate
Maine National Bank
In memory of Nancy St. John
David and Janet Comeau
In memory of Charles R. Donnell, Trustee 1907–1935
In memory of Florence Donnell Watson, Corporator 1932–1962

DONORS

Mr. and Mrs. Douglas H. Mott
M. Cynthia and Robert J. Footer
Susan and James Hummer
Joseph and Margaret B. Allen
Mary Gesner Clarke
Paul H. and Joanna W. Dumdey
Mr. and Mrs. Robert Bygrave
Joseph P. and Louisa P. Malizia
Mr. and Mrs. S. Theodore Bertocci
Terrance and Sally Gray
W. Hallam Bonner
Charles and Eugenie Arbuthnot
Mary Jo and John Heyl
Esther F. Fletcher
Albert B. Moore
Betsy and Dan Donovan

Thomas E. Anglim, D.D.S.
David and Nancey Calhoun
Clifford M. and Alice D. Pye
Janet B. and Lynn M. Bussey
Granville Colby
Spencer L. French
Steen Co., Inc.
Bisson Moving and Storage Co.
Mr. and Mrs. William F. Mussenden
Janice A. and Donald M. Povich
"Brother" Bill and Janet Bodwell
Judith E. and Thomas H. Barrington
Addiella D. Palmer
Central Maine Power Co.
Dorothy T. Wyman
H. Christie and Ralph L. Snow
Raymond W. and Ruth Farnham
New Meadows Inn
In memory of Lorna S.M. Newcomb and Herbert B. Lilly, Sr.
Thatcher B. Pinkham, Jr.
Mr. and Mrs. Lincoln T. Ravenscroft, Jr.
Jay and Alice Sperling
William A. Bruce
Ray and Barbara Lebel
Mr. and Mrs. William Potter
Shirley J. Lewis
Gordon H. Falt, Jr.
Linwood E. and Barbara G. Temple
Mr. and Mrs. James H. Riley
Capt. and Mrs. George L. Bliss
Mr. and Mrs. William P. Drake
William E. Howell, D.D.S.
Lynn M. Bussey
Laurene L. Mattor
Mr. and Mrs. Malcolm R. Varney
Abbot and Eileen W. Fletcher
George M. Carlton, Jr.
Daniel R. Donovan
Douglas B. Rink
Evelyn Percy
Lloyd and Collette Coombs
Mr. and Mrs. Leon B. Pennell
Almena J. Thurston
Casco Northern Bank
Florence W. Jewell
In memory of Louis P. Nelson

Bibliography

Note: All Interviews Were Conducted by the Authors.

Additon, Loring R. Interview. Sabattus, ME, August 1987.

Aldridge, Richard, ed. *Memories of Morse, 1904–1979: A Seventy-Fifth Year Tribute to Morse High School in Bath, Maine*. Brunswick, ME: Brunswick Publishing Co., 1979.

Anderson, Martin. *The Federal Bulldozer: A Critical Analysis of Urban Renewal, 1949–1962*. Cambridge: M.I.T. Press, 1964.

Architectural Tours: Walking and Driving in the Bath Area (brochure). Bath: Sagadahoc Preservation, Inc., n. d.

[Atwood, John; Blackwell, John T.; and Young, Leo]. *City of Bath, Maine: 1959 Citywide Planning Guide Summary*. [Bath]: Bath Planning Board, 1959.

[Atwood, John; Blackwell, John T.; and Young, Leo]. *1959 Bath Downtown Plan*. [Bath]: Bath Planning Board, 1959.

Baker, William Avery. *A Maritime History of Bath, Maine and the Kennebec River Region*. 2 vols. Bath: Marine Research Society of Bath, 1973.

Barnes, Albert F., ed. *Greater Portland Celebration 350: A Commemorative Edition*. Portland, ME: Gannett Books, 1984.

Bath Business Guide. Bath: New England Supply Co., 1946.

Bath Daily Times, 1934–1967.

Bath Directory, Including Arrowsic, Georgetown, Phippsburg, West Bath, Woolwich. Published biannually. [Beverly, MA]: Crowley & Lunt, 1926–27—1953–54.

Bath Independent, 1936–1961.

Bath Iron Works Corporation: A Congoleum Company. Bath: Bath Iron Works, n. d.

Bath, Maine Centennial, 1847–1947. Bath: Bath's Centennial Committee, 1947.

Bath Urban Renewal Authority. *Documents Relating to Downtown Bath Urban Renewal Project, Project No. Maine R-5*. Bath: Bath Urban Renewal Authority, [1965].

Bath Urban Renewal Authority. *Investment Opportunities in Bath, Maine* (brochure). Bath: Bath Urban Renewal Authority, n. d.

Bath Water District. *The Seventh Report of the Trustees of the Bath Water District, 1938*. Bath: Bath Water District, 1938.

Blackmer, Rev. Franklin H. *Notes About Churches in the Lower Kennebec Valley, 1607–1976* (mimeographed publication). Bath: Greater Bath Council of Churches, 1976.

Hunter, Stanley R. and Vivian. Interview. Woolwich, ME, February 1987.

Hutchinson, Gloria. "New Dawn for Bath." *Down East*, February 1980, pp. 76–91.

Huxtable, Ada Louise. *Will They Ever Finish Bruckner Boulevard?* New York: Macmillan, and London: Collier-Macmillan, 1971.

Industrial Products and Services, Bath Iron Works Corporation. Bath: Bath Iron Works Corporation, 1980.

Isaacson, Dorris A., ed. *Maine: A Guide 'Down East.'* American Guide Series. 2d ed. Rockland, ME: Courier-Gazette, 1970.

Jackson, Gregory; Masnick, George; et al. *Regional Diversity: Growth in the United States, 1960–1990*. Boston: Auburn House Publishing Co., 1981.

Jacobs, Jane. *The Death and Life of Great American Cities*. New York: Random House, 1961.

Jones, Herbert. *Portland Ships are Good Ships*. Portland, ME: Machigonne Press, 1945.

Kay, William. Interview. Bath, August 1987.

Kendall, Glenn. "Study of School Community: Summary of Results of Workshop Course conducted at Bath by Prof. Glenn Kendall, Winter of 1945–1946" (typescript [copy], 1946). Patten Free Library, Bath.

Kennedy, Roger G. *American Churches*. New York: Stewart, Tabori & Chang, 1982.

Kenney, Norman C. and Virginia. Interview. Bath, August 1987.

King, David A. Interview. Bath, October 1987.

Kirkpatrick, Howard W. Interview. Woolwich, ME, April 1987.

Kouwenhoven, John A. *The Beer Can by the Highway: Essays on What's "American" about America*. Garden City, NY: Doubleday, 1961.

Kulski, Julian Eugene. *Land of Urban Promise: Continuing the Great Tradition. A Search for Significant Urban Space in the Urbanized Northeast*. Notre Dame, IN: University of Notre Dame Press, 1967.

Larrabee, John, comp. Scrapbooks on the History of Bath, 1946–1978. Patten Free Library, Bath.

Laverty, Dorothy Bowler. *Millinocket: Magic City of Maine's Wilderness*. Freeport, ME: Bond Wheelwright Co., 1973.

Leamon, James S. *Historic Lewiston: A Textile City in Transition*. Auburn, ME: Central Maine Vocational and Technical Institute for the Lewiston Historical Commission, 1976.

LeClair, Henry A. Interview. Bath, July 1987.

A Legacy of Pride . . . A Future of Promise: The First Hundred Years of Bath Iron Works. [Bath]: Bath Iron Works, n. d.

Lemont, Levi P. *1400 Historical Dates of the Town and City of Bath, and Town of Georgetown, from 1604 to 1874, Together with the Address of Francis Winter, . . . July 4, 1825*. Bath: Published by the Author, 1874.

Lipfert, Nathan and Janine. Interview. Bath, October 1987.

Lipfert, Nathan. "The Shipyard Worker and the Iron Shipyard." *The Log of Mystic Seaport*, Fall 1983, pp. 75–87.

Longley, Diane G.; and Young, Arthur H. *Steel Over the Kennebec: Building a Maine Bridge*. Bath: Published by the Authors, 1978.

Luke, Roger M. Interview. Bath, February 1987.

Maine Department of Economic Development. *Industrial Resources of Southwestern Maine*. Augusta, ME: Department of Economic Development, n. d.

Maine Division of Economic Opportunity. *Profile of Poverty in Maine: A Data Source*. [Augusta, ME]: Executive Department, Maine Division of Economic Opportunity, 1973.

Maine Flood Disaster of Friday, the 13th of March, 1936 (tabloid commemorative). Portland, ME: Gannett Publishing Co., 1936.

Maine Maritime Museum Photograph Files. Maine Maritime Museum, Bath.

Marentette, David B. "An Historical Geography of Bath, Maine: 1600–1920." Doctoral thesis (typescript [copy]). University of Oregon, 1983.

Martin, Kenneth R.; and Lipfert, Nathan R. *Lobstering and the Maine Coast*. Bath: Maine Maritime Museum, 1985.

Martin, Thomas J.; Gamzon, Melvin A.; et al. *Adaptive Use: Development Economics, Process, and Profiles*. Washington, DC: ULI-The Urban Land Institute, 1978.

Mayer, Martin. *The Builders: Houses, Neighborhoods, Governments, Money*. New York: W. W. Norton, 1978.

McCabe, Willard H. Interview. Bath, June 1987.

McCarthy, Joe, and the Editors of Time-Life Books. *New England: Connecticut, Maine, Massachusetts, New Hampshire, Rhode Island, Vermont*. New York: Time Inc., 1967.

Mellon, Gertrud A., and Wilder, Elizabeth F., eds. *Maine and Its Role in American Art*. New York: Viking Press, 1963.

Melman, Seymour. *Profits Without Production*. New York: Alfred A. Knopf, 1983.

Melnicove, Mark; and Merriam, Kendall. *The Uncensored Guide to Maine*. Augusta, ME: Lance Tapley, Publisher, 1984.

Michaud, Charlotte; Janelle, Adelard; and Leamon, James. *Historic Lewiston: Franco-American Origins*. Auburn, ME: Central Maine Vocational and Technical Institute for the Lewiston Historical Commission, 1976.

Miller, Alan Robert. *The History of Current Maine Newspapers*. Lisbon Falls, ME: Eastland Press, 1978.

Morse, Henry Franklin. *One Yankee Family: Being about Ten Generations of One Family, 1635–1969, that Migrated to New England and Made Homes in a Wilderness*. New London, CT: H. F. Morse Associates, 1969.

Morse High School Graduation File, 1887–1964. Alumni Room, Morse High School, Bath.

Morse High School Yearbook. Published annually. Bath: Morse High School Senior Class, 1936–1947.

Morse, John G., Jr. Interviews. Phippsburg, ME, February and June 1987.

Morse, John G., Jr.; and Pohl, William. "Logs, Ice, and Ships." *Down East*, February 1980, p. 86 ff.

Mulligan, Leonard C. Interview. Bath, June 1987.

Mussenden, William F. Interview. Bath, February 1987.

National Trust for Historic Preservation. *Economic Benefits of Preserving Old Buildings*. Washington, DC: Preservation Press, 1976.

National Trust for Historic Preservation. *Preservation: Toward an Ethic in the 1980s*. Washington, DC: Preservation Press, 1980.
Niss, Bob. *Faces of Maine*. Portland, ME: Guy Gannett Publishing Co., 1981.
Notebook of Morse High School Activities and Awards, 1927–1964. Alumni Room, Morse High School, Bath.
O'Rourke, P. J. "Let the Sixties Die." *Rolling Stone*, 24 September 1987, pp. 114–16.
Owen, Henry Wilson. *The Edward Clarence Plummer History of Bath, Maine*. Bath: The Times Company, 1936.
Owen, Henry Wilson. Research Notes on the History of Bath. Maine Maritime Museum, Bath.
Owings, Nathaniel Alexander. *The American Aesthetic*. Photographs by William Gannett. New York: Harper & Row, 1969.
"*Paper Talks" In the Bath-Brunswick Area*. Bangor, ME: Credit Unions of the Bath-Brunswick Area, n. d.
Patten Free Library, 1847–1952. Bath: Patten Free Library, 1952.
Peirce, Neil R. *The New England States: People, Politics, and Power in the Six New England States*. New York: W. W. Norton, 1976.
Phillips, Judy. "Will the Real Hyde School Please Stand Up?" *Kaleidoscope* (Morse High School magazine), [1983], pp. 21–23.
Pohl, William L. *The Voice of Maine*. Photographs by Abbie Sewall. Thorndike, ME: Thorndike Press, 1983.
Purington, William C. *A Look into West Bath's Past*. [West Bath, ME]: Published by the Author, 1976.
Reed, Parker McCobb. *History of Bath and Environs, Sagadahoc County, Maine, 1607–1894*. Portland, ME: Lakeside Press, 1894.
Reed, Richard Ernie. *Return to the City: How to Restore Old Buildings and Ourselves in America's Historic Urban Neighborhoods*, Garden City, NY: Doubleday, 1979.
Reidel, Carl H., ed. *New England Prospects: Critical Choices in a Time of Change*. Hanover, NH: University Press of New England, 1982.
Rich, Louise Dickinson. *The Coast of Maine: An Informal History*. Rev. ed. New York: Thomas Y. Crowell, 1962.
Rich, Louise Dickinson. *The Kennebec River*. New York: Holt, Rinehart and Winston, 1967.
Ring, Harry E., Jr. Interview. Bath, June 1987.
Robinson, John. *Highways and Our Environment*. New York: McGraw-Hill, 1971.
Rosen, Robert E. *John Dos Passos: Politics and the Writer*. Lincoln: University of Nebraska Press, 1981.
Rubin, Harold J. Interview. Bath, June 1987.
Sagadahoc County, Maine. Bath: Sagadahoc County Commissioners, n. d.
Sagadahoc Preservation, Inc., comp. Clipping Scrapbooks.
Saltonstall, Richard, Jr. *Maine Pilgrimage: The Search for an American Way of Life*. Boston: Little, Brown, 1974.
Scott, R. L. "Of Ships and Shipbuilders." *The Orange Disk*, September–October 1967, pp. 30–31.
Sewall, William D.; and Henderson, Melvin B. Interview. Bath, May 1987.

Shepard, Charles A., Jr. Interviews. Bath, April–May 1987.

Small, Raymond C. Interview. Bath, May 1987.

Snow, Ralph Linwood. *Bath Iron Works: The First Hundred Years*. Bath: Maine Maritime Museum, 1987.

Southern Mid Coast Regional Planning Commission. *Housing Data Book*. Bath: Southern Mid Coast Regional Planning Commission, 1976.

Southern Mid Coast Regional Planning Commission. *Housing: Goals, Policies, and Recommendations*. Bath: Southern Mid Coast Regional Planning Commission, 1976.

Southern Mid Coast Regional Planning Commission. *Housing Plan: Background Information*. Bath: Southern Mid Coast Regional Planning Commission, 1976.

Souvenir of Bath, Maine, 1915. Bath: Bath Times Printshop, 1916.

Spear, Arthur G. *I Bought a White Elephant in Maine: An Adventure in Homes*. N. p.: Published by the Author, n. d.

Spear, Donald A. Interview. Bath, June 1987.

Spear, Donald A., comp. Scrapbook on Morse High School Athletics, 1943–1947. Alumni Room, Morse High School, Bath.

"Spiffing Up the Urban Image." *Time*, 23 November 1987, pp. 72–76, 77ff.

Stinson, Carl W. Interview. Bath, August 1987.

Stover, Elford A. Sr. Interview. Bath, February 1987.

Stover, Elford A., Jr. Interview. Bath, July 1987.

Swearingen, David L. Interview. Brunswick, ME, May 1987.

Tabulae (Morse High School yearbook). Published annually. Bath: Morse High School Senior Class, 1949–1952.

Tardif, Dominique J. Interview. West Bath, April 1987.

Taylor, Toni. "High School Graduation, Bath, Maine: 'Like a Mighty Army . . . ' " *McCall's*, June 1943, pp. 14–15.

Temple, James W. Interview. Wiscasset, ME, February 1987.

Temple, Linwood E. Interview. Bath, April 1987.

Temple, Linwood, E., comp. Personal File on Bath Waterfront Park.

Thompson, Deborah, ed. *Maine Forms of American Architecture*. Camden, ME: Down East Books, and Waterville, ME: Colby Museum of Art, 1976.

The *Times Record* (Brunswick, ME), 1967–1986.

The *Times Record* Photograph Files. Brunswick, ME.

Topsham, Maine: 200th Anniversary. Topsham: Topsham Bicentennial Committee, n. d.

Tozer, Eliot. "Bath, Maine." *Yankee*, December 1986, pp. 58–66, 126 ff.

20 Questions & Answers on Urban Renewal (brochure). Washington, DC: Urban Renewal Administration, Housing and Home Finance Agency, 1963.

Urban Policy Group, Advisory Council on Historic Preservation. *Remember the Neighborhoods: Conserving Neighborhoods through Historic Preservation Techniques*. Washington, DC: Advisory Council on Historic Preservation, 1981.

Urban Renewal: A Socialist Scheme to Confiscate Private Property (brochure). New Orleans: The Independent American, 1959.

The Urban Renewal Fact Sheet on Federal Assistance to Communities for Urban

Renewal and Related Activities. Washington, DC: Urban Renewal Administration, Housing and Home Finance Agency, 1962.

Van Note, Bartlett M. Interview. Bath, July 1987.

Weaver, Robert C. "Urban Renewal Is Dispossessing Its Critics." *Washington Post*, 5 April 1964.

Wilson, James Q., ed. *Urban Renewal: The Record and the Controversy*. Cambridge: M.I.T. Press, 1966.

Ziegler, Arthur P., Jr.; and Kidrey, Walter C. *Historic Preservation in Small Towns: A Manual of Practice*. Nashville: American Association for State and Local History, 1980.

Zorach, William. *Art is My Life: The Autobiography of William Zorach*. Cleveland: World Publishing Co., 1967.

INDEX